Performance-related p

Teachers' pay settlements have long been an emotive subject, but recent changes in salary structures and introduction of appraisal systems have brought new controversy. The central point of contention is the link between appraisal and pay, and the question of whether teachers should be rewarded for quality performance by increases in salary. Opinions are divided, but with performance-related pay schemes already in operation across the private and public sector, the introduction of similar schemes in education seems to some to be inevitable. *Performance-related Pay in Education* looks in detail at the background to and growth of performance-related pay schemes, and attempts to shed some light on the controversy. The book explores the ways in which such systems have been introduced in the United States, not usually successfully, and how payment systems are changing in Europe. It also looks at lessons which can be learned from the ways in which pay structures in industry function, and how these might be applied in an education context. Most importantly, there are case studies of the first performance-related pay schemes for headteachers to be set up in the UK, in which the teachers concerned reflect on their experiences. In conclusion, Harry Tomlinson considers the attitudes of teacher unions, the Interim Advisory Committee, and the government in an environment where improved performance and value for money seem to be crucial.

Harry Tomlinson is Principal of Margaret Danyers College, Cheadle Hulme, Stockport, Chair of the Manchester Branch of the British Institute of Management, and Treasurer of the Secondary Heads Association.

EDUCATIONAL MANAGEMENT SERIES
Edited by Cyril Poster

Staff Development in the Secondary School
Chris Day and Roger Moore

Challenges in Educational Management
W. F. Dennison and Ken Shenton

Preparing School Leaders for Educational Improvement
K. A. Leithwood, W. Rutherford and R. Van der Vegt

Support for School Management
A. J. Bailey

Restructuring Universities: Politics and Power in the Management of Change
Geoffrey Walford

Education and the US Government
Donald K. Sharpes

Managing the Primary School
Joan Dean

Evaluating Educational Innovation
Shirley Hord

Teaching and Managing: Inseparable Activities in Schools
Cyril Wilkinson and Ernie Cave

Schools, Parents and Governors: A New Approach to Accountability
Joan Sallis

Partnership in Education Management
Edited by Cyril Poster and Christopher Day

Management Skills in Primary Schools
Les Bell

Special Needs in the Secondary School: The Whole School Approach
Joan Dean

The Management of Special Needs in Ordinary Schools
Edited by Neville Jones and Tim Southgate

Creating an Excellent School: Some New Management Techniques
Hedley Beare, Brian Caldwell and Ross Millikan

Teacher Appraisal
Cyril and Doreen Poster

Time-constrained Evaluation
Brian Wilcox

Performance-related pay in education

Edited by
Harry Tomlinson

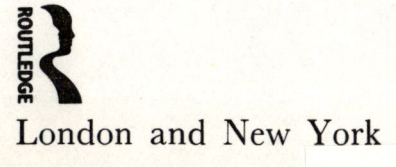

London and New York

First published 1992
by Routledge
11 New Fetter Lane, London EC4P 4EE

Simultaneously published in the USA and Canada
by Routledge
a division of Routledge, Chapman and Hall, Inc.
29 West 35th Street, New York, NY 10001

© 1992 Harry Tomlinson

Phototypeset by Intype, London
Printed and bound in Great Britain by
Biddles Ltd, Guildford and King's Lynn

All rights reserved. No part of this book may be reprinted or
reproduced or utilized in any form or by any electronic,
mechanical or other means, now known or hereafter
invented, including photocopying and recording, or in any
information storage or retrieval system, without permission in
writing from the publishers.

British Library Cataloguing in Publication Data
A catalogue reference for this title is available from the British Library
0-415-06967-X

Library of Congress Cataloging-in-Publication Data
Performance-related pay in education / edited by Harry Tomlinson.
    p. cm. — (Educational management series)
  Includes bibliographical references and index.
  ISBN 0-415-06967-X
  1. Teachers—Salaries, etc.—Great Britain. 2. Merit pay—Great
Britain. I. Tomlinson, Harry, 1939– . II. Series.
LB2844.G6P47 1992
331.2'813711'00941—dc20   91-41537
                                                                    CIP

Contents

List of figures and tables vii
List of contributors viii
Foreword xii

1 Performance-related pay in the 1980s: the changing climate 1
  Harry Tomlinson

2 Teachers' salaries 22
  Joanna Le Métais

3 Performance-related pay for teachers: the American experience 34
  Stephen L. Jacobson

4 Performance-related pay in the context of performance management 55
  Helen Murlis

5 Performance-related pay in IBM 73
  Gordon Sapsed

6 The history of teachers' pay negotiations 88
  Rene Saran

7 Teachers' pay and personal professional development 114
  Alan Marr

8 School teacher appraisal: for monetary reward, or professional development, or both? 131
  John Heywood

Contents

9 Performance management and performance-related pay in an education department 151
David Cracknell

10 Experience in schools: case study I
Kemnal Manor School for Boys 164
John Atkins

11 Experience in schools: case study II
City Technology College, Kingshurst 177
Valerie Bragg

12 Performance-related pay for teachers in the 1990s 184
Harry Tomlinson

Index 208

Figures and tables

4.1 Salary increase matrix 61

4.2 Performance management: main stages in cycle 66

5.1 A structure or series of salary ranges for each level, with the IBM objective near the mid-point of each range 78

5.2 Employee progress through the salary range 83

TABLES

6.1 Major Burnham settlements: the salaries structure 98

6.2 Increases in pay and incentive allowances 1988–91 102

9.1 Summary of responses to postal inquiry of education departments 153

9.2 East Sussex performance rating and reward scale 154

10.2 Kemnal Manor use of time for appraisal and performance-related pay interviews and observations per annum 166

11.1 Salary scales at the City Technology College, Kingshurst 182

12.1 Additional increments for headteachers 195

Contributors

John Atkins was born in London, and educated at Latymer Grammar School. He took his degree at Goldsmiths' College. He spent sixteen years teaching in the former Inner London Education Authority. Starting in Wandsworth, he worked his way up from probationer to senior teacher in one boys' school. He followed this by gaining valuable management experience at deputy head level at a mixed comprehensive school in Brixton. During this time he studied part-time for the Open University Advanced Diploma in Educational Management. John was appointed to his present post, as Head of Kemnal Manor School, in the London Borough of Bromley in January 1990.

Valerie Bragg is Principal of The City Technology College, Kingshurst, Britain's first city technology college. After education at Leicester and London Universities, her varied career in education has included being a Head of Sixth Form, and Head of Stourport-on-Severn Comprehensive School. She is a governor and Chair of the Audit Committee at Birmingham Polytechnic, and holds a number of directorships in enterprise companies. She has been involved in varied industrial work experience. Her innovative role has inevitably meant considerable involvement with the media, and a consequential membership of many committees and working parties.

David Cracknell is group director, Educational Services, for Cheshire County Council; until the end of the 1990 he was deputy county education officer in East Sussex, where performance management and performance-related pay had been under development for some time. He has taught in schools and in a college of education and worked as an education officer in Warwickshire, Leeds and Wakefield. Alongside a number of national commitments, he is active in the Society of Education Officers, particularly in the Industry Committee which has provided him with opportunities to develop a business perspective on performance-related issues.

John Heywood attended Manchester Grammar School as a scholar. After the Royal Navy he read Theology at Oxford. After teaching in a northern grammar school he had experience as a househead in a Coventry comprehensive and as deputy head of a new comprehensive outside Birmingham. For fifteen years he was head of a Cambridgeshire comprehensive village college. In 1989 he became Cambridgeshire teacher appraisal co-ordinator. He is Chair of the Salaries and Conditions of Service Committee of the Secondary Heads' Association, which he represented on the Appraisal National Steering Group. Among his interests are politics and he was Labour Party parliamentary candidate for Mid-Bedfordshire in 1987.

Stephen L. Jacobson is an Assistant Professor in the Department of Education Organization, Administration and Policy at the State University of New York at Buffalo. He received his PhD from Cornell University in 1985, and his doctoral thesis, 'Alternative practices of internal salary distribution and their effects on teacher recruitment and retention', won the 1987 Jean Flanigan Dissertation Award for Outstanding Research in the Field of Educational Finance. His work on teacher compensation has been widely published. Dr Jacobson recently co-edited a text on administrator preparation entitled *Educational Leadership in an Age of Reform*. His presentation at the International Intervisitation Programme in Manchester, UK, 'Future US Educational Leaders', will appear in the forthcoming volume *Leadership Development for Education*.

Joanna Le Métais has been Head of EPIC Europe (Education Policy Information Centre) and National Head of the EURYDICE education policy information network for England, Wales and Northern Ireland since 1984. EPIC provides an information service to senior policy-makers and in other member states of the EC through the EURYDICE network. She was educated in the Netherlands, Australia, England and France and was Head of Foreign Languages Department in a comprehensive school before working in local authority administration. Now a member of the Institute of Directors, she has published numerous papers on education policy and carried out research on the impact of teacher mobility (Association of Education Committees Trust), and factors affecting mobility within the EC, sponsored by the Commission of the EC and the National Foundation for Educational Research (NFER).

Alan Marr taught Art and Design in the former Inner London Education Authority before his wider interest in curriculum innovation and professional development took him into research and evaluation. His chapter is based upon the ESRC-funded 'Teachers' Jobs and Lives Project' which he initiated and conducted in collaboration with Dr Maggie McClure at the Centre for Applied Research in Education at the University of East Anglia. He is currently the Gulbenkian Research Fellow at the Polytechnic of East London completing the evaluation of the residency programme which is part of the BA Fine Art and Design Course.

Helen Murlis was recently appointed Director in the Compensation Practice of Hay Management Consultants. Immediately prior to this, when she was principal consultant and leading remuneration specialist at KMPG Peat Marwick McLintock, she set up and ran the Incomes Data Services Top Pay Unit between 1980 and 1985. Her experience has included reward strategy reviews for major clients in both the public and private sectors as well as providing detailed advice on pay issues from the shop-floor to the boardroom. With Michael Armstrong she is co-author of *Reward Management*, the standard UK text on salary policy development and practice. Helen is a regular columnist for *Personnel Management*; she is a founder member and on the Steering Committee of the Institute of Personnel Management Compensation Forum.

Gordon Sapsed spent twenty-four years with IBM in various personnel management and management development roles. His later career with IBM was as a consultant both within the company and with IBM's customers and suppliers. Prior to the IBM he had ten years as a civil service research physicist, taught at the Royal Naval College, Greenwich, and was an education and safety manager in a Merseyside shipyard. He is now a management and personnel consultant, a frequent speaker at international conferences and a contributor to various journals. He is a visiting fellow at the London School of Economics and Southampton University Management School.

Rene Saran is Visiting Fellow in Policy Studies at the Institute of

Education, University of London. She recently held a Leverhulme Emeritus Fellowship for research on the implementation of the imposed teacher contract of employment. Publications include *The Politics Behind Burnham* (1985; 1989 2nd edn) and *Public Sector Bargaining in the 1980s* (1988). She was joint editor of *Research in Education Management and Policy: Retrospect and Prospect* (1990), and chairs the Research Committee of the British Educational Management and Administration Society (BEMAS).

Harry Tomlinson is Principal of Margaret Danyers College, Stockport. After working abroad and in Lincolnshire, Essex and Walsall he has been headteacher and principal of three other institutions, all of which have closed due to reorganizations. He is treasurer of the Secondary Heads' Association and Chair of their Equal Opportunities Working Party, Chair of the Manchester Branch of the British Institute of Management, and regional secretary of the British Educational Management and Administration Society (BEMAS).

Foreword

There is no doubt that performance-related pay is a highly controversial issue, which makes this book both timely and important. Its editor, Harry Tomlinson, has drawn together a wide range of contributions from industry, from local government, from the academic world and of course from education. There are, not surprisingly, conflicting views, all of which need to be heard and heeded if school teachers and managers, governors, LEA officers and teacher unions are to make sound judgements over the possibilities for relating pay to performance now both implicit and explicit in the current conditions of service and the pay awards.

The argument against using teacher appraisal as a means of judging a teacher's suitability for salary enhancement has, in this symposium, both an ardent advocate and an equally ardent opponent. For a third contributor the main issue is low teacher morale which, he argues, relates far less to salary than to the general low esteem in which politicians in particular hold teachers, whatever they may say on public occasions. The conditions under which teachers in other European countries work and the pay they receive for what they are contracted to do are also fully explored by another writer. What happens in some areas of industry and local government is also aired by other contributors. The editor himself sets the historical scene in the opening chapter and attempts a forecast of what the future may hold in the final chapter.

I welcome this book into the education management series in the expectation that it will be much read and the issues that it raises hotly debated.

Cyril Poster
Series editor

Chapter 1

Performance-related pay in the 1980s
The changing climate

Harry Tomlinson

Performance-related pay is in essence an individualized system of payment linking all or part of the reward of each individual employee to his or her performance, though compromises relating to group or organizational performance are an occasional extension. There has been a massive increase in its application throughout the public sector, particularly for managers. In the 1980s there have been quite legitimate financial, political and legislative pressures which have led to value-for-money and market-forces arguments becoming more powerful, and necessarily so, as perhaps they always should have been. Government has succeeded in changing the climate to one more focused on quality, excellence, accountability and performance, and contributed purposefully to this very significant change. Though performance-related pay was initially mainly confined to managers it is spreading quickly down the old hierarchies and undermining them.

The most common ways of assessing performance are by the use of rating scales and by measuring performance against objectives. Rating scales, which are much less frequently used, normally include several elements of job performance, and require both quantitative and qualitative judgements. A particularly significant and difficult qualitative judgement, for example, is often made about effectiveness of relationships with colleagues. Scales usually have four, five or six points ranging from excellent to unsatisfactory. An overall score, giving appropriate weightings to the different components, is computed. The more sophisticated of these are behaviourally anchored. Rating scales might be considered inappropriate for a task as complex as teaching, but might be necessary if fixed proportions of teachers only were to be allowed particular salary increases.

The measurement of performance against targets which can be financial, task-based or quality-based in the wider world, is more suitable for education provided the targets are carefully selected. The targets, which are set at the start of the performance year, reflect the principal accountabilities of the job. The additional amounts which can be earned, particularly in schemes which are based on performance assessment, can be very large, as much as 30 per cent, or substantially more for the anomalous but widely publicized company chairmen, whose salaries rarely appear to drop when the company's performance deteriorates. They can take the form of annual bonuses, extra increments on an incremental scale – the higher reaches of which may be available only to those who perform consistently well – and a higher percentage annual increase.

Introducing performance-related pay is without doubt an act of faith based on the assumption that people will perform more effectively if offered the financial incentive to do so. This does not imply that teachers are motivated only by money, and this is certainly allegedly a crucial issue. Some headteachers are paid more than four times the salary of newly qualified teachers, and there is presumably a motivational rationale for this very significant difference in pay which is not only about responsibility. Performance-related pay emphasizes personal accountability, rather than merely status or seniority. Many organizations, like schools and colleges, are becoming leaner and flatter management structures in order to improve effectiveness, with reduced promotion opportunities for responsibility as a consequence. Eight salary scales for secondary schools are clearly unnecessary, indeed absurd if they are for responsibility. Performance appraisal, the consequential training, career development and performance-related pay will give a clearer direction to schools, and will make them responsive and flexible enough to meet new challenges. The significance of this consequence of performance-related pay is often insufficiently recognized by those who see it only as a means for paying better teachers more. Performance-related pay is part of a necessary change to school and college culture, if standards are to be raised significantly without a massive and possibly wasteful input of new resources. The change needs to be from one which lists all the staff qualifications in the school brochure to one which is genuinely self-critical, and is about much higher standards, thus justifying additional resources.

Performance rewards can reflect short-term or long-term performance. They have been used, very infrequently, to recognize the success of whole organizations, rather than teams or individuals. A performance-related pay system must, however, match the culture and value systems of the organization. There are those who argue that this is precisely why it is inappropriate for schools. The deputy general secretary of the NAS/UWT (National Association of Schoolmasters Union of Women Teachers), O'Kane, believes that there is an understandable unwillingness on the part of headteachers and governors to make a distinction between the work of one classroom teacher and another. This unwillingness might, on the other hand, be characterized as a serious abdication of management responsibility. He argues that the incentive post system itself is no more than a monument to those who believe that without stratification and hierarchy schools would collapse into chaotic anarchy. For him this is not about unions demanding the triumph of mediocrity at the expense of excellence. The NAS/UWT, in common with other teacher unions, wants a highly motivated energetic teaching force, just as others do. This, O'Kane suggests, will come from paying all teachers a reasonably decent salary, with one hierarchical level of teachers only between the standard scale teacher and the deputy head and headteacher, regardless of quality of performance. After the entry grade for new teachers, an appraisal system would provide the basis for the NAS/UWT collegiate approach.

There is a coherence and rationale here which deserves consideration. It is unclear why increments would continue to be appropriate. They are presumably based on the assumption that performance improves equally with each year's experience for all teachers. There is obviously no evidence to substantiate this. If there were no increments many teachers would reach their maximum salary in their twenties. There is an idealism or naïvety about these proposals. There is an assumption built in that all teachers will genuinely welcome equal pay not only regardless of the quality of their teaching, but also regardless of the responsibility they carry out. It is also assumed that this will not lead to a levelling down process.

Obviously no teachers want a superficial judgement made about the quality of their performance. However, a soundly based analysis of classroom performance and of the teacher's effectiveness in carrying out responsibility which rewards excellence through increased pay is more rational than the assumption that excellence will emerge simply from treating everyone the same. Certainly Her Majesty's Inspectorate (HMI) reports insist that many teachers frequently do not have high enough expectations of pupils, and that this is the major cause of underachievement. It might not be inappropriate, if somewhat grandiose, to suggest that the collapse of the bureaucratic centralist East European economies is a testimony to the mistaken assumptions which underlie the NAS/UWT model. It is precisely this very different culture of performance, possibly based on Japanese-style total quality management and not necessarily the Japanese education system, which we have to create in schools to achieve the massive increase in standards which is necessary, and achievable. The cornerstone for a well-designed performance-related pay system is that there is a correct salary for every teacher, both externally competitive and internally equitable, reflecting the level of responsibility, experience and individual performance.

EFFECTIVE INCENTIVE SCHEMES

In 1988 at a conference I attended entitled Effective Incentive Schemes, there were contributions from a wide range of highly successful industrial and commercial undertakings. These case studies, from manufacturing, financial services, engineering, retailing, electronics, leisure and insurance, demonstrated that incentive schemes were widely recognized as necessary and appropriate. The emphasis was on implementing, improving and managing the incentive schemes to improve the company's results by designing performance-linked reward schemes which directly matched business objectives. The parallel in the education service would be a concentration on improving standards from much more sharply focused school improvement and development plans, and even local education authority (LEA) policy-making.

The emphasis on improving incentive schemes had changed over recent years from scheme design to implementation. There was a recognition that every scheme had to be continually developed and revitalized. This is why for teachers they will have to be very flexible and school-based. Business priorities have to be determined, and they are complex and changing, as they are in schools, so there can be no once-and-for-all centrally planned scheme. Inadequate performance-related pay schemes were shown to hide the real ingredients of performance, and to be driven by scheme design rather than business need. This has been the major problem with the US schemes for merit pay for teachers discussed by Stephen Jacobson in Chapter 3. There was no pretence that dilemmas relating to payment system could be simply resolved, but there has to be a payment system, and this seemed to be the best. There are no panaceas to bridge the gap between theory and practice for performance-related pay. Schemes require careful implementation but nevertheless quickly become obsolescent. There is, in industry as in teaching, the real problem of balancing intrinsic and extrinsic rewards for work, but that does not mean that extrinsic rewards can be ignored. A reward system should reinforce good performance, even if this is not necessarily the ideal place to start. All payment systems have flaws and may produce unintended or undesired behaviour. The present pay system for teachers rewards those who leave the classroom and become administrators, and thus works actively against encouraging excellence in classroom performance. There is clearly no simple relationship between pay and motivation. Indeed the performance appraisal process in theory may arguably be as important as the pay system, but pay must genuinely reflect value to the organization. Performance requirements will change over time and differ within the same organization, and hence must normally be individually based. Given all this I would still argue that the present payment system for teachers is much less efficient in directing teacher salary resources, and certainly in determining a culture for whole system improvement, than one which is based on performance-related pay.

An incentive should link defined levels of performance to defined levels of pay. The formula must generate sufficient variation in reward for variation in performance to provide motivation. It must be communicated clearly and regularly enough for employees to understand what performance is expected of them. The formula must be based on criteria the employee knows how to influence directly. The evidence suggests that bonuses range from 10 per cent for junior managers to 25 per cent for chief executives, and teaching in a classroom is a highly complex managerial task, though it is infrequently recognized in these terms. In industry, decisions have to be made about eligibility. At present the local authority formal procedures for performance-related pay in place for teachers apply to headteachers only, with deputy heads as a possible development. It should be made clear that the headteachers who negotiate arbitrary pay rises for themselves and sometimes their deputies, using the flexibilities within the Interim Advisory Committee Report (IAC 1991) where there is no apparent relationship to performance inevitably create problems in their schools. Excluding other teachers from taking part in the new pay flexibilities will cause discontent and demotivation for all those not involved. Universal participation is preferable, and will become the case within a few years for teachers. Whether there should be variation by seniority, with higher proportionate increases at more senior levels to reflect the more identifiable impact of the performance of senior managers in teaching also, is not yet determined.

There can also be variation by function. Some jobs are more geared to short-term achievement, and therefore a reduced base salary could be appropriate in return for greater bonus opportunity. This may well be appropriate for classroom teachers. It will require great care to ensure long-term parity and to protect benefit entitlement levels. It is important to set a base performance at which base salary is appropriate, before considering what performance level is appropriate for additional incentive payment, particularly for teachers. There is sufficient flexibility for additional payments for teachers in the new structure. All this theory, based on both research and experience, is directly relevant to the emerging schemes for performance-related pay for teachers.

ESSO

Despite the supposed difficulties, many companies were linking performance appraisal not only to reward but also to ongoing career appraisal. ESSO called this dual process personnel assessment and career development counselling (ESSO 1988). This is a co-operative process with the subordinate taking an active role in analysing present performance, developing objectives and improvement plans, and defining interests regarding future assignments. ESSO make clear that both positive feedback and constructive criticism are more readily accepted and effective when given on a regular basis. This may imply a weakness in the teacher appraisal scheme if it is too rigidly adhered to as a formal process. Coaching or counselling is seen as a joint responsibility in the personnel development discussion. It is designed to improve performance. Counselling discussions should be consistent with information used in making performance assessments. Judging is solely a managerial responsibility, which involves assessing the performance and promotability of the subordinate. This will be how appraisal and performance-related pay will be distinguished in schools. How direct the link is between the two will depend on experience. The ESSO personnel development discussion is followed by the performance assessment discussion. Many of the dimensions on the performance assessment and counselling work sheet relate equally to aspects of the teacher's role. *Acquiring and Maintaining Job and Professional Knowledge, Interpersonal Skills* and *Initiative and Adaptability* are the first three of twenty-one dimensions which are evaluated. Each of them is examined for how significant it is for the particular post, and how effectively requirements have been met.

TEACHERS AND INCENTIVES

The new salary structure imposed in 1987 placed teachers on a single main scale, consisting of eleven points. The promotional structure based on a movement to a higher scale was replaced by a system of incentive allowances. Scale 2 teachers lost an allowance, and perhaps status; scale 3 teachers received a scale B incentive allowance; scale 4 teachers received a scale D incentive allowance, and senior teachers a scale E incentive allowance. There were in addition scale A and scale C incentive allowances interposed. What was unclear was how these incentives were to be significantly different from the allowances they replaced. Were they about incentives at all?

The Effective Incentive Schemes conference had been about matching business priorities and compensation, developing a profit-seeking culture, incentive pay for maximizing sales-force potential, setting targets and measuring results, structures for increasing teamwork effort, reward schemes for long-term profitability, refining existing incentive schemes, and integrating career development and performance appraisal. This is the kind of language which needs to be accepted much more readily by those developing teachers' pay policies if we are to raise standards and, I suspect consequentially, pay.

This culture implies very different values from those assumed by the National Union of Teachers (NUT) when, in 1991, it consulted its members about incentive allowances (NUT 1991). Teachers' pay, the NUT assumes, should reward job size, with additional payments made solely on the basis of extra duties and responsibilities, regardless of how well they are carried out. The NUT has consistently opposed all forms of merit pay. There is a clear concern that, if two-thirds of teachers hold an incentive allowance, this would change the perception of the payment system from one which rewards additional duties to one that equates with length of service, merit or performance-related pay. Whether five allowances is an appropriate number, if one is dealing solely with additional duties, is certainly questioned in the consultation document. Too many allowances will serve to depress the value and significance of the standard scale, but a reduction in the present five levels of allowance may mean again that some teachers will feel that their contribution and particularly their status have been devalued. The A allowance, which was 3.8 per cent of the top of the main scale in 1987, increased to 6.9 per cent by December 1991, while the respective movement in the value of an E allowance has been from 31.6 per cent to nearly 41 per cent. The 1991 increase, despite its deferment to December, raises both the number of allowances available, as well as the relative value of the individual allowances by 30 per cent. This massive transfer within the salary bill would seem to be inappropriate if all that is happening is that more teachers are being awarded allowances for extra responsibility with the effect of increasing stratification and hierarchy, particularly in the flatter management structures which are emerging in schools.

The NUT is critical of the NAS/UWT collegiate approach, which they interpret as based on an unjustified belief that such an approach would motivate teachers, raise morale, and restore enthusiasm and professionalism. The NUT suggests, quite rightly, that this does not provide a proper career structure, but fails to make the case for an alternative career structure. The issue of career development planning remains unresolved for young teachers who are seeking to develop strategies to establish their careers, given a lack of clarity about the concept of career. It is not clear whether the NUT's ideal model would involve something not dissimilar to an extension of the incremental system, where teachers are paid more for having experience, and for obtaining responsibility regardless of how well they carry out that responsibility. The NUT does describe the present system as confusing and unsatisfactory but only because the criteria for awarding discretionary payments and incentive allowances should, according to the IAC, be different. There is a real problem about the different models of teachers' careers that are assumed by both unions, neither of which seems to be fully thought through. They are both perhaps increasingly unrelated to the salary structure in place, the changed nature of teachers' careers, and appear to have internal contradictions.

The NUT opposes a direct link between appraisal and pay. Government policy it sees as being quite clearly in favour of a strong and direct relationship. Howarth, under-secretary of state for education at the time, speaking at an NUT conference on teacher appraisal on 30 January 1990, said that the government did not envisage a direct or automatic link between appraisal and pay. The appraisal process ought to be taken into account in any decisions about pay which are related to performance, including the award of incentive allowances. The draft regulations for appraisal published in April 1991 suggest that consultation with parents and others 'will often be appropriate for the appraisal of headteachers, but is less likely to be appropriate in the case of other teachers' (DES 1991b). This was significantly altered in the subsequent Statutory Instrument, where it was stated that it is likely in the case of headteachers, but unlikely for other teachers except in special cases. It is not clear to me how crucial this consultation actually is, but it is sensible to use all relevant information to make appraisal even more effective. It clearly will not be long before those applying for posts of responsibility, if they continue to exist, or even incremental enhancement, attach their appraisal reports as the best possible evidence of their performance.

For the NUT, appraisal should result in better and more effective teaching. It is designed to make teachers better professionals and to raise their expectations through a professional process conducted by professionals. The nature of professionalism, which is undefined and unclear, remains for the NUT unquestionably a good thing. The appraisal process must be beyond reproach, within an agreed national framework, based on classroom observation and on an agreed job description. The significance of classroom observation and the process by which it can be evaluated is not discussed. Appraisal must be discrimination free and apply to all, from probationers to headteachers. There must be proper outcomes with teachers recognizing when they need to put in an effort to improve and with an established right to support and training. The NUT perhaps implies that not all teachers need to improve. The appraisal process must have public confidence and enhance the professional status of teachers. It should ensure value for the money, time and effort invested in it. Public confidence would, in practice, be enhanced by the apparently unacceptable wider involvement of other teachers, parents, LEA officers and advisers, and governors. Indeed, confident teachers of older students will want students to be involved, as they are in higher education, in their evaluation.

Much of this NUT commentary on appraisal and the incentive system would seem extremely valuable, but for them, perhaps inevitably, it should have no link with merit pay. I suspect that this means it should have no link with performance-related pay, which is perhaps different, or with promotion to a higher incentive allowance based on merit. Merit pay is what you deserve because of what you are as a result of your achievement; performance-related pay, however, is for what you have achieved in the previous year. The difficulty is that we are moving into a new political environment discussed elsewhere, with accelerated incremental progression, incremental enhancement, increased numbers of incentive allowances, and headteachers and governors deciding how to use budgets of up to £2 million to improve the effectiveness of schools. To ignore appraisal, not to use it as directly as possible, would seem absurd. It is not two-tier pay leading us back a hundred years to payment by results in a new guise, though results do need to be taken into account, in context. Nor is it a beauty contest, a recipe for civil war in the staffroom, with parents and governors as judges as de Gruchy (NASUWT) insists (*Guardian* 24 April 1991), if information relevant to the school teacher's performance is obtained. This desperate defensiveness further undermines attempts to make teacher professionalism widely and genuinely accepted. Performance-related pay is not about teachers' pay being decided by the performance of pupils, disregarding the many varied factors which influence and impede the effectiveness of a teacher. However, the performance of pupils and at certain levels their judgement should be taken into account, as should for example the views of advisers and inspectors. Perhaps the teacher unions need to have more confidence in the quality of performance of their members, and their ability to improve, than appears to be the case.

In 1989 there were four significant publications which, independently, but more or less directly, discussed the issue of performance-related pay in the education service.

TOWARDS A SKILLS REVOLUTION

The Vocational Education and Training Task Force of the Confederation of British Industry produced a report (CBI 1989) which was about targets and action for all, setting world-class targets, putting individuals first, improving employers' performance, and making the market work. It was both visionary and imaginative. The CBI recognized the importance of the education service for achieving the radical transformation of industrial performance which they judged to be essential if Britain was to improve its economic performance. In order to mobilize the teaching force to help achieve this change of culture, the CBI sought

> changes to the pay and reward structure, to create a high performance, high pay service so that it is possible to attract and keep the most talented. The emphasis will probably need to shift towards greater local determination of pay. At the same time the morale and motivation of teachers is the key to the success of current education reforms.
>
> (CBI 1989)

While recognizing the importance of increasing and directing pay for teachers to improve morale and motivation, the CBI failed to appreciate the alarm that the apparently straightforward suggestion of paying teachers for performance might create. There was the folk memory of payment by results. The relationship of motivation to a proposed reward structure was not examined, and is central, particularly because many teachers genuinely do not believe that classroom performance can be evaluated. This is clear despite very strong evidence from HMI, in many reports of both excellent and very inadequate teaching. The CBI belief was that standards would be raised by 'ensuring that all teachers meet the required quality standards, through regular assessments, performance related payments, and flexible refresher and retraining schemes' (CBI 1989: 41). Teachers may be suspicious about whether high performance can be evaluated, but they are even more so about whether high pay would be a consequence. Scepticism about a national scheme would be justified, but there is also a fear of school-based schemes which are the inevitable alternative, because of the fear of arbitrary headteacher patronage. Appraisal should prevent this.

PERFORMANCE-RELATED PAY: A PUBLIC SECTOR REVOLUTION

Rycroft (1989) interpreted what was happening for the British Institute of Management. When the director-general introduced his booklet he said:

> The greatest benefits of individual performance pay are that it enables the organization to indicate to its employees what its priorities are, by weighting rewards for achievement in those areas. From an individual's point of view performance pay creates a direct link between their daily labours and the rewards they receive. It allows them to identify areas where they are underperforming.
>
> (*Management News* May 1989)

This language might concern teachers because of the earlier approach of the government to appraisal. However, this is the obvious and possibly the only way to improve individual performance. Confidence in the appraisal process would make self-criticism possible, and teacher confidence must be re-established. It is very difficult to understand how the consequential commitment to working hard at improvement will be so greatly increased if performance-related pay is totally ignored.

Rycroft looks at the issue in a very broad historical context which deserves consideration. Britain's role as leader of the industrial revolution and the development of a strong trade union movement led to the growth of collective bargaining in the nineteenth century. Management negotiating pay and conditions with the work-force as a whole was the conventional wisdom for over a century, though in other countries different relationships developed. This system was perhaps appropriate for mining, steelmaking, shipbuilding, manufacturing and other large labour-intensive industries employing huge numbers of unskilled or semi-skilled people, but it had its consequences after the Second World War. Whether it was ever appropriate for teachers, if they wished to interpret professionalism as is commonly assumed, is at least questionable.

Technological advance more recently has led to the replacement of unskilled and semi-skilled workers by smaller numbers of highly skilled and skill-flexible workers. Each recession accelerates this process. Organizations have become stretched horizontally with a wide range of more flexible employees, offering unique skills and specializations. This is perhaps not yet the case in teaching, though secondary schools have started to evolve in this way, and the language of core and peripheral workers is becoming significant. The development of new professions and the growth in specialized qualifications have allowed individuals to identify to their employers more accurately their abilities. This language is appropriate for schools, particularly for the changing roles of senior management. It is suggested that employees are starting to see collective bargaining as increasingly irrelevant to their needs, and detrimental to their aspirations. I suspect there is increasingly a crisis of identity for the larger teacher unions with the traditional distinctions between them no longer valid, and certainly not significant for their members. The changing membership of teacher unions can be interpreted in this way. If teachers now offer varied individual skills, these should be recognized and the rewards should be commensurate with those skills. This language is precisely that which teachers will use purposefully when they understand the value of their individual forms of expertise, as well as the variation in the quality of performance.

The Conservative government has brought in both trade union and employment legislation. The reduction of the power of trade unions to call strikes, to discipline members and regulate their internal affairs has accelerated the decline in collective bargaining and the influence of trade unions. Teacher unions are only very slowly coming to terms with this, as was shown by their reactions to the proposed Pay Review Body. Individuals now have access to industrial tribunals which may be more effective in guaranteeing or asserting rights in the 1990s than using the power of the trade union to fight for justice. There is a growing gap between individual aspirations and the ability of the traditional collective structures to respond to them. In addition, the government has been anxious to contract the boundaries of the monolithic, inflexible and inefficient state, and to ensure that what was left was better managed. This was the rationale. The intention of privatization was to develop new forms of efficiency, though the large privatized monopolies remain monolithic. Local authorities have had to open up their services to tender. This might indeed be part of a process which could lead to their disappearance. The assumption that the Conservative governments were attacking the education service, however, was all too frequently simply unquestioned. This was true about both local authorities and teacher associations, despite the fact that, for example, until 1991 the pupil–teacher ratio was constantly improving.

The management consultancy development in the 1980s was built upon the development of performance measurement and reward systems in education as elsewhere. If collective incomes policies were not to restrain inflation, then performance and profit-related pay became not only realistic, and more prevalent, but also an economic necessity. With over 400,000 teachers such developments are inevitable for teacher pay. Organizational structures have changed in the outside world, and are beginning to do so in education. The line management and human resource function has become eroded by the increased efficiency of communication made possible by information technology, as it will be increasingly in schools. The flatter organizational profile means that new methods of assessing responsibility and performance will have to be found. The procedures and structures in teaching are outmoded. Performance measurement and performance reward, which do have a beneficial effect on recruitment and retention, are being used in business to help solve the consequences of the demographic time-bomb, as they will be to solve teacher shortages.

We have to deal with issues relating to teachers' pay not with systems and attitudes remaining from the nineteenth century, but, in the word of *Future Shock* (Toffler 1973), with systems appropriate for the 1990s and further into the future. If we fail to recognize the inevitability of performance-related pay, we will not so quickly relate it purposefully to appraisal and school development plans, and delay the chance to raise teacher pay as well as pupils' educational performance. It may not be over-ambitious to consider the implications for national economic performance.

PAYING FOR PERFORMANCE IN THE PUBLIC SECTOR: A PROGRESS REPORT

Incomes Data Services and Coopers & Lybrand describe, without qualification:

> a rapid growth of performance-related pay schemes . . . in the

Civil Service, the NHS, local government, and the quasi-autonomous government organizations. . . . The Government has been a major influence in the Civil Service and the NHS, where performance pay has been part of a new performance culture, essential to Government plans for greater 'value for money' and 'management accountability'.

(IDS 1989)

Value for money in the education service needs to be considered. It is not that teachers are not working hard enough. Many of them are working too many hours but insufficiently efficiently and effectively. There needs to be greater accountability, and the improvement in educational standards which shows signs of faltering needs to be accelerated.

Their six key research findings were as follows.

1 Performance pay is being introduced into the public sector as part of a wider process of organizational change in the public sector, with an emphasis on devolved management control and the fostering of a performance culture.
2 Performance pay is largely confined to managerial staff at present. The major exception is the Civil Service.
3 The overwhelming majority organized target-based appraisal schemes, with the emphasis on the mutual setting of targets between the appraiser and the appraisee. For many organizations this process was considered more important than any link with pay.
4 There are two strategies for developing performance pay arrangements. The evolutionary approach involves adapting existing salary structures, for example by adding extra, performance-based increments, or making incremental progression dependent on performance. This is clearly happening in teaching. The revolutionary approach means replacing existing salary structures with completely new arrangements.
5 There are three main types of performance pay systems: incremental based schemes; salary range schemes; and those based on spot salaries with one-off lump sums. All of these are now available in teaching.
6 Experience in the United States shows the need for caution. The subordination of performance assessment to financial considerations, such as fixed budgets or quotas, can have a negative effect. There is a danger that when many teachers achieve high

targets, as they will, there will not be sufficient money to pay the teachers initially.

This research foreshadowed the changes which are occurring in the education service.

PERFORMANCE-RELATED PAY: AN UPDATE

The LACSAB Research Paper, *Performance-Related Pay: An Update* (LACSAB 1989), saw performance-related pay as serving a number of management purposes: employee motivation, improved management and communication, establishing equity in employee rewards, a solution to recruitment and retention problems, and fostering the performance culture. LACSAB was providing a checklist for local authorities introducing performance-related pay, including the details of the technicalities involved in the preparation, design, implementation, and control and review of schemes. The case studies presented showed the categories of employees covered, the methods of performance assessment, the size and form of performance payment and the control and management of the scheme. Performance-related pay was very obviously being used increasingly, particularly at senior levels, in local authorities.

The assessment of performance must be rigorous. The manager has to develop explicit objectives and standards of performance. Such assessment will in practice generate systematic information, not just on how individuals are performing, but on the performance of the whole organization. Equity in the rewards given requires both a good design and clear communication, monitoring, an appeals procedure, and procedures for dealing with poor performers. There was a recognition that the existing culture of local government, the ethic of public service, might be lost. The language of bureaucratic inefficiency was unsurprisingly not discussed. However, by providing an incentive, sharpening objectives and importing the principle of payment based on individual performance, the new performance culture was expected to foster economy, efficiency and effectiveness in the delivery of services, and better use of resources as it must in schools.

In 1989 it was clear that the continued ignoring of performance related pay for teachers was becoming absurd.

THE SCHOOL EFFECT

In *The School Effect: A Study of Multi-Racial Comprehensives*, Smith and Tomlinson (1989) showed again that schools were important for pupil performance, and very different in their effectiveness. There really are good and less good schools in terms of adding value, and the significant differences are not widely recognized or understood. Their research project followed pupils throughout their secondary school careers. Performance was regularly tested to measure progress. Interviews with children and their parents provided additional information. Smith and Tomlinson conclude:

> If schools were improved only within the current range of performance of urban comprehensive schools, this would be enough to radically transform the standards of secondary education.
> (Smith and Tomlinson 1989)

Teachers are still not convinced that this is the case. Perhaps only when those who are achieving these standards are recognized and rewarded appropriately will the system respond strongly. This may well now happen if the White Paper *Education and Training for the 21st Century* (DES 1991a) is implemented. It will be relatively simple to measure added value for sixth-form colleges, particularly for Advanced Level students. Indeed this may be a basis for the funding they receive from the Regional Councils.

Research on school effectiveness has shown that schooling has not been effective as a means of reducing inequality. Until recently the school effectiveness tradition had not been primarily concerned with improving personal development and relating this to economic performance. The problem has been that school effects appear small in relation to the very wide range of highly stable individual differences. Nevertheless these school differences can in practice be very large in terms of the standards of education the schools are delivering. It is also clear, despite the justifiable concern about whether SATs are necessary, that teachers often seriously underestimate the ability of their pupils. Ball (1991) sees the low self-esteem for those for whom schooling has meant an experience of boredom, irrelevance and failure as one of five impediments to the establishment of a learning society of the future, characterized by success in securing both high standards and low levels of failure. He also comments on the inadequacy of the theory and practice of learning with which we are working. Learning itself, I suspect, may well be better understood and then improved as we learn from the appraisal process.

School Matters (Mortimore *et al.* 1988), a parallel research project on primary school, examined given and policy variables at school and class level. The given variables at school level included resources; the policy variables at school level were the headteacher's style of leadership, the type of organization, the involvement of staff, the curriculum, rewards and punishments, parental involvement with the school, equal opportunities, the school atmosphere. The given variables at the class level included, for example, the age, social class and ability composition of the class; the policy variables were the aims and planning of the teacher, the teacher's strategies and organization of the curriculum, management of the classroom, including rewards and punishments, classroom atmosphere, the level and type of communication between teacher and pupils, parental involvement and record-keeping. All this is about improving the education children receive, and provides a preliminary basis for headteacher and teacher performance-related pay.

They identify twelve key factors that lead to an effective school. Some of these might well be incorporated in any appraisal observation.

> The amount of teacher time spent interacting with the class (rather than with individuals or groups) had a significant positive correlation with progress.... It was the number of interactions involving the whole class, rather than any attempt to teach the whole class as one unit [which had beneficial effects].
> (Mortimore *et al.* 1988: 228)

This has obvious implications for assessing and improving teaching effectiveness if this information is genuinely included in appraisal.

Rutter *et al.* (1979) found one general theory, that while individual teachers do vary in their effectiveness, there is something called the school ethos, a set of school-wide influences which make it more or less likely that teachers will teach in an effective manner. This will relate to the performance of the headteacher. In addition there were a number of specific theories. Most significantly, as shown in the Mortimore research, the way teachers manage the classroom is inevitably crucial to effectiveness in secondary schools also. This, Rutter argues, is essentially a matter of maximizing the amount of time pupils are engaging in useful learning or practice. Teachers do this, for example, by engaging pupil attention, securing orderly behaviour and managing their behaviour so as to maximize the amount of useful contact with each member of the class. He points out that this perhaps obvious theory has important policy implications, since teachers are given little instruction in classroom management, and are not helped to develop these skills on the job often throughout a whole career in the classroom. If performance is to improve this must be one area on which appraisal and improvement must concentrate.

All this research needs to be used if we are to reward improved teaching based on the evidence from classroom observation. Smith and Tomlinson (1989: 301) showed that there were also very significant differences in performance at department level. Despite the anxiety about payment by results of an unsophisticated kind, these differences do raise the issue of whether there should be differential payments for very significant variations in quality of performance. A pupil of average ability at the end of the second year would attain a Grade 3 CSE in English in one school. The same pupil would have achieved a Grade B GCE in another school. A boy of above average ability would achieve at best a Grade 4 CSE in Mathematics in one school. The same boy would have achieved a Grade B/C GCE at another school. The evidence presented for these unacceptable differences is in my judgement incontrovertible. If this is the case then departments and the teachers in them are demonstrably performing with very variable degrees of unrecognized success. This incremental improvement is clearly large enough to be highly significant for its effect on what each individual is actually achieving, if small in comparison with the differences between individuals. It could be paralleled by very obvious measures of added value in comparing GCSE and Advanced Level performance in schools. There is also very considerable evidence that a higher proportion of children could be required or expected to compete at a significantly higher level in all phases of education. Low teacher expectations are a real issue, and related to motivation and pay.

Schools can now very easily measure the relative performance of departments and inform teachers, parents and governors of these results. An analysis against national norms is also feasible. Few yet do so, because the measurement of performance by teachers is not yet taken sufficiently seriously, possibly because of all the problems caused by the massive and largely irrelevant overtesting which has been required by the government at Key Stage 1.

This would have provided so many data which would have been incomprehensible, as well as wasting time when children might be learning. Nevertheless parents need much better and fuller information than they are at present receiving. It might ironically actually delay the advent of pay based on the genuine performance which the government thinks it demonstrates. Maughan *et al.* (1990) have shown that schools can improve their examination results and attendance without any change in intake ability. In one of the six schools in their study these rose from relatively poor to at or above the expected levels for the local division and the LEA as a whole, over a five-year period, and in pupils of all abilities. This particular evidence suggested that improved attendance results from school-wide processes for all students, but that improved examination results might take place only at some ability levels.

Smith and Tomlinson (1989: 303) showed, again quite conclusively, that parents' attitudes and views about schools vary widely from one school to another. They are, however, surprisingly little related to their own child's attainment, and not at all related to their child's progress. This also applies to the child's enthusiasm for school, and the parent's assessment of how happy the child is. If parents are to make judgements about the effectiveness of their child's school, this shows precisely how 'the results of national testing will be seriously misleading' (Smith and Tomlinson (1989: 303). The new statistical techniques available would make it possible to make valid comparisons between schools that are widely different in the attainment and social class of the children entering them. At present parents cannot identify the schools that are doing well in terms of pupil progress, and the panoply of testing imposed will actually confuse the issue further because of a failure to allow for social class. At present teachers likewise make inadequate judgements about pupils and headteachers make oversimplified judgements based on inadequate evidence about teacher performance.

Children who are failing at school, are poor at reasoning and unable to express themselves are unlikely to be creative, constructive, spiritual or good at teamwork. The argument that there is an overemphasis on academic success as measured by tests, as opposed to more important educational growth, assumes that the two are not complementary, or indeed necessarily and mutually reinforcing. Rutter demonstrated that they certainly occur together. Those who make good progress in school work also tend to participate in a range of school activities outside the classroom. The standards in all schools need to improve. Though teachers' morale is low, despite government assertions to the contrary, it may be a consequence of a lack of belief in improvement rather than a reaction to all the changes which have been imposed in an attempt to galvanize the system into taking improvement seriously. Paying teachers well, particularly those who ensure that children learn particularly effectively, and changing the culture so that standards are raised substantially, are increasingly essential.

REFERENCES

Ball, C. (1991) *Learning Pays: The Role of Post-Compulsory Education and Training*, London: Royal Society of Arts.
CBI (1989) *Towards a Skills Revolution*, London: Confederation of British Industry.
ESSO (1988) *Supervisors' Guide to Performance Assessment and Counselling*, London: ESSO.
DES (1991a) *Education and Training for the 21st Century*, London: HMSO.
—— (1991b) *School Teacher Appraisal: Circular* (draft), London: DES.
Guardian (1991) Teacher appraisal: a beauty contest, *Guardian* 24 April.
IAC (1991) *Fourth Report of the Interim Advisory Committee on School Teachers' Pay and Conditions*, Cm 1415, London: HMSO.
IDA (1989) *Paying for Performance in the Public Sector*, London: Incomes Data Services and Coopers & Lybrand.
LACSAB (1989) *Performance-Related Pay: An Update*, London: Local Authorities Conditions of Service Advisory Board.
Maughan, B., Pickles, A. and Rutter, M. (1990) 'Can schools change?', *School Effectiveness and School Improvement* October.
Mortimore, P., Sammon, P. *et al.* (1988) *School Matters: The Junior Years*, Wells: Open Books.
NUT (1991) *Incentive Allowances: A Consultative Document*, London: National Union of Teachers.
Rutter, M., Maughan, B., Mortimore, P. and Ouston, J. (1979) *Fifteen Thousand Hours*, Shepton Mallet: Open Books.
Rycroft, T. (1989) *Performance Related Pay: A Public Sector Revolution*, London: British Institute of Management.
Smith, D. J. and Tomlinson, S. (1989) *The School Effect: A Study of Multi-Racial Comprehensives*, London: Policy Studies Institute.
Toffler, A. (1973) *Future Shock*, London: Pan.

Chapter 2

Teachers' salaries

Joanna Le Métais

My work on teacher training and the employment and management of teachers in the context of increasing mobility within the European Community has involved discussions with teachers and their employers throughout Europe. In every country, one question recurs: how do teachers' salaries in our country compare with those in other countries?

While cross-national comparisons are always complex, involving as they do differences in values, traditions and structures, comparisons of salary are notoriously difficult. Even where the rate of exchange and deductions are standardized, there remain the comparisons of the teachers' standard of living with that of other employees in the public and private sectors who have equivalent qualifications and experience.

This chapter will first examine the prescribed duties and responsibilities of teachers in a number of European countries. It will go on to describe the framework and components of the basic salary, the scope for classroom teachers to increase their income and the opportunities for promotion to more senior posts. Finally, the recently revised salary structure of French teachers will be described as an example of the issues raised.

TEACHERS' RESPONSIBILITIES

The initial training, qualifications and recruitment of teachers in other member states of the European Community are described elsewhere (Le Métais 1991a; 1991b) and will not be treated in detail here, other than to say that there are considerable variations both in the level of education and in the age of those admitted to the profession. For example, while a primary school teacher in

Italy may be as young as 18, a secondary school teacher in Germany may be ten years older before she has completed the academic and professional education and the 18–24 month period of supervised practical teaching, which precede qualification. Most secondary school teachers overseas are several years older on appointment than probationers in the UK.

All teachers are expected to prepare lessons, teach, set and correct homework and assess their pupils' progress; but the nature and emphasis of other, often implicit, responsibilities may vary considerably. For example, the pastoral role performed by British teachers is only just emerging in other countries. Thus we see a lighter teaching load for class teachers in Norway, mainly for recording attendance and co-ordinating reports on pupil progress, or for those undertaking student guidance in Germany. On the other hand, the requirement that pupils who fail to achieve a given overall standard repeat a year involves teachers in continental Europe in an annual review of all pupils. This judgemental role is one of the reasons why permanent teaching posts in Germany are reserved for German nationals.

The teacher task is frequently defined in terms of hours per week. Although their contract may be expressed in terms of hours, the virtual absence of non-contact time means that for primary school teachers this is equivalent to the total school hours. For secondary teachers, the number of hours may vary according to teachers' corps (e.g. France between fifteen and twenty-six) or school type (e.g. Belgium between twenty-two and thirty-three; Germany between twenty-four and twenty-eight). In Denmark, the teachers' load is defined as 1,080 teaching periods per year, plus four days for in-service training, planning meetings and the like. Italian teachers are required to undertake directed duties and consultation with colleagues for up to twenty hours per month, but there is no effective check on whether these duties are carried out.

The teaching load may be reduced according to the teachers' age, years of service, or alternative responsibilities. In Germany teachers over 50 teach two periods fewer and those over 60 teach four periods fewer per week. In Denmark teachers over 60 benefit from a reduction of up to 108 periods per year, according to total teaching load. In Greece teachers with six years' service teach nineteen periods instead of twenty-one, while after twelve years' service this is reduced to eighteen periods per week. In Denmark there is an extensive system of reductions for responsibilities such as supervision and setting up the equipment for physics lessons. Allowance is also made for setting and marking written work, according to the subject, the level and the number of pupils.

Since many teachers are not required to remain at school when not teaching, their lessons may be grouped to avoid gaps. It is not unknown for *agrégés* in France to complete their entire teaching commitment in three days per week. (An *agrégé* is a teacher who has passed the highest examination for recruitment of teachers.) Another consequence of a contract expressed in terms of class-contact time is that cover for absent colleagues, supervision during breaks between lessons and extra-curricular activities are carried out only in return for separate payment. Primary teachers are eligible for overtime payment only if they undertake supervisory or extra-curricular duties outside school hours. However, full-time secondary school teachers in France, Italy, the Netherlands and Norway may legitimately augment their income in this way, or even by a regular commitment to teach in excess of twenty-six periods (the Netherlands) and eighteen periods (Italy). The basic teaching load in Luxembourg and Norway is variable, depending on the level and discipline. All overtime earnings in Norway are taxed at a higher rate.

In-service training (INSET) is increasingly stressed as part of the teachers' professional responsibility to keep abreast of rapid change and it may be used as a criterion for discriminating between applicants for promotion. It often takes the form of sustained study to achieve a recognized qualification which will lead to an immediate salary increase, as in France or Norway, or open up access to better paid posts, as in Belgium and the Netherlands. Belgian teachers who undertake INSET lasting at least twenty-four hours benefit from a reduction of their workload by one hour per week.

SALARY FRAMEWORK

In many European countries, teachers are subject to the regulations governing public servants and are paid on special public service scales or on specific points of the public service salary spine. The scope for salary negotiations and for raising the status of teachers, as compared with other public servants, varies. However, two points may be made in response to the view that UK teachers would fare better if their salaries were linked to those of civil servants. First, in every country visited by the author, teachers felt that their salaries did not reflect their responsibilities and their contribution to society: Norway and Portugal are only two of the countries where teachers have taken industrial action in support of their pay claim in recent years. Second, despite the fact that outsiders frequently consider them to be highly regarded and well paid, teachers in Germany, who can neither negotiate their salary nor take strike action, complain about their position relative to other civil servants with comparable qualifications.

England and Wales are apparently unique in having a single salary structure for primary and secondary teachers. Elsewhere, teachers are divided into corps according to their qualifications. Teaching posts are categorized by school type (general, technical, vocational or special education), phase (primary, lower secondary, upper secondary, higher) and discipline. Appointment to a teaching post depends on qualifications but teachers of a given corps are often eligible to teach in more than one school type. For instance, in France teachers holding an *agrégation* usually teach in a *lycée*, but they may be appointed to a *collège* or apply to teach at a university. In Luxembourg those qualified to teach general subjects at secondary level may spend some time teaching in technical secondary schools before a vacancy arises in a more prestigious classical secondary school.

In both of these cases, the teachers are paid according to their qualifications, irrespective of the status of the post. A slightly different position arises in the Netherlands. Although qualifications govern access to posts and salary, an upper secondary (*1e Graads*) teacher appointed to a lower secondary post is paid according to the salary scale for *2e Graads* teachers.

COMPONENTS OF THE BASIC SALARY

A teacher's salary in all the countries studied is composed of three elements: the salary scale appropriate to the teacher's qualifications or post, the incremental point to which she has progressed by virtue of seniority or performance and any supplementary payments to which she is entitled. In determining the teacher's initial placement on the scale, the teacher's age, formal education, military service, where applicable, and employment experience in teaching or industry are among the factors taken into consideration.

The effect of inflation on a teacher's salary is recognized in several countries by periodic adjustments of salaries to rises in the cost-of-living index (Belgium, France, Luxembourg) or by supplementary allowances (Denmark, Italy). In Denmark, updated salaries are published every six months while in France and Luxembourg the process is facilitated by expressing teachers' salaries in terms of a salary point, to be multiplied by the current cost-of-living index.

Incremental increases

As might be expected, there is wide variation in the number of increments and the speed of progress. While the French scale has only 11 increments, the Danish public sector salary spine comprises 53 scales of which scales 1–32 have between 2 and 6 points and scales 33–53 are single point scales. Additional increments are earned annually (the Netherlands), biennially (Denmark, Germany), triennially (Spain) or at variable intervals depending on the salary scale, the length of service or performance. Italian teachers on scale 7b receive biennial increments, while those on scales 6 and 7 have two triennial, followed by six biennial increments. Each of these increments represents 8 per cent of the initial salary. Belgium, France and Luxembourg are examples of systems where the intervals between increments lengthen as a teacher's career progresses. Only France introduces a performance-related element into the payment of increments.

Supplementary payments

It is in the supplementary payments that the greatest variation occurs between member states. While some supplements are paid in recognition of special difficulties, as in educational priority areas, additional responsibilities or overtime, teachers may also receive allowances which bear no direct relation to the responsibilities of their post. Thus they may be entitled to additional payments by virtue of being an employee (holiday pay), a public servant (pension contributions), resident in a particular geographical area (urban allowances), newly appointed (starting-up allowances) or because they have dependants (family allowances).

In the Netherlands, those paid above a certain salary level must subscribe to private health insurance but employees receive a contribution towards their premium which varies with the number of dependants. Teachers receive 6 per cent of their salary. In Germany teachers have a non-contributory pension scheme.

Holiday and annual bonus

This may be calculated as a percentage of the net (Denmark) or gross (the Netherlands) salary, a fixed sum (Germany) or a combination of both (Belgium). An annual bonus comprising a fixed sum plus 2.5 per cent of the gross October salary is paid to teachers in Belgium, while those in Germany and Italy receive a thirteenth-month's salary in November and December respectively.

Geographical allowances

Payments analogous to the London Allowance are a common feature. In Denmark teachers are placed in one of six bands and receive supplements ranging from 5.15 to 17.9 per cent of their basic salary. These benefits are progressively reduced by 5 per cent per incremental point from scale 23 and cease when the teacher reaches scale 31 point 41. In France two zones grant entitlement to an additional 3 and 1 per cent respectively. However, these are being replaced by fixed allowances, integrated into the pensionable salary. A special 3 per cent allowance is paid to German teachers working in Berlin, or seconded from Berlin.

Family allowances

German civil servants are placed in one of three salary bands (single; married, or single-parent families; married with children) and receive an allowance for each child up to a maximum of six children. Like other employees, teachers receive family allowances on a sliding scale (France) or at a fixed percentage of their salary (Luxembourg 7.2 per cent). In Italy, following the birth of a child, a teacher may receive an immediate increase of 2.5 per cent which is incorporated into the next standard (8 per cent) increment.

General income supplements

Special support is given to Belgian teachers on the lower salary scales in the form of a residence allowance (single teachers) or a housing allowance (married teachers). In Denmark teachers qualify for a pensionable supplement on a sliding scale, ranging from 81.5 per cent of lowest salary to 14.7 per cent of highest salary. An additional general allowance is paid to teachers on scales 35–40.

Long-service allowances

These may be paid to experienced teachers who do not receive any other allowances, for example, a Danish *magister* with twenty-one years' service who does not receive any other supplements. These may be temporary in nature and withdrawn when a higher salary rate reached.

The salary and allowances of individual teachers are protected against the effects of falling rolls or redeployment (Germany, Italy, the Netherlands).

POST-RELATED INCREASES

In anticipation of formal promotion basic scale teachers may enhance their income by

1 teaching in an educational priority school or area, or one where there is a teacher shortage (France, the Netherlands)
2 teaching in a residential school where accommodation is provided (France, Germany, Luxembourg) or in prison schools (Germany)
3 qualifying for overtime, through extra teaching or other activities (France, Italy, the Netherlands, Norway)
4 special duties: undertaking additional responsibilities is one means whereby teachers can supplement their income, although in some countries the increased workload is balanced by a reduction in their teaching load rather than by an increase in salary; activities which qualify include co-ordination of subject areas or pilot projects in experimental education, providing vocational guidance, serving on boards or committees, supervising initial training or INSET activities
5 additional qualifications may lead to an immediate increase in

salary in France, Ireland and Luxembourg; alternatively, they may grant access to different categories of post with the higher salary scales
6 participation in INSET (Italy).

CAREER DEVELOPMENT AND PROMOTION PROSPECTS

Most schools have very few posts of responsibility as we know them, other than deputy head and headteacher. An exception is the German *Gymnasium*, where there are four levels of responsibility above the basic grade: *Oberstudienräte, Studiendirektoren, Studiendirektor* and *Oberstudiendirektor*.

The limited scope for promotion may be one reason for long-service payments made to experienced teachers who have not achieved promotion (for example, in Denmark), for the *hors classe* grade in France or for the supplement which brings teachers aged 55 in Luxembourg to the top of the scale. However, well-qualified teachers may, and do, apply for administrative, inspectorial or advisory posts at national or regional level.

CASE STUDY: FRANCE

Permanent teachers are recruited to one of a number of civil servant corps by means of competitive examinations (*concours*) specific to the level and subject discipline. The corps determines the type of establishment in which they are entitled to teach, their salary, conditions of service and promotion opportunities. There is at present a single corps of primary teachers (*instituteurs*) but secondary teachers may be *professeurs agrégés, professeurs certifiés (CAPES)* and *professeurs de lycée professionnel (PLP* – vocational education).

Permanent appointments are limited to the number of expected vacancies and suitable candidates may be rejected once the limit is reached. However, the converse does not apply and, even when there is a shortage, some applicants may be rejected. In 1989 the number of teachers appointed as a percentage of applicants in each *concours* ranged from 10 to 55 per cent while the number of vacancies remaining varied from 0 to 64 per cent. For example, there were 11,105 applicants to fill 3,120 posts at *CAPES* level in the humanities. Although 2,279 (20 per cent) applicants were successful, 27 per cent of posts remained unfilled. These posts are filled on fixed-term contracts and unsuccessful applicants must reapply if they wish to secure a permanent appointment and the advantages which accompany it.

Current shortages, together with the increase in suitably qualified teachers required to meet the government's declared objective of raising the *de facto* school-leaving age to 18 for 80 per cent of students by the year 2000, have resulted in reforms in teacher training and in the salaries, conditions and career prospects for teachers. These are outlined in *Profession professeur*, as part of a major recruitment campaign (Ministère de l'éducation nationale 1989).

Teachers' responsibilities

The teacher's specific duties are to teach for the number of hours appropriate to her grade, not to undertake other paid work without the approval of the authorities and to maintain neutrality in accordance with the non-denominational character of public education. The teacher's responsibility to communicate cannot be quantified but requires her to participate in meetings with pupils, parents, colleagues and so on.

Components of the basic salary

The basic salary is calculated by multiplying the relevant incremental point by the cost-of-living index (*indice de rémunération nouveau majoré*). To this is added a graduated family allowance paid to all employees and a regional allowance. Teachers in Paris receive half the cost of the monthly season ticket.

Post-related increases

A teacher may be called upon to teach for two hours in addition to the contractual minimum if the interests of the service require it. Overtime is payable for teaching in excess of fifteen periods (*agrégé*), eighteen periods (*certifié*) or twenty-six periods (*PLP*). Teachers of physical education or art teach for an additional two periods. For each hour's additional teaching per week, there are supplements according to the category to which the teacher belongs.

Since participation in class councils to discuss pupils' work and consultations with colleagues have been defined as basic responsibilities, the supplements formerly paid for these activities have been incorporated into the revised salary scales.

Performance-related elements

A teacher's performance can increase her income by enhancing her progress up the incremental scale or by enabling her to transfer to the *hors classe* scale. The rate at which increments become payable varies according to the corps to which a teacher belongs, to the career stage and to individual performance. Rapid progress is possible in the early years, to encourage graduates into the profession. Subsequent progress is made at three rates: *grand choix*, *petit choix* and *l'ancienneté*, which are linked to performance. Each year, the headteacher appraises all her staff and notifies them of their grade. Teachers are placed in rank order and classified as *grand choix*, *petit choix* or *ancienneté*. The *grand choix* (maximum 30 per cent of total staff) and *petit choix* taken together may not exceed 71 per cent of the total.

Once a teacher has reached increment 7, she can be recommended for transfer to the *hors classe* scale, on the basis of experience and performance. Only 15 per cent of the teachers are admitted to this scale at any one time but the effect of retirements means that the majority of teachers may expect to progress to this scale at some time during their career.

Career development and promotion prospects

Teachers are entitled to apply for leave to undertake in-service training, to upgrade their existing qualifications or to take a conversion course for a different discipline. The *congé mobilité* provisions allow teachers to undertake one year's paid study in preparation for a public service *concours* in education or for employment outside teaching.

Teachers may progress to a higher category of teacher by means of the internal *concours* which provides a privileged route to public sector appointments for those already in the public service. One of the main objectives is to enable holders of the *CAPEGC* (a non-graduate qualification for secondary teachers) to upgrade their qualification to the level of the *CAPES*.

Profession professeur highlights the following career opportunities, most of which are achieved by means of a further *concours:*

1 promotion to deputy head or headteacher
2 teaching at university level
3 secondment to a teaching post overseas, or to administrative, research and documentation posts
4 appointment to the local inspectorate
5 appointment to a post in the Ministry of Education or in one of the national bodies specializing in educational research, information and documentation or comparative education.

Future developments

New university-based initial teacher training at *Instituts Universitaires de Formation des Maîtres*, piloted in 1990, will be generally introduced in 1991. Although differentiated training will lead to specialized qualifications for the primary or secondary sector, teachers will enjoy parity of salary. The introduction of a unified salary scale raises the salary and status of primary teacher salaries to that of certificated secondary teachers, although primary school teachers will teach for longer hours than their secondary counterparts. The grade of *agrégé* will remain unaffected. Secondary school teacher unions have perceived this loss of differential as a reduction in the status of their members. The wider consequences remain to be seen, but it is at least possible that potential secondary teachers, seeing no financial disadvantage, may opt for the primary phase instead. One contributory factor may be the fact that primary teachers may be redeployed only within the *département*, while secondary school teachers could be redeployed anywhere within the country.

CONCLUSION

The salary, status and conditions of teachers reflect their qualifications and consequently the age of the pupils they teach. Those who teach academic subjects to the upper secondary age group enjoy greater prestige than both teachers of technical and vocational subjects, irrespective of pupil age, and primary school teachers. The outstanding exception to this rule applies to teachers in the vocational secondary schools (*Berufsschule*) in Germany, whose training and salary equal those of the grammar school teachers.

The incorporation of all teachers into a single scale as in England and Wales appears to reduce the wide salary ranges common in other countries. The new salary arrangements in France perpetuate the status of the *agrégé*. However, secondary school teachers fear that the considerable enhancement of primary teacher salaries will be at their expense.

Although the trend towards accountability in education is growing throughout Europe, there is little evidence of performance-related pay other than that resulting from promotion to a more senior post or scale.

NOTE

While the provisions in this chapter apply equally to men and women teachers, for convenience of reading and given the preponderance of female teachers in most countries, the terms she/her/hers have been used throughout.

REFERENCES

Le Métais, J. (1991a) *Initial Teacher Training in the European Community* Slough: EPIC Europe/NFER.
—— (1991b) *The Recruitment and Management of Teachers in the European Community*, Slough: EPIC Europe/NFER.
Ministère de l'éducation nationale (1989) *Profession professeur*, Paris: Ministère de l'éducation nationale.

Chapter 3

Performance-related pay for teachers
The American experience[1]

Stephen L. Jacobson

In 1983 a series of reports critical of the state of education in the USA, the most notable being *A Nation At Risk*, the report of the National Commission on Excellence in Education, triggered what has come to be known as the 'first wave' of American educational reform.[2] There was consensus among these reports that reforming teacher compensation was central to school improvement. Specifically, the reports urged that teacher salaries, particularly at the entry-level, must become more competitive with those offered in other professions if public education were to attract and retain high calibre individuals. Boyer, for example, argued:

> Our society pays for what it values. Unless teacher salaries become more commensurate with those of other professions, teacher status cannot be raised; able students cannot be recruited.
> (Boyer 1983: 168)

Of the various compensation reforms proposed, performance-related pay, more commonly known as 'merit pay' in the USA, stirred the most heated debate. These proposals explicitly linked salary differentials to performance, even though there was only limited empirical support for the premise that monetary incentives effectively motivate teachers to improve the quality of their work. Although some argue that teachers are no different from workers in other occupations where money has been used effectively as an incentive (Casey 1979), the weight of the evidence suggests that teachers are motivated more by the content and process of their work than by the opportunity for extra compensation (Goodlad 1983; Johnson 1984; 1986).

Advocates of performance-related pay, such as former President Ronald Reagan, argued that schools would improve only if teachers were 'paid and promoted on the basis of their merit and competence'.[3] Opponents countered that merit pay plans were nothing new to American education, and that this approach to teacher compensation has a well-documented history of failure (Cohen and Murnane 1985; Lipsky and Bacharach 1983; Urban 1985). As Murnane and Cohen (1985: 3) observed, 'The history of merit pay suggests that while interest in paying teachers according to merit endures, attempts to use merit pay do not'.

The purpose of this chapter is to examine the major issues and problems surrounding the use of performance-related pay as drawn from the American experience. The chapter begins with a conceptual analysis of merit pay that is informed by perspectives from industrial psychology and labour economics. Next follows a brief history of the use of performance-related pay in American education, as well as a working definition of merit pay in its contemporary context. Central to this discussion is a typology of performance criteria used to identify meritorious teaching, a typology developed originally by Monk and Jacobson (1985a). As we shall see, merit pay in the USA has become a catch-all designation for a variety of compensation plans that use differing performance criteria to determine teacher salary differentials.

THEORETICAL PERSPECTIVES ON PERFORMANCE-RELATED PAY

Johnson (1984: 176) pointed out that the revival of interest in performance-related teacher pay in the USA had broad appeal among the American public because it appeared to fit neatly with popular conceptions of how a free enterprise system ought to work. Specifically

> If teachers are paid competitively on the basis of performance, they will work harder. The system will reward effective teachers and encourage them to remain in classrooms while nudging ineffective, unrewarded teachers to leave.

The apparent simplicity of how performance-related pay works belies a rather complex set of relationships that exists between teacher behaviour and the availability of rewards. These conceptual underpinnings are perhaps best explained by Vroom's Expectancy Theory (1964).

Expectancy theory

Vroom's model of employee motivation describes the processes that link behaviours to rewards and suggests that performance can be influenced positively by monetary incentives only if the following conditions exist:

1. Workers have a high expectancy that meritorious performance can be achieved through increased effort.
2. Workers believe that a high instrumentality exists between meritorious performance and the likelihood of reward.
3. Workers find monetary rewards attractive.

Advocates of performance-related pay for teachers assume implicitly the existence of the first and third conditions, that is that meritorious teaching can be achieved through increased effort, and teachers find monetary rewards highly attractive. Once a highly instrumental relationship between superior performance and increased monetary rewards has been established, merit pay proponents predict that teachers will increase their efforts, and thereby improve their performance, in order to obtain these highly desired rewards. One might argue as well that, if these conditions hold, unless performance is rewarded monetarily teachers will withhold their effort. This argument represents the fundamental criticism of compensation plans that do not reward performance directly.

Yet one can use the expectancy approach to provide alternative explanations for why teachers might withhold effort, even when instrumentality between performance and monetary reward is high. Specifically, Vroom's theory suggests that on-the-job experience provides individuals the opportunity to re-evaluate their subjective estimates of the relationship between effort and performance. If, for example, teachers come to believe that certain conditions of school employment, such as overcrowded classes, limited or outdated materials, misdirected curricula goals, prevent the translation of increased effort into improved performance, then the motivation to raise one's level of effort will diminish. Thus, even if the instrumentality between performance and reward is high, the *sine qua non* of performance-related pay, it is conceivable that if teachers' expectations are that increased effort does not result in improved performance, low expectancy will cause teachers to withhold effort.

An alternative explanation for why high instrumentality between performance and reward need not increase effort has to do with the relative attractiveness of money as an incentive. If money is not the primary motivator of teacher behaviour, as merit pay advocates assume, then the expectancy approach would predict little change in teacher effort. In other words, people should not be expected to work harder for rewards they do not find especially attractive. This issue is examined in greater detail later in the chapter in the section on Herzberg's two-factor theory.

Equity theory

Advocates of performance-related pay also use compensatory fairness or equity as a rationale for their proposals. Equity theory advances the notion that fairness in compensation exists when employees believe that 'what is' is 'what should be'.[4] Stated another way, workers believe that their pay is fair when equals are rewarded equally, and unequals are rewarded unequally. Advocates of performance-related pay in the USA contend that meritorious teachers are dissatisfied with the uniform salary schedules that predominate in US schools because teachers identical in experience and education are paid the same regardless of differences in performance. In other words, in some cases the uniform salary schedule allows unequal effort to yield equal reward, and in others, equal effort to yield unequal reward such as when teachers equally meritorious are nevertheless compensated differentially because of differences in experience and education. This is seen to be particularly troublesome to high-calibre junior faculty members, who are often paid substantially less than senior colleagues who may not perform as well.

Supporters of performance-related pay argue that these inequities, inherent in uniform salary schedules, drive good teachers from the profession, encourage poor ones to remain, and discourage high-quality individuals from entering. Making salary performance-based, advocates argue, will drive poor teachers from the profession, since teaching will no longer be financially rewarding for them, and encourage high-quality teachers to enter and remain, since teaching will now equitably reward their efforts. Yet the strength of this position, as with the expectancy approach, depends upon how central monetary incentives are to teacher behaviour. Are teachers primarily motivated by money?

The two-factor approach

Perhaps the best-known theory of employee motivation is Herzberg's two-factor approach (1966) which suggests that worker behaviour is influenced by two categories of rewards: motivators and hygiene factors. Herzberg defines motivators as rewards intrinsic to the content of one's work; rewards that stimulate psychological growth, a necessary precondition for job satisfaction and enhanced performance. These intrinsic motivators include achievement, recognition, responsibility, advancement and the work itself.

Hygiene factors, on the other hand, are rewards extrinsic to the content of work, and act not as a curative, but rather as a preventive. In other words, improving hygiene factors, such as salary, may help to reduce job dissatisfaction by making the conditions of work less unpleasant, but because these rewards do not promote psychological growth, Herzberg contends they will have little effect on increasing effort. Therefore, while pay incentives may prevent job dissatisfaction, they cannot be used to improve performance. Instead, Herzberg's work suggests that policy-makers wishing to improve teacher performance should be less concerned with salary and more attentive to making intrinsic rewards available. Indeed, when teachers have been asked to self-report their reward preferences, they typically focus on teaching's intrinsic benefits. For example, Lortie (1975) found that the most frequently reported attractors to teaching were the opportunity to work with children and the belief that teachers provide an important service to society. Although Lortie recognized that normative expectations of teachers as dedicated professionals may inhibit their acknowledging the extent to which material benefits influence behaviour, intrinsic rewards consistently rank higher than monetary gain in teacher opinion surveys (Feistritzer 1986). In fact, studies of the effects of extrinsic rewards on motivation suggest that pay incentives could even undermine performance if money becomes more important than the content of the work itself (Deci 1976). In other words, teachers might begin looking for self-serving, opportunistic ways of obtaining rewards with a minimum of effort.

It is important to note that while the two-factor approach suggests that pay incentives do not motivate improved performance, there is a growing body of empirical evidence to support the notion that monetary rewards can play an important role in improving teacher recruitment, retention, and attendance (Monk and Jacobson 1985b; Jacobson 1988; 1989a; 1989b; 1990; 1991). In other words, money may influence the participation of high-quality individuals in teaching, but not their level of engagement.

A very different perspective on performance-related pay, one that focuses as much on the organization as on the individual, is provided by a branch of micro-economics that Murnane and Cohen (1985) call the contracts literature.

The contracts literature

This suggests that an organization's approach to compensation should depend upon the nature of the work required of its employees. The usefulness of the contracts literature is that it stresses the importance of organizational trade-offs between the benefits of employee performance gains and the costs of performance evaluations. This benefit-cost analysis is based on three assumptions

1 Workers' preferences are not completely consonant with the employing organization's goals. If there are no adverse consequences for them, workers prefer to work less hard than the organization would like.
2 Monitoring the output of individual workers or the actions of individual workers is costly.
3 Imperfect monitoring will induce workers to attempt behaviour that makes them appear productive relative to other workers, but in fact is contrary to the goals of the organization.

(Murnane and Cohen 1985: 3–4)

Applied to pay incentive plans in education, the contracts literature focuses on the criteria used for performance evaluation. Murnane and Cohen suggest that performance-related pay plans that reward teachers on the basis of student gains on standardized tests are analogous to piece-rate compensation, that is a payment algorithm that attaches a unit price to each unit of performance output measured. Murnane and Cohen contend that piece-rate compensation works best in industries where a worker's output can be measured easily and at low cost, such as the number of shirts ironed by a laundress.

Murnane and Cohen suggest that the benefit of piece-rate compensation is that it provides workers with incentives to find new ways to increase production, while the cost of piece-rate compensation is that these new production methods can include opportunistic behaviours, such as neglect of machinery, as employees reallocate their time in an attempt to increase output. Applied to teaching, opportunistic teachers desirous of performance incentives may choose to attend only to cognitive aspects of student performance, while ignoring students' affective needs. Murnane and Cohen feel that teaching does not satisfy the conditions under which piece-rate compensation works most effectively, and they suggest that performance-related pay based on standardized test scores will tend to narrow the curriculum to only those subjects tested. Even without a direct tie to salary, test scores used to determine school performance substantially shift the focus of administrators and teachers, as Corbett and Wilson (1989) found in Maryland and Pennsylvania:

> Most of their professional time became devoted to test-related activities, to the exclusion of other staff development and improvement initiatives.
> The test becomes foremost in at least the minds of the staff. The end result is that the major emphasis in the school becomes to improve the next set of scores rather than some longer-term, more general goal of improving student learning. Thus, the indicator of performance becomes the goal itself.
> (Corbett and Wilson 1989: 36–7)

The contracts literature further suggests that, due to their inherent vagueness and subjectivity, performance-related pay plans that reward on the basis of classroom evaluations will fare no better than plans that reward student outcomes. Murnane and Cohen (1985) suggest that:

> Merit pay is efficient when the nature of the activity in which workers are engaged is such that supervisors can provide relatively convincing answers to the following two questions posed by workers:
>
> 1 Why does worker X get merit pay and I don't?
> 2 What can I do to get merit pay?
> (Murnane and Cohen 1985: 11–12)

The imprecise nature of teaching makes these questions difficult for supervisors to answer and produces a number of dysfunctional side-effects including

1 teachers who become angry when supervisors cannot identify specific actions that will result in meritorious performance
2 teachers who are unwilling to discuss classroom problems for fear that they will hurt their chance for merit
3 teachers who are dissatisfied with their evaluation, since teachers typically rate their own performance higher than do their supervisors
4 disagreement over whether the best teacher or the teacher whose performance is the most improved should be rewarded.

Murnane and Cohen (1985: 16) argue that performance-related pay plans that reward teacher evaluations lower faculty morale and change the principal or headteacher's role from 'being a coach into being a referee'.

Unlike the expectancy, equity, or two-factor theories, in which the success or failure of performance-related pay plans are seen to depend upon the perceptions of individuals, the contracts literature indicates that these plans are inappropriate in public education because they are simply too costly. Whatever gains are realized in terms of improved performance are quickly lost as a result of the dysfunctional consequences to teacher morale. Murnane and Cohen conclude that the goal of putting the power of money into improving teachers' performance is misguided.

THE HISTORY OF PERFORMANCE-RELATED PAY IN THE USA

Recent interest in performance-related pay belies the fact that monetary incentive plans have been used frequently in the USA over the past century (Urban 1985). The use of performance-related pay appears to have peaked during the early 1920s when perhaps as many as 40 per cent to 50 per cent of the USA's school districts had so-called 'merit' plans in effect. But, during the 1930s, performance-related pay slowly gave way to the uniform salary schedule, due, in part, to the fact that merit was more often determined by a teacher's sex and/or level of instruction than by level of performance.

The crisis in US education spawned by the Soviet Union's successful launching of Sputnik in the late 1950s renewed public interest in compensating teachers on the basis of their performance. As a result of this interest, 11.3 per cent of US school districts with student enrolment greater than 6,000 had performance-related pay plans by 1968. But, once again, these plans were abandoned as unworkable, with difficulties in measuring performance and teacher union opposition commonly cited as the principal reasons for their failure (Bacharach et al. 1984). Porwoll (1979) found that in 1978, only 4 per cent of US school districts still had a performance-related pay plan in effect. By 1979, only 33 of the USA's largest public school districts (districts serving communities with a population greater than 30,000), had performance-related pay in operation, down 80 per cent from 170 districts in 1959 (Porwoll 1979). Even in private schools, where union opposition would typically be less of a factor, the National Catholic Education Association (1985) found that pay incentive plans were the exception rather than the rule, with only 7 per cent of Catholic high schools using merit pay in 1983.

By 1985 over 99 per cent of US teachers were employed in school districts that utilized uniform salary schedules. In fact, that same year, Murnane and Cohen (1985) could identify only seven districts in the USA with student enrolment of more than 10,000 that had both used performance-related pay for at least five years, and also paid awards of at least $1,000. These surviving plans existed in wealthy districts that were able to hire teachers selectively, pay them well, and provide excellent working conditions. Two characteristics typical of these surviving programmes were that merit awards were given inconspicuously and every teacher received an award of some size. Although inconspicuous awards distributed among all staff may reduce competition and make everyone feel special, these are hardly the programme characteristics performance-related pay advocates envision. Indeed, Murnane and Cohen note that the merit pay plans in these districts do not appear to have an effect on the way teachers teach.

OPERATIONALIZING PERFORMANCE-RELATED PAY

Under a 'pure' performance-related pay system, teachers' salary differentials would be determined exclusively on the basis of differences in their performance. Recognizing that teacher union opposition makes the prospects of totally dismantling uniform schedules highly unlikely, recent proposals in the USA have recommended pay incentives that would supplement, rather than supplant, existing salary schedules. Thus merit pay in the USA means awards over and above those provided by the uniform schedule, and though other incentives, such as sabbaticals, tuition assistance and/or attendance at professional conferences can be offered, merit pay awards usually take one of two forms: a temporary salary increase that is a once per year bonus for which a teacher competes on an annual basis, or a permanent salary increase, that is a monetary award that, once earned, becomes part of the teacher's base salary, regardless of subsequent performance.

Merit pay awards are usually used to recognize individual achievement, although they can also be presented in recognition of meritorious performance by an entire instructional unit. By shifting pay incentives from the individual to the instructional team, group incentives are intended to reduce teacher competition, a factor often cited as a detriment to school improvement.

The next question that schools must address is how meritorious performance is to be identified and measured. This is a question that is not easily answered and one which goes to the heart of most problems with performance-related pay plans.

What counts as meritorious performance?

A thread common to almost all performance-related pay proposals in the USA is the belief that teachers' salaries should reflect their contribution to the educational enterprise. Unfortunately, there is considerable disagreement among proposals as to what legitimately counts as merit. As Monk and Jacobson observed

> Some writers use the term 'merit pay' but disagree over how merit should be assessed. Others eschew the use of the term, but nevertheless propose what amounts to a plan of differentiated payment based on an assessment of teachers' contributions.
>
> (Monk and Jacobson 1985a: 223)

Although the presage criteria used by uniform schedules may be objectionable to merit pay advocates, years of experience and educational training are easy to measure. Furthermore, as Lipsky and Bacharach (1983: 7) note, 'the selection of performance criteria for use in merit-pay plans is a process fraught with peril'.

To address this issue, Monk and Jacobson developed a typology of performance criteria recommended by 'first wave' US merit pay proposals as contributions worthy of additional remuneration. These performance criteria include

1 quantity of work
2 level of efficiency
3 teacher effectiveness or level of accomplishment
4 the importance of the accomplishment.

The quantity of a teacher's work

Among the most commonly recommended monetary rewards in 'first wave' proposals were salary add-ons based upon some measure of the quantity of an individual's work. For example, in 1983 Tennessee's 'Master' teachers had the opportunity to accept ten, eleven or twelve month contracts that provided 15 per cent, 35 per cent, and 60 per cent pay supplements respectively (Stedman 1983). Although extra pay for extra work incentives hardly represent a departure from traditional compensation practice, Murnane and Cohen (1985) found that the opportunity for these rewards was characteristic of the few enduring merit pay plans in the USA. These authors suggest that the success of this approach is that it allows teachers with additional financial needs the opportunity to meet those needs. Yet the potential effectiveness of extra pay for extra work incentives, particularly those offered as contract extensions, may be of limited use since most (79 per cent) public school teachers in the USA would rather teach ten months than twelve months, even if there were the opportunity for other professional activities (Feistritzer 1986).

A variation on the quantity of work theme is the use of pay incentives to reduce rates of teacher absenteeism. A number of school districts in Western New York have used salary bonuses to reward teachers with exemplary attendance (Jacobson 1989a; 1989b; 1991).

The level of teacher efficiency

Some times called 'old style' plans (Bhaerman 1973), this approach ties teacher salary to supervisor observations. As Monk and Jacobson (1985a) contend

> This input-based approach to the measurement of teacher efficiency has gained widespread use in American education.

> Much of what now passes for teacher evaluation relies heavily on the use of periodic classroom observation.
>
> (Monk and Jacobson 1985a: 226)

Note that the efficiency approach assumes positive correlations between identifiable teacher behaviours and levels of student achievement. Checklists of teacher behaviours often include classroom organization and management, in-service growth, professional attitude, school community service, and even personal fitness and appearance. This approach is often criticized as stifling creativity since teachers are under considerable pressure to conform to supervisors' perceptions of good teaching. For example, if their supervisor emphasizes discipline, teachers may feel that they have to be more attentive to keeping students seated and silent than to what they learn.

While substantive questions can be raised as to which teacher behaviours, if any, are significantly related to student achievement, one must recognize that, even if such questions could be resolved, performance-related pay plans based upon evaluations are rewarding the potential rather than the accomplishment of high student achievement.

Teacher effectiveness or the level of accomplishment

Whereas 'old style' merit pay as efficiency rewards the process of teaching, 'new style' merit pay as effectiveness rewards the product: teacher performance is evaluated by the level of student accomplishment on standardized tests. As Murnane and Cohen (1985) observed

> The attractiveness of this strategy is that the evaluation problem is solved by actually measuring certain dimensions of each teacher's output, and thereby avoiding the subjectivity of the evaluations under old style merit pay.
>
> (Murnane and Cohen 1985: 5)

Although performance-related pay based upon level of accomplishment is arguably less subjective than performance as efficiency, the use of student outcomes is often criticized because of the difficulty inherent in disentangling an individual teacher's contribution to a child's achievement from other influential factors such as the contextual effects of other students in the classroom and the socio-economic status of the child's family.

As noted earlier in the contracts literature discussion, a common criticism of this 'new style' approach is that it may foster opportunistic behaviour, such as encouraging teachers to teach exclusively to the test or focus only on those students they believe will do well on the test.

The importance of the accomplishment

This approach rewards salary differentially on the basis of differences in the market values of teachers' duties and responsibilities. Monk and Jacobson (1985a) point out

> The teacher need not work harder, may not be more efficient, and need not accomplish more. The relevant points are that (1) the teacher makes a different contribution, and (2) the market value of the various possible contributions can vary.
> (Monk and Jacobson 1985a: 227)

The teacher career ladder, which can be viewed as a variation on the performance-related pay theme, falls under this dimension. Career ladders are compensation systems that create a staged profession in which an individual proceeds from an apprentice to a master. Applied to education, as teachers move up the career ladder their professional responsibilities and compensatory rewards increase.

Although career ladders became the hallmark recommendations of such 1986 'second wave' reports as those by the Holmes Group (1986) and the Carnegie Forum on Education and Economy (1986) the Congressional Merit Pay Task Force developed the following 'model' teacher career ladder in 1983:

- *Apprentice teacher* an individual with a degree from an accredited institution of higher education, who has met all state requirements for initial certification could begin teaching at $15,000
- *Professional teacher* a fully certified teacher with five years' experience, some in-service training or post-graduate course work, and at least four positive annual evaluations, would receive a base fifth-year salary of $20,000
- *Senior teacher* a certified Professional teacher with a Master's

degree in his or her area of concentration, and at least eight out of ten positive annual evaluations, would receive a base tenth-year salary of $30,000
- *Master teacher* a certified Senior teacher with additional study beyond the Master's degree and more than ten years of consistently positive evaluations, who has demonstrated 'best practice' and is willing to accept in-service or summer training responsibility for other teachers, would receive $35,000 and a minimum $10,000 annual bonus for continuing positive evaluations and in-service contribution.

(US House of Representatives 1983)

Scarcity bonuses also fall under the heading of pay incentive plans that reward the importance of an accomplishment. For example, differential pay may be offered teachers in subject areas where shortages exist, such as mathematics or science, or so-called 'combat' pay to teachers willing to work in less desirable schools, such as those that serve large numbers of disadvantaged students.

Rewarding the importance rather than the level of an accomplishment is criticized for being less an attempt to make salaries performance-based than market-sensitive. As a result, if there were a greater supply of history than physics teachers, this approach would allow a mediocre physics teacher to be paid more than an excellent history teacher. This is hardly the outcome that US proponents of performance-related pay envisaged.

In order to overcome potential problems created by any one of the reward categories listed above, some performance-related pay plans have taken to incorporating multiple performance criteria. Houston's Second Mile Plan, for example, offered the following incentives in 1982:

1 *Outstanding educational progress* $800 per teacher in schools that exceed predicted gains on standardized achievement tests
2 *High-priority location* as much as $2,000 per teacher willing to work in schools that have a high concentration of educationally disadvantaged students
3 *Critical shortage* bonuses for teachers of subjects where shortages exist, e.g. $800 for mathematics or science, $600–900 for special education, and as much as $1,000 for bilingual education
4 *Professional growth* $300 for each six credits of college coursework (or seventy-two hours of in-service training) related to a teacher's area of instruction

5 *Attendance* $100 per day for unused absences up to five, thus a teacher with perfect attendance earns an additional $500.

(Miller and Say 1982)

PERFORMANCE-RELATED PAY IN PRACTICE

With all the public attention given to merit pay at the time of the 1983 reform reports, surprisingly few US teachers were subsequently compensated in this manner. In a nation-wide survey of public and private school teachers in 1987–8, the National Center for Educational Statistics of the US Department of Education (NCES 1990) found that of the USA's more than 2 million public school teachers only 2 per cent received individual pay awards for exceptional performance and 3 per cent received group awards for school-wide performance improvement. An additional 2 per cent received scarcity bonuses: 1 per cent for teaching in a shortage area and 1 per cent for teaching in a high-priority location. Data from private school teachers (just over 300,000 nation-wide) suggest only slightly more reliance on performance-related pay with just 4 per cent receiving individual awards for exceptional performance, 4 per cent group awards for school-wide improvement, and 3 per cent scarcity bonuses: 2 per cent for shortage areas and 1 per cent for high-priority location.

These findings suggest that, in practice, the notion of awarding teachers for exceptional performance, as promoted by 'first wave' merit pay advocates, appears not to have gained much of a foothold in the USA. On the other hand, findings from the same survey indicate that the 'second wave' reforms of the Holmes Group (1986) and the Carnegie Forum on Education and Economy (1986) have been implemented more broadly. Specifically, these reports recommended the use of career ladders to expand teachers' responsibilities to include mentor and master teacher roles. The NCES (1990) survey revealed that in 1987–8, 9 per cent of public school teachers had been rewarded for serving as a master or mentor teacher and 16 per cent had received a career ladder salary increase, while 7 per cent of private school teachers had received an award for serving as a master or mentor teacher and 14 per cent had received a career ladder salary increase.

By expanding the role of teachers, particularly in terms of decision-making, these recommendations were more consonant with the underlying tenets of the two-factor approach than were proposals of the 'first wave'. They intentionally broaden the scope of compensation reform to include the motivating effects of intrinsic benefits. In *A Nation Prepared: Teachers for the 21st Century* (Carnegie 1986), the Carnegie Task Force was quite explicit in addressing these intrinsic needs:

> Giving teachers a greater voice in the decisions that affect the school will make teaching more attractive to good teachers who are already in our schools as well as people considering teaching as a career.
>
> (Carnegie 1986: 24)

In order to accomplish this, the Carnegie Task Force called for the creation of a cadre of Lead teachers within each school that would be responsible for setting school-wide performance criteria, developing curriculum, and even hiring and dismissing personnel. This restructuring of teachers' roles would enable individuals to advance in the profession without having to move out of the classroom. And, while the Lead teacher concept recognizes the motivational potential of giving teachers the opportunity to translate insights acquired through experience into educational policy, the Carnegie report also recognized the importance of pecuniary rewards, noting that 'higher teacher pay is an absolute prerequisite to attracting and keeping the people we want in teaching'. Under a hypothetical salary structure designed by the Carnegie Task Force, Lead teachers would earn as much as $72,000 per year, a salary level now available to a select group of outstanding Lead teachers in Rochester, New York.

While there is evidence to suggest that career ladders and job expansion are more likely to be successful than merit pay plans (Astuto 1985; Malen *et al.* 1988), career ladders are not without problems themselves. MacPhail-Wilcox and King (1988: 111), for example, found that in some districts 'career ladders can breed suspicion, aggressive and circumventing behaviors and strikes'. The key issue, once again, appears to be the criteria upon which movement up the ladder and increased salary are based. The more the plans reward subjective assessments of performance, the more difficulty they encounter. The more that the plans reward role differentiation and increased responsibility, the more acceptable they appear to be and the greater their likelihood of success.

CONCLUSIONS

In this chapter, performance-related pay was examined from a variety of theoretical perspectives that focused on both the individual and the organization. The central premise of performance related pay – that pecuniary rewards can effectively motivate teachers to improve their performance – is based upon the assumption that teachers are primarily motivated by money. Yet the theoretical underpinnings of teacher motivation suggest that the quality of teacher performance is more a function of intrinsic reward than salary. Therefore, increased recognition and responsibility may do more to promote enhanced performance than do increases in pay. But even if teachers were motivated primarily by money, performance-related pay would still be inappropriate because teaching does not satisfy the production conditions under which this type of piece-rate compensation works most effectively. The products of teaching are not easily tallied in a ledger. Focusing only on those products that can be quantified may result in opportunistic behaviour, the cost of which can easily override potential gains in performance. Due to teaching's imprecise nature, focusing instead on classroom evaluations may also produce dysfunctional effects such as adversarial relationships between teachers and supervisors. Indeed, pay differentials based on inherently subjective evaluations could ultimately produce inequities as egregious as those found under the uniform salary schedule.

Examining performance-related pay in practice revealed that it has been more a subject of debate than a reality in the USA. Pure systems are non-existent and the characteristics of the few supplemental merit plans that do exist hardly exemplify the vision of performance-related pay advocates. Difficulties in measuring performance accounted for the demise of most plans, yet there is little to suggest any less confusion in identifying meritorious teachers now than in the past. Indeed, common performance criteria suggest that meritorious teaching means different things to different people.

Although there is little to encourage the belief that performance-related pay plans can effectively improve teacher performance, advocates of merit pay in the USA are probably correct when they argue that the US public would be more willing to support higher teacher salaries if salary increases were somehow pegged to improved student performance. This quid pro quo virtually assures continuing interest in performance-related pay schemes. Yet performance-related pay in the 1990s will probably be very different than merit pay in the 1920s and 1960s. A restructured profession through the use of career ladders may well be the predominant mechanism. Teacher productivity as measured by student performance will probably represent only one part of an overall teacher compensation algorithm, and productivity would be measured by school-wide student performance, thus providing group rather than individual rewards. Other factors that will likely be used to differentiate teacher salaries include level of certification, job function and seniority. Under proposed and existing career ladders, teachers progress through a sequence of stages, some requiring advanced certification, but at each new level teachers assume new job functions and responsibilities, with salaries increased accordingly and additional increments accrued through seniority.

Another factor that will undoubtedly foster continued interest in performance-related teacher pay is a growing movement in the USA towards greater school choice for parents. It is argued that educators will become far more attentive to programme quality if schools are forced to compete among themselves for students and the fiscal resources they bring with them. Since exceptional teachers are often viewed as the glue that holds good programmes together, schools with high-quality faculties will be magnets for parents seeking to get the most for their educational dollars. Making schools market-sensitive may allow teachers to capitalize on their reputations in a manner that is simply not possible in the present context. Pushing this scenario a bit, one might envision 'star' teachers, that is teachers who can attract students to the schools in which they work, negotiating incentives into their contracts that would pay off on the basis of enrolment. In the USA, where astronomical salaries are paid to box office stars in the worlds of sport and entertainment, teachers might come to view performance-related pay as a form of educational free agency.

NOTES

1 An earlier version of this chapter, entitled 'Merit pay incentives in teaching,' appeared in L. Weis, P. G. Altbach, G. P. Kelly, H. G. Petrie and S. Slaughter (eds) (1989) *Crisis in Teaching*, Albany,: State University of New York Press. The present chapter is printed by permission of the State University of New York Press.
2 Among other 'first wave' reports were E. Boyer (1983) *High School: A*

Report on Secondary Education in America, New York: Harper & Row; Task Force on Education for Economic Growth (1983) *Action for Excellence*, Denver Col.: Education Commission of the States; C. E. Feistritzer (1983) *The Condition of Teaching*, New York: Carnegie Foundation; J. Goodlad (1983) *A Place Called School*, New York: McGraw-Hill; National Science Board Commission on Precollege Education in Mathematics (1983) *Educating Americans for the 21st Century*, Washington, DC: National Science Foundation; T. R. Sizer (1983) *Horace's Compromise*, New York: McGraw-Hill; Task Force on Federal Elementary and Secondary Education Policy (1983) *Making the Grade*, New York: Twentieth Century Fund.
3 Speech at Seton Hall University, South Orange, NJ, May 1983, reported in S. M. Johnson (1984) Merit pay for teachers: a poor prescription for reform, *Harvard Educational Review* 54 (May): 175.
4 For a more complete elaboration of Equity Theory, see J. S. Adams, 'Injustice in social exchange, in L. Berkowitz (ed.) *Advances in Experimental SocialPsychology*, vol. 2, (1965) New York: Academic Press; or K. E. Weick (1966) *Equity and the perception of pay*, Administrative Science Quarterly 11: 415–18.

REFERENCES

Adams, J. (1965) Injustice in social exchange, in L. Berkowitz (ed.) *Advances in Experimental Social Psychology*, vol. 2, New York: Academic Press.

Astuto, T. (1985) *Merit Pay for Teachers: An Analysis of State Policy Options*, Educational Policy Studies Series, Bloomington, Ind: Indiana University.

Bacharach, S., Lipsky, D and Shedd, J. (1984) *Paying for Better Teachers: Merit Pay and its Alternatives*, Ithaca, NY: Organizational Analysis and Practice.

Bhaerman, R. (1973) 'Merit pay? No!', *National Elementary Principal* 52: 63–9.

Boyer, E. (1983) *High School: A Report on Secondary Education in America*, New York: Harper & Row.

Carnegie (1986) *A Nation Prepared: Teachers for the 21st Century*, New York: Carnegie Forum on Education and Economy.

Casey, W. (1979) Would Bear Bryant teach in the public schools?, *Phi Delta Kappan* 60: 500–1.

Cohen, D. and Murnane, R. (1985) *The Merits of Merit Pay*, Project Report no. 85-A12, Stanford Education Policy Institute, Palo Alto, Calif: Stanford University.

Corbett, D. and Wilson, B. (1989) Raising the stakes in statewide mandatory minimum competency testing, in J. Hannaway and R. Crowson (eds) *The Politics of Reforming School Administration*, Philadelphia, Pa: Falmer Press.

Deci, E. (1976) The hidden costs of rewards, *Organizational Dynamics* 4: 61–72.

Education Commission of the States (1983) *Action for Excellence*, Denver, Col: ECS.
Feistritzer, E. (1983) *The Condition of Teaching: A State by State Analysis*, New York: Carnegie Foundation.
—— (1986) *Profile of Teachers in the US*, Washington, DC: National Center for Education Information.
Goodlad, J. (1983) *A Place Called School*, New York: McGraw-Hill.
Herzberg, F. (1966) *Work and the Nature of Man*, New York: Crowell Publications.
Holmes Group (1986) *Tomorrow's Teachers*, East Lansing, Mich: Holmes Group.
Jacobson, S. (1988) The distribution of salary increments and its effect on teacher retention, *Educational Administration Quarterly* 24: 178–99.
—— (1989a) The effects of pay incentives on teacher absenteeism, *Journal of Human Resources* 24: 280–6.
—— (1989b) Pay incentives and teacher absence: one district's experience, *Urban Education* 23: 377–91.
—— (1989c) Merit pay incentives in teaching, in L. Weis, P. Altbach, G. Kelly, H. Petrie and S. Slaughter (eds) *Crisis in Teaching*, Albany, NY: SUNY Press.
—— (1990) Change in entry-level salary and the recruitment of novice teachers, *Journal of Education Finance* 15: 408–13.
—— (1991) Attendance incentives and teacher absenteeism, *Planning and Changing* 21: 78–93.
Johnson, S. (1984) Merit pay for teachers: a poor prescription for reform, *Harvard Educational Review* 54: 175–85.
—— (1986) Incentives for teachers: what motivates, what matters, *Educational Administration Quarterly* 22: 54–79.
Lipsky, D and Bacharach, S. (1983) The single salary schedule vs. merit pay, *NEA Research Memo*, Washington, DC: National Education Association.
Lortie, D. (1975) *Schoolteacher: A Sociological Study*, Chicago, Ill: University of Chicago Press.
MacPhail-Wilcox, B. and King, R. (1988) Personnel reforms in education: intents, consequences, and fiscal implications, *Journal of Education Finance* 14: 100–34.
Malen, B., Murphy, M. and Hart, A. (1988) Restructuring teacher compensation systems: an analysis of three incentive strategies, in K. Alexander and D. Monk (eds), *Attracting and Compensating America's Teachers*, Cambridge, Mass: Ballinger.
Miller, L. and Say, E. (1982) This bold incentive pay plan pits capitalism against teacher shortages, *American School Board Journal*: 24–5.
Monk, D. and Jacobson, S. (1985a) Reforming teacher compensation, *Education and Urban Society* 17: 223–36.
—— (1985b) The distribution of salary increments between veteran and novice teachers: evidence from New York State, *Journal of Education Finance* 11: 157–75.
Murnane, R. and Cohen, D. (1985) *Merit Pay and the Evaluation Problem*,

Project Report no. 85 A14, Stanford Education Policy Institute, Palo Alto, Calif: Stanford University.
National Catholic Education Association (1985) *The Catholic High School; A National Portrait*, Washington, DC: NCEA.
National Center for Educational Statistics (1990) *Selected Characteristics of Public and Private School Teachers 1987–88*. Washington, DC: US Department of Education.
National Science Board Commission on Precollege Education in Mathematics (1983) *Educating Americans for the 21st Century*, Washington, DC: National Science Foundation.
Porwoll, P. (1979) *Merit Pay For Teachers*, Arlington, Va: Educational Research Service.
Sizer, T. (1983) *Horace's Compromise*, New York: McGraw-Hill.
Stedman, C. (1983) Tennessee's master plans for teachers, supervisors, and principals, *Journal of Teacher Education* 34: 55–8.
Twentieth Century Fund (1983) *Making the Grade*, New York: Twentieth Century Fund.
US House of Representatives (1983) *Merit Pay Task Force*, Washington, DC: US Government Printing Office.
Urban, W. (1985) Old wine, new bottles? Merit pay and organized teachers, in H. Johnson, Jr (ed.) *Merit, Money and Teachers' Careers*, Lanham, Md: University Press of America.
Vroom, V. (1964) *Work and Motivation*, New York: Wiley.
Weick, K. (1966) Equity and the perception of pay, *Administrative Science Quarterly* 11: 415–18.

Chapter 4

Performance-related pay in the context of performance management

Helen Murlis

Pay systems in the UK have been subject to a revolution during the 1980s. The dominant theme of that revolution has been performance-related pay. The changes, practices and lessons that will be considered in this chapter are, of course, part of a wider change process: the updating and sharpening of British management practice to face the demands of competing in a global market-place. The search for greater clarity and focus over what has to be done to improve both individual and organizational performance has been intensive and this continues. Recognizing and rewarding performance improvements has become accepted as an essential part of this broader picture.

HISTORICAL CONTEXT

Performance-related pay is not a new phenomenon and it certainly did not start with the arrival of the Thatcher government in 1979. In various forms, some no doubt more acceptable than others, the idea goes back to the beginning of paid employment. What distinguishes the systems that have been implemented in the 1980s, and perhaps the more acceptable approaches of earlier years, is the attempt to link pay to a 'rational' basis of performance assessment of some kind. What undoubtedly and deservedly gave performance-related pay a bad name in the past was a lack of judgemental framework, abuse of discretionary managerial power, a 'bias for the blue-eyed boy' and the imposition of systems into environments where there was a fundamental lack of trust between managers and those whose salary progression was in their power. No wonder performance-related pay got a bad name! No wonder too that many attempts to introduce performance-related pay in the early 1980s, and even now in environments where the idea is new, have been met with such fear and mistrust. People who have been subject to arbitrary, unfair and what they sometimes perceived to be punitive 'merit pay' systems take a long time to forgive and try again. Sometimes organizations have to deal with the experience and prejudices of more than one generation at the time they embark upon change. In the academic environment, it is important to be aware that there is a body of older management research that mapped the unfortunate results of old performance-related pay systems, especially shop-floor, payment-by-results systems, spelling out their demotivational effects as a warning to future generations to avoid the divisiveness, unscrupulous manipulation and resentment that these earlier researchers uncovered.

So why, at the beginning of the 1980s, did the UK private sector start on its wholesale move towards performance-related pay? Inevitably, perhaps, the answer lies in top management beliefs and behaviour. For this group in the UK, as in the USA and elsewhere in the developed world, performance-related pay seems an obvious and necessary move. As the group which believes it has ultimate control over profitability and other key measures of corporate success, top executives see every reason to link their own rewards to performance improvements achieved by their organization.

As soon as the voluntary incomes policies of the previous Labour government were overturned in 1979, they started putting this philosophy into practice with the introduction of bottom-line-driven incentive schemes for directors. The pace of implementation was slow at first, but it gathered speed as the recession of the early 1980s eased. Setting themselves more or less stretching targets in terms of measures such as profit before tax, earnings per share growth, return on assets and cash flow, top executives in the private sector engineered the delivery of cash bonuses reflecting the level of their individual and collective achievement. From the timid 10 per cent of basic salary bonus payouts of the early 1980s, more aggressive schemes changed to pay 30 per cent, 50 per cent or even 100 per cent bonuses for exceptional achievement. Not all of these schemes were particularly well designed or run strictly according to the rules of implementation. Some were too simplistic or built round individual targets rather than emphasizing team as well as individual contributions. Some overdelivered or underdelivered payments and some were just too open to manipulation by scheme members: the 'crime' of budgeteering, that is, of fixing targets against measures to maximize payout in a way that does not best serve business interests.

What the best of them achieved, according to evidence collected in a survey by Hay Management Consultants in 1988, was the benefit of a notable change and improvement in the nature of debate at board level as to what in considerable and concrete detail constituted good corporate performance and what strategies and actions were needed to ensure the probability of success. Whatever the realities of executive incentives, those who liked them believed that the principle of distinguishing between good and poor performers and paying accordingly should be extended as far down the organization as possible. For the most part they accepted that they could not expect to achieve this without implementing some form of performance appraisal to provide a sound basis for assessing the level of achievement scheme either as a new initiative or to replace the typically looser appraisal processes then used for staff development purposes.

Such moves were encouraged by the government, the Institute of Directors, the CBI and other management bodies who believe that there is a clear relationship between money and motivation which should feature in pay systems in terms of performance rewards. They believe too that such rewards usefully emphasize personal accountability as well as providing a greater return on organizations' investment in payroll costs.

MANAGEMENT RATIONALE

Many senior managers welcomed these developments because they enabled them to use pay as a management tool and as a means of communication to individual employees on the need continuously to seek performance improvements. They also enabled limited pay increase budgets to be spent more effectively, by focusing payments on the better performers and enabling poor performance to be penalized by lower or even zero payments.

During the 1980s many organizations became both leaner and flatter in shape. Promotion opportunities diminished substantially and the traditional motivational lure of vertical career progression receded and started to lose its gloss. For many organizations performance-related pay therefore also provided a means of rewarding continued good performance in jobs where there were few or no promotion opportunities, not only as a replacement for them, but also to reward people for acquiring and using new skills.

EMPLOYEE DEMAND

Not all of the pressure for performance-related pay has come from management. The perception of equity in employment appears to be changing. Many employees in the 1980s became disgruntled with pay systems based on fixed increments which meant that they were paid the same amount for being in the same job or grade for the same amount of time as their peers regardless of contribution. Some of those in the private sector who had been forced into such systems by the exigencies of incomes policy in the 1970s felt insulted that those whom they perceived as the 'timeservers and shirkers' in their midst could earn as much as those whose effectiveness and commitment had delivered tangible performance improvements. The offer and implementation of pay differentials for better performance in this environment would inevitably have a positive motivational impact. Add to that the prospect of greater clarity and focus on business direction and better trained managers to monitor and appraise performance and develop their people as well as to deliver performance-related rewards and there is considerable appeal. This has been the message in well-communicated performance-related pay schemes in the private sector: it is one that has often been welcomed, even if some organizations' ability to deliver well-managed systems has not always proved as good as the promise.

WHAT KINDS OF PERFORMANCE-RELATED PAY HAVE BEEN IMPLEMENTED?

There are four principal forms of performance-related pay currently in use in the UK: merit pay systems, incentives and bonuses, equity shares, and profit shares. This section deals with each in turn, together with examples of their use and the pros and cons of operating them.

Merit pay systems

By far the most common form of performance-related pay, merit pay systems now cover most managers and specialists in the private sector in the UK as well as increasing numbers of support staff. Incidence of individual merit pay on the shop-floor is also growing, notably in advanced manufacturing environments and among the subsidiaries of Japanese and US parent companies. Merit pay is typically given in the form of an annual increase in basic salary which is consolidated for pension purposes but it can also be given as non-consolidated annual bonuses. More frequent payment, for example every six months, is normally confined to younger employees, those in training schemes and those in areas of market scarcity where, perhaps unwisely in terms of the message this gives, pay movement to meet market movement sometimes gets mixed up with merit-based progression.

The mechanisms for operating merit pay systems change along a continuum from fixed increments which vary in size with performance rating to payments decided by a manager who has total freedom to distribute merit awards from an agreed salary increase budget. The typical payment systems along this continuum are as follows.

Fixed performance-related increments within a salary scale or on a pay spine

This form of merit pay is usually the first move for organizations changing from fixed incremental payment systems. For this reason, it is common in the public sector and among more traditional private sector employers, particularly for clerical and other support staff. Actual payments are typically distributed as:

Performance rating	*Increment(s)*
Outstanding	2
Highly competent	1.5
Competent	1
Developing	0.5
Marginal	0

In these systems annual market and cost-of-living adjustments are typically paid to all staff, often as the result of collective bargaining. The allocation of performance ratings will generally be subject to guidelines which specify the expected proportion of individuals likely to be given each rating. Rigid, forced-choice distributions which allow only, say, 5 per cent of staff to be rated as excellent are still used but have fallen into some disrepute. Most organizations permit some flexibility while monitoring performance ratings carefully for consistency and to ensure sensible cost control. Hard lessons have been learned in this area to which we return later in this chapter.

The main advantage of this approach is its simplicity to explain and operate. It is, however, inflexible, allowing for no fine gradations of performance reward and, unless a merit bar, that is, a salary level above which only good performers can progress, is imposed at some place in a salary scale, all employees, whatever their real contribution, will eventually reach the top.

Variable performance-related increases which reflect service, experience and performance

This approach is based on the belief that it is right to pay higher increases to those who perform well when relatively new to the job. It reflects recognition of the learning curve, which normally rises steeply at the beginning and then tails off. Payments are usually allocated in relation to a merit matrix. Figure 4.1 illustrates this for pay scales that stretch between 80 per cent and 120 per cent of a midpoint and for an overall pay increase budget of 9 per cent which includes annual market movement. Like the first system this approach is normally underpinned by guidelines on the allocation of performance ratings. This method enables some manipulation of the increases in the central squares of the matrix, that is those most commonly used to contain expenditure while recognizing justifiable deviations from the original performance guidelines. Merit matrices have been widely used in many sectors of the UK economy including areas of the public sector such as local government.

Like fixed increments they are relatively easy to explain and operate. The problems come when excellent performers reach the top of scale with no prospect of further merit pay, or when the system is challenged because the learning curve philosophy which underpins it is inappropriate. Properly designed, the system avoids paying less satisfactory performers at the top end of their scale and in fact prevents them from getting there.

Position in range

Performance assessment	80–88%	89–96%	97–104%	105–112%	113–120%
Outstanding 1	18%	15%	13%	11%	9%
Highly competent 2	15%	13%	11%	9%	8%
Competent 3	12%	10%	9%	8%	7%
Developing 4	8%	6%	4%	0%	0%
Marginal 5	0%	0%	0%	0%	0%

Figure 4.1 Salary increase matrix
Note: The figures used in each box of the matrix are for illustrative purposes only, to demonstrate the principles of how the matrix would work. In this example a market movement of 9 per cent has been assumed.

Increases paid in relation to performance rating in addition to market movement

This approach allows considerable management discretion in relation to actual payment levels but still provides a cost-of-living element, often called a general increase, for all staff. It is still commonly used where annual pay negotiations are part of the picture and where the general increase and perhaps even the merit budget are negotiated. Research by Incomes Data Services Top Pay Unit in the ten years since its *Monthly Review of Salaries and Benefits* was first published indicates that, whatever the underlying rate of market movement or inflation, merit budgets have normally been in the range 2.5 – 3.5 per cent of the payroll.

Such systems have proved usable in fairly heavily unionized

environments because, despite the possibility of some performance differentiation – delivering perhaps an extra 8–10 per cent on top of a general increase to the excellent – purchasing power is protected. Their principal disadvantage is that many organizations feel that they do not deliver powerful enough performance messages, especially at more senior levels, and that they prevent more flexible use of payroll budgets. For these reasons the use of this approach has declined markedly in the UK since the mid–1980s in favour of the approach outlined below.

Increases related purely to personal performance

Often called 'merit only' increases, these systems typically provide for increases that range from zero for poor performers up to 15 per cent or even 20 per cent or more for outstanding performers. They are now the norm for most managers and professionals in the private sector. Increases are given generally in relation to guidelines which link amounts to performance ratings, but in a growing number of organizations, managers are left free to award increases as they see fit within a given payroll budget. Even where this freedom is well established, checks for consistency of treatment are normal. In well-run schemes, managers are given annual briefings on the objectives and operation of the system, its values and the messages to employees that need to be put across. Consistency, fairness and the need to make defensible judgements are normal core values alongside the requirement to provide significant rewards for exceptional performance and acceptable rewards that motivate the 60–70 per cent of good, reliable core performers on whom all organizations depend.

The main advantage of this approach is the flexibility it gives to individual managers to reward their staff together with real accountability for the use of pay to reward achievement. The main problems encountered stem from two sources. First, many managers used to having pay decisions made mainly by the personnel function find the freedom hard to get used to. They typically need a lot of guidance and advice in the first and sometimes further years following the introduction of the scheme.

Second, reasonable consistency may be far harder to achieve, especially where strong directors play organization politics to get a disproportionately large merit budget and so look after their own people at the expense of others. The latter is normally a response to severe market pressure which can be controlled by the use of good market monitoring as the basis for developing market responses such as pay supplements which prevent unwanted mixing of performance rewards with market premiums.

INCENTIVES AND BONUSES

Incentive or bonus payments are cash lump sums which are typically paid in addition to merit increases. Although the terms *bonus* and *incentive* tend to be used interchangeably, it is important to be clear that they can have two separate meanings. In its purest definition an incentive is a payment given to recognize the achievement of an agreed and specific target: hard financial targets such as a given profit figure or percentage earnings per share increase, or soft targets such as recruitment of a given number of graduates in a specified mix of specialisms or the creation of a management succession plan. Incentives can be geared to give x per cent of salary for y or z level of target achievement. Good targets are specific, measurable, agreed, realistic and easily trackable by the individuals to whom they apply so that they can work out exactly and without difficulty how their incentive payments are adding up during the year. Increasingly, at top executive levels in the UK, incentives are being set on a longer term basis, often to reinforce the need to achieve a corporate strategic plan that looks three or more years into the future. In this case payments will be in the form of either cash or share options and may be deferred.

Bonuses, by contrast, are usually paid as rewards once success has been achieved and may be discretionary or be relatively unrelated to specific targets. They can be paid annually or be one-off payments designed to reward particular achievements such as completing an important project, for example the implementation of a new computer system, ahead of schedule. Merit bonuses are sometimes used to supplement merit payment systems either as rewards for good performers who have reached the top of their salary scale, or to provide additional rewards without adding to consolidated basic salary costs. Merit bonuses tend, typically, to be of a similar size to the performance-related pay increase that an individual might otherwise have received.

To be effective bonus and incentive payments need to be significant in relation to the level of achievement. It is worth remembering that, in general, people use bonus money in different ways from the money they get as pay increases. A cash injection that pays for a dishwasher, a weekend in Paris or a family holiday will be remembered for what it delivered. If the amount feels derisory after tax has been paid, then it cannot be expected to have much motivational value. Where only a small or relatively small bonus is appropriate, experience suggests that it may be better to go for a non-cash reward. Vouchers for meals out for two, for consumer durables or, more flexibly, for purchases in a local department store can be greatly appreciated in the right circumstances and be seen as real recognition for achievement.

Equity shares – alignment with shareholder interests

Although the distribution of shares is not currently an option in the UK education system, it should be borne in mind that the private sector does issue shares and/or share options with a view to sharing success. Unless they are granted for the achievement of specific targets, the allocation of shares is not, however, really a reward for performance. But performance-related share option allocation is beginning to happen at board level in the UK, often as part of a long-term incentive strategy. Organizations in the public sector that compete for top-level talent need to be aware that executive share options can deliver substantial opportunities for capital accrual to individuals, that they are perceived as a mark of status and are therefore often an expected part of the executive remuneration package. They align the executive's interests more closely with those of shareholders, or they should, and can act as useful means to retain key people. Attempts at recruitment from the private to the public sector may need to take this into account.

Profit shares – a share in success

Profit-related pay, be it Inland Revenue approved (that is tax-free within limits set out most recently in the Finance Bill 1991) or otherwise, is normally used as a means of rewarding employees for their collective contribution to corporate profits. It is essentially a share in success and its principal use is for its communication value. It is a means of reaffirming the need for effective work and commitment at all levels and has been widely used by banks and other financial institutions as well as by the manufacturing sector.

Although Inland Revenue approved profit-related pay schemes are not available to the public sector in general and schools in particular, the concept of sharing gains in efficiency with staff may be transferable for schools which achieve beyond their school plan within budget. Its cultural and political acceptability in this context remain to be explored.

THE LINKS WITH PERFORMANCE MANAGEMENT

One of the major lessons emerging from the application of performance-related pay during the 1980s is the need for effective performance management to underpin the pay system. A good working definition of performance management is that it is 'the process that links people and jobs to the strategy and objectives of the organization'. Good performance management is about operating a process which increases the likelihood of achieving performance improvements. Current thinking in this area indicates that performance management needs to be practised by the integrated operation of four processes. Figure 4.2 illustrates how these work together. In outline the processes are planning for performance, managing performance, appraising performance and rewarding performance.

Planning for performance

Planning involves matching individual accountabilities in each job or role against organizational or departmental plans, reaching agreement about individual targets and the way work is to be done with jobholders and identifying the knowledge and skills required to achieve the standards needed. Out of this process should come a performance contract between individual and organization in which each is clear about what is needed in each aspect of an individual's job to deliver performance improvements. It will typically include a personal development plan.

Managing performance

This is essentially about tracking performance against targets through the year on a regular basis and as a normal part of the everyday management process. It is a joint process in which jobholders and their managers maintain a dialogue about progress

A process for making sure that people:

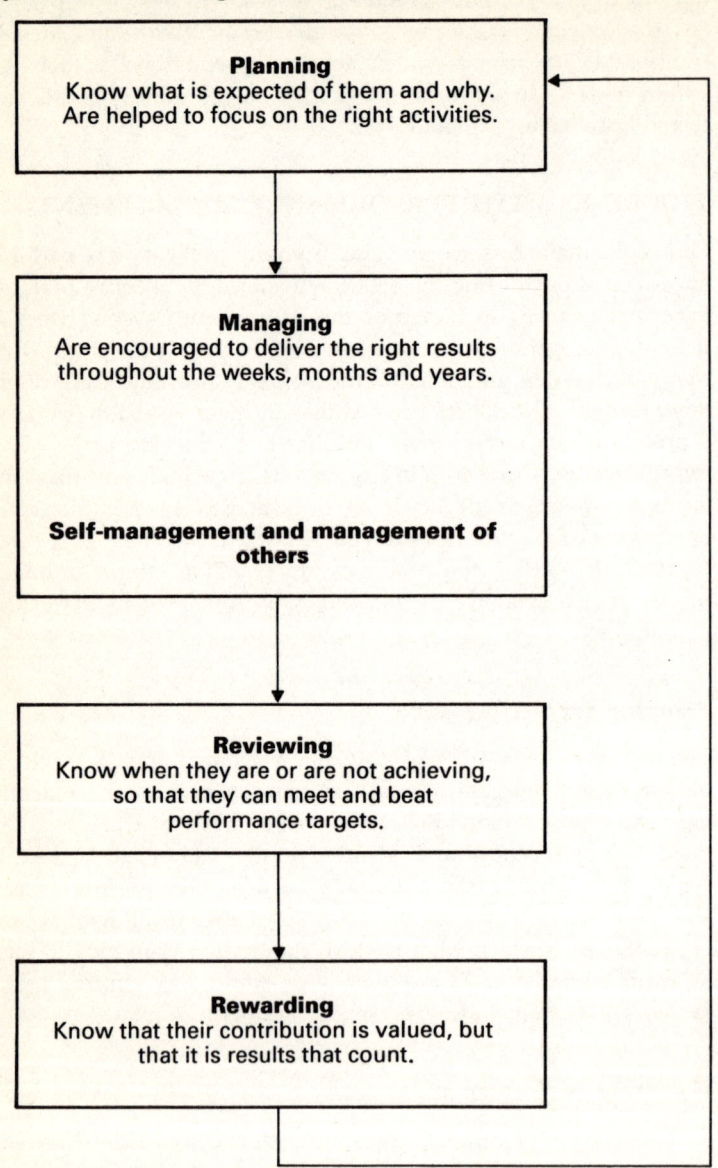

```
┌─────────────────────────────────────────┐
│              Planning                   │
│  Know what is expected of them and why. │ ←┐
│  Are helped to focus on the right       │  │
│  activities.                            │  │
└─────────────────────────────────────────┘  │
                    │                        │
                    ▼                        │
┌─────────────────────────────────────────┐  │
│              Managing                   │  │
│  Are encouraged to deliver the right    │  │
│  results throughout the weeks,          │  │
│  months and years.                      │  │
│                                         │  │
│   Self-management and management of     │  │
│                 others                  │  │
└─────────────────────────────────────────┘  │
                    │                        │
                    ▼                        │
┌─────────────────────────────────────────┐  │
│              Reviewing                  │  │
│  Know when they are or are not          │  │
│  achieving, so that they can meet and   │  │
│  beat performance targets.              │  │
└─────────────────────────────────────────┘  │
                    │                        │
                    ▼                        │
┌─────────────────────────────────────────┐  │
│              Rewarding                  │  │
│  Know that their contribution is        │  │
│  valued, but that it is results         │  │
│  that count.                            │  │
└─────────────────────────────────────────┘  │
                    │                        │
                    └────────────────────────┘
```

Figure 4.2 Performance management: main stages in cycle

and what needs to be done either individually or in terms of the interdependencies between jobs to make it more likely that agreed targets will be achieved or exceeded.

Appraising performance

This is the formal process of assessing and rating whole-job performance and progress against the performance contract. This stage should be the combination of a series of discussions throughout the year so that there are no surprises for the jobholder or manager in the reviewing session. The essence of a good review is that it should be a positive and constructive professional discussion between manager and jobholder and the beginning of a new performance contract for the year to come.

Rewarding performance

This means placing value on the performance achieved either through the performance-related pay system or through other major forms of recognition such as training, career progression, broadening assignments, mentoring, the provision of improved equipment and other measures. Thus pay comes at the end of the cycle, recognizing the reality that pay systems do not manage people or performance: only managers can achieve this!

APPRAISAL SYSTEMS: THE PROBLEMS

Traditional appraisal systems have all too often failed because they were implemented in ignorance of the principles outlined above. The main causes of failure appear to be:

- ownership of the system by personnel rather than line management
- perception that the system is just another piece of bureaucracy, a chore to be added to an already overloaded schedule
- inadequate or non-existent training of managers and staff in the objectives of the systems and, more particularly in the skills involved in operating an effective performance management process of planning, managing and reviewing performance, processes which many managers initially find very difficult and for which they need continuing support to get right

- use of performance-rating systems which are either ill defined or inept or which use language of scoring/systems which tend to demotivate, often because they use language redolent of school reports, for example, 'satisfactory', 'B+'
- over-complexity of documentation, trying to do too much in one system and failing to make the paperwork user-friendly
- ugly, unappealing supporting literature and appraisal forms: failure to deliver to employees the same quality of writing and design as is given, as a matter of course, to customers
- failure of top management to become personally involved with and drive the process; performance management is just as important at board level as lower down and gaps in this area quickly affect credibility and the ultimate sustainability of the system
- failure to understand just how much new systems need to be supported and nurtured after the first phases of implementation: systems need to have their successes communicated and built upon.

THE CONFLICT BETWEEN RATING AND COST CONTROL

Rating drift – the tendency of managers to be 'soft' with performance scores causing more high ratings to be given than is realistic – is a difficult and sometimes intractable problem. The best cure is prevention, by managing the way ratings should be used, communication in detail of the circumstances in which each rating should be allocated, and managing employee expectations accordingly. If rating drift has set in, firm discipline needs to be applied. One common way of tackling this is to change the rating definitions used, improve their clarity and so, effectively, reposition the scheme. Another approach, rather than simply issuing guidelines on the expected range of rating distributions, is to ask managers to rank their staff in overall performance order and then distribute merit pay in different amounts to different groups in the order that emerges, for example, 20 per cent increases to the first two in a list of twenty, 15 per cent to the next four, 10 per cent to the next ten, 7.5 per cent to the next two and 5 per cent to the remaining two. To reinforce the values of the organization some organizations set rules for ranking. One organization known to me set its rankings in 1989 in relation to the following criteria:

- contribution beyond expectations as set out in agreed targets
- contribution to the work of others, that is better teamworking
- contribution to change, since there was a culture-change programme going on at the time.

PROSPECTS FOR THE 1990s: THE LESSONS SO FAR

It should be clear from what has been said so far that performance management and performance-related pay are not quick fixes. They are processes which take time, care and investment to get right and maintain. The lessons of the 1980s are mainly about going away and trying to do better next time. There is no suggestion that the idea should be abandoned, since no other process in isolation is likely to deliver for the UK the improved performance it needs to compete in the global market-place and survive the challenges of the 1990s. In summary, experience from many sources indicates that the following lessons are important:

- Although pay systems do not of themselves manage people or performance, they have value in any organization as a cutting edge for change and in the introduction of a sharper performance focus.
- New systems need to match the culture and values of the organization. For those in education, this means that the pay and performance management systems operated in industry cannot be translated wholesale. They must be modified, adapted, even rethought, to match the special demands of schools and other educational institutions.
- Designing new systems is an iterative process that has to be tested and developed against the background in which they must work. It is not possible simply to take a design or a set of performance measures from one environment and expect them to work effectively in another.
- Performance rewards need to be closely linked to the milestones that mark the achievement of an organization's strategy; by doing so they underpin it and improve the chance of success.
- Processes for monitoring, evaluating and reviewing the performance management and pay systems need to be implemented from the start to help manage expectations about what those systems will and will not deliver.

- Performance rewards are not easily justifiable or credible without properly conducted appraisals.
- Performance rewards cannot be used to make up for the deficiencies of seriously uncompetitive basic salaries. This always causes more problems than it solves: money at risk needs to go on top of a sensible even if not extravagant base.
- A mechanistic approach to target setting tends to focus only on the bottom line, important though that is. Qualitative targets are as important as quantitative ones: quality can be about effective teamwork, people management, levels of service, customer satisfaction and loyalty and other 'soft' issues needed to ensure delivery of the 'hard' targets.
- Change should be managed at a pace the organization can cope with. New systems can rarely be implemented quickly: it may take several years to embed performance management and implement performance rewards in an organization of any size.
- Above all, it is critical to have top management involvement in the process, not just to launch it, but to drive implementation. Directors who 'walk as they talk' are worth a dozen company videos of the chief executive saying how good the innovation is, but not, afterwards, being seen to do very much to contribute to the process.

Many performance management and performance-related pay systems underachieve not because of flaws in design but because communication was not as effective as it should have been. Consistent, credible messages need to be given regularly about why the processes are being introduced, how they are working, what the particular performance messages are for this year and other issues which help maintain interest in and commitment to them.

In conclusion, it needs to be stressed that this is an area where there is a considerable mismatch between the simple and appealing theory of paying more to people who perform better and the hard reality of delivering processes that really motivate and deliver improved performance. It is much more difficult to achieve that than most people imagine and requires a strategic and thoughtful approach. Experience from the few reviews of systems after implementation conducted by independent outsiders suggests that employees would rather have performance-related pay systems and try to improve them than return to a world where mediocrity is as likely to be recognized in the pay system as excellent performance.

Well-implemented performance management and performance-related pay systems deliver a number of benefits:

- increased clarity and focus about what the organization has to deliver to achieve and maintain success
- a positive and constructive change in the nature of debate on performance and performance improvement within the organization at all levels
- effective use of the process by managers to communicate key messages about business direction
- more effective use of the pay budget
- increased motivation among all who perform competently
- more honest and positive management of poor performers.

The challenge for most organizations in the 1990s is not therefore whether to introduce performance-related pay and performance management, but how to do it better and how to ensure that it becomes an integrated part of the overall management process.

REFERENCES

Armstrong, M. and Murlis, H. (1991) *Reward Management: A Handbook of Remuneration Strategy and Practice*, 2nd edn, London: Kogan Page.
Bowery, A. (1989) *Managing Salary and Wage Systems*, Aldershot: Gower.
Brading, L. and Wright, V. (1990) Performance related pay, Factsheet 30, *Personnel Management*, June.
Carrington, L. (1989) Not written on tablets of stone, *Personnel Today* 26 September: 27–8.
Fowler, A. (1988) New directions in performance pay, *Personnel Management*, November: 30–4.
Greenhill, R. (1990) *Performance Related Pay for the 1990s*, London: Director Books.
Incomes Data Services (1985), Top Pay Unit *The Merit Factor: Rewarding Individual Performance*, London: IDS in association with the Institute of Personnel Management.
—— (1988) Top Pay Unit *Paying for Performance*, London: IDS.
—— (1989) *A Guide to Performance Related Pay*, Public Sector Unit, London: IDS.
—— (1990) Top Pay Unit *Putting Pay Philosophies into Practice*, London: IDS.
LACSAB (1990a) *Handbook on Performance Related Pay*, Report no 2, London: Local Authorities Conditions of Service Advisory Board.
—— (1990b) *Performance Related Pay in Practice: Case Studies from Local Government*, Report no 3, London: Local Authorities Condition of Service Advisory Board.

Murlis, H. (1987) Performance related pay in the public sector, *Public Money* March.
—— (1988) Merit payment systems: the lessons so far, *Manpower Policy and Practice* Spring.
—— (1990) Just rewards, *Pensions and Employee Benefits* February.
Ranking, N. (1988) Performance and pay: making the connection, *Manpower Policy and Practice* 3(3): 23–38.
Rock, M. L. and Berger, L. A. (eds) (1991) *The Compensation Handbook: A State of the Art Guide to Compensation Strategy and Design*, New York: McGraw Hill.
Smith, I. (1991) *Incentive Schemes, People and Profits*, 2nd edn, Kingston upon Thames: Croner.
Vizie, R. (1990) Failing the test, *Personnel Today* 28 August: 22–3.
(No author, no date), Disclosing the results of performance related pay reviews, *IDS Report* no. 570: 25–6.
(No author) (1989) Rewarding excellence, *Employment Digest* no. 274, 4 September: 4–5.
(No author) (1990) Paying for performance at the London Business School, *IDS Top Pay Unit Review* August: 2–4.
(No author) (1990) Performance related pay, *Employment Digest* no. 302, 10 December: 4–5.
Widespread coverage of both public and private sector performance-related pay systems as they are implemented and evolve are covered in the publications of Incomes Data Services (IDS Report, IDS Studies, 105 Top Pay Unit Review) and in those of Industrial Relations Services (Industrial Relations Review and Report, Pay and Benefits Bulletin).

Chapter 5

Performance-related pay in IBM

Gordon Sapsed

IBM's Merit Pay system must be looked at in the context of the company's overall management system and in particular the employee-manager relationship and the appraisal process. In this chapter the background to the company's human resource management will first be outlined. The practices described are those current in the United Kingdom, although there is little variation from country to country.

THE COMPANY

IBM United Kingdom Limited is a subsidiary company of the International Business Machines Corporation. There are IBM subsidiary companies in more than 130 countries, employing approximately 370,000 people, as at the end of 1990. The employees are normally nationals of the country in which they are employed and there is considerable autonomy at country level.

The company is in the business of applying advanced information technology to help solve the problems of business, government, science, defence, education, medicine and other areas. IBM offers customers solutions that incorporate information systems, software, communications systems and other products and services to address specific needs. These solutions are provided both by IBM directly and through the company's business partners, who include dealers, agents, value-add remarketeers and software houses.

In the UK IBM has about 17,000 employees, of whom approximately half are in marketing, sales and service branches throughout the UK, including a series of high-tech learning centres. Manufacturing activities absorb another 20 per cent, administration approximately 20 per cent and research and development the remaining 10 per cent. Almost half of IBM's UK employees have a first degree or equivalent qualification.

Approximately 250 of IBM UK's employees are full-time instructors and specialists in education. Their activities include training and development for IBM employees from the UK and abroad, dealer and business partner education and customer education.

BASIC COMPANY PRINCIPLES

The overall philosophy governing the way in which IBM conducts its business was developed in the 1930s and has been written about by a number of internal and external observers (Watson and Petrie 1990; Rogers and Snook 1986; Maisonrouge 1988).

The company's booklet *Employment with IBM*, which is given to all new employees, opens with

> IBM is often cited as a company that strives hard for – and thrives on – success; sets high standards of quality and ambitious targets; looks for opportunities; is always prepared to review its methods and practices; and believes in the highest professional and business ethics. These are qualities IBM demands of itself as a business, encourages in its people and builds into its employee relations system and its personnel practice.

At the heart of the company's philosophy are three basic beliefs:

1 respect for the individual
2 customer service
3 pursuit of excellence.

It has been said on several occasions, most recently by the current IBM corporate chairman John Akers, that IBM is prepared, in developing its business, to change any of its policies and practices except the basic beliefs. *Respect for the individual* provides the fundamental basis for IBM's practices in the area of employee development, performance management, reward and recognition.

Notable among the consequences are individual merit pay, single-status benefit programmes and the company's full employment practice. The commitment to full employment has caused extensive retraining, redeployment and relocation and has enabled the company historically, on a world-wide basis, to provide employment security for all employees maintaining a satisfactory job performance.

The IBM management system

IBM has only one supervisory job title, that of manager. There are no supervisors, foremen, charge-hands or other supervisory grades. A typical manager has ten to twenty people in blue-collar or clerical job areas and five to fifteen people in professional job areas. The manager's role includes recruitment, training, performance planning, performance evaluation, salary progression and career development planning for each of the employees reporting to him or her. In several of those roles the responsibility is partially shared with the next level of management, particularly with regard to equity and maintaining standards across the organization.

Single status

All employees of IBM have essentially the same employment terms and conditions, which offer the same personnel policies and practices with only occasional differences such as part-time or fixed-time term contracts, shift-working or overtime arrangements. An appraisal and counselling process, applicable to all employees and an associated merit pay system has been in place in the UK for more than twenty-five years.

Employee benefits – pensions, medical cover, vacation entitlement, life assurance and so on – are the same for all IBM employees, although there are service-related entitlements associated with some benefits. At the time of writing there is a company car scheme for senior-level employees as part of the compensation package.

Employee relations and communication

Internal communication is regarded as very important. There are a variety of channels including notice boards, internal newspapers and magazines, video, closed circuit television and an internal electronic mail network. The primary medium for communication, however, is through the employee-manager relationship.

All company information is normally routed to employees through their manager. Important topics and issues are discussed in departmental meetings, which are usually held monthly, and in one-to-one discussion sessions. Most employees in professional areas will have a scheduled weekly or fortnightly individual discussion session with their manager at which job-related or even personal concerns may be discussed. Support staff from departments such as Personnel, Medical, Safety or other areas may be consulted, but the manager is always the starting-point for any topic. Other communication channels encourage the formal or informal escalation of issues to more senior management, if necessary.

The dual ladder

In many areas of IBM's business, high level technical expertise and specialist experience are required. Job levels and salaries of some employees in such departments may be higher than that of the department manager. The manager is responsible for performance planning and assessment of all employees in that department and for setting their salaries. This dual ladder concept allows careers for suitably qualified individuals to progress to the most senior levels in the company structure, without managerial responsibility. It is likely, however, that an individual possessing the necessary communication skills and business acumen required at higher levels will have had some managerial experience en route.

OVERALL PHILOSOPHY ON PAY

Throughout the world IBM's overall philosophy is to pay salaries which are competitive in the relevant labour market and which reflect the job responsibilities of the individual. The system, although it varies in minor detail from country to country, also provides pay for performance with that job.

The outside market

IBM compares itself with other companies through participation in salary surveys in which information is exchanged on salaries paid for similar jobs. Comparisons are made with companies that IBM competes with for business or for employees, as well as other leaders in industry or commerce. These companies are typically well managed and have good overall pay and benefits practices.

IBM also participates in salary and benefits surveys covering specialist careers and professions such as Accountancy, Personnel, Legal and Occupational Health.

In making comparisons great care is taken to ensure that like is being compared with like. To ensure that job comparisons are well understood line managers accompany personnel staff in the discussion and comparison process. Factors such as low-interest loans, bonuses, company cars or housing must also be taken into account where they form part of the other organization's total compensation offering.

Salary ranges

The salary survey data are compared to actual salaries being paid by IBM. These comparisons, together with forecasts of likely future market-place movements, enable IBM to establish objective midpoints for future salary ranges. The ranges are built around those midpoints, defining the maximum and minimum salary payable at IBM for each job level. There is considerable overlap between job levels, enabling consistently high performers at one job level to achieve higher salaries than low performers at the level above (see Figure 5.1).

Job responsibility

IBM uses a system of job evaluation to assess the relative worth of each job to the company. The system used by IBM throughout the world is a weighted points system, similar to the HAY-MSL system. It uses two sets of factors, one for managerial and professional jobs and another set of the lower-level technical and clerical jobs.

Job evaluation at IBM is totally independent of the current jobholder. It is concerned solely with measuring the responsibilities associated with the job. Each job level covers a wide variety of jobs and a broad band of responsibilities. Typically a graduate joining IBM direct from university might expect to be promoted to a new job level three or four times in a lifetime career. There are intermediate job levels accommodating specialist roles, between the main career levels, giving a total professional structure of about eight levels.

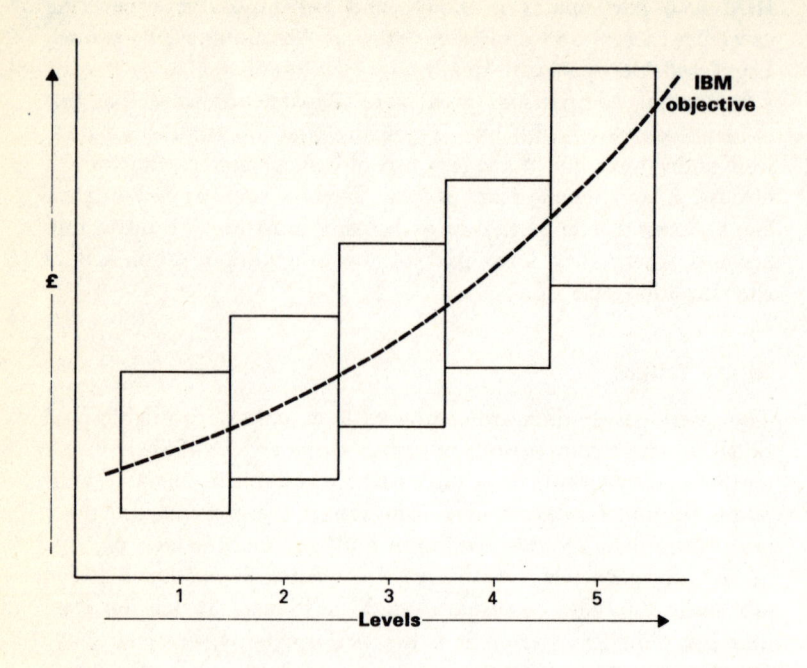

Figure 5.1 A structure or series of salary ranges for each level, with the IBM objective near the mid-point of each range

PERFORMANCE PLANNING

The IBM UK performance appraisal system has been reviewed and modified about every five years during the twenty-five years of existence. In its early years the system was based on the employee's manager completing an appraisal of traits such as dependability, loyalty and so forth. That system was replaced by an objective-setting system in the late 1960s. Changes in the 1970s encouraged more specific measurement targets and performance indicators.

The present system requires the manager and the employee to develop job objectives, usually five to ten in number, based on an annual cycle. A plan is initially set for six months if the employee is in a new job. The degree of employee involvement in defining objective varies. A new employee, or someone moving to a new areas of the business, may depend heavily on the manager to define a work plan. More experienced employees will often take the leading role in proposing objectives both for work to be accomplished and for their own development. The manager's manager also reviews the objectives, proposed measurements and the priority rankings when agreed by the employee and the manager, coming back to them if there is some cause for concern.

Each objective is accompanied by performance criteria defining how the objective will be measured. It is this aspect of performance planning which has, over the years, proved the most challenging and is the most frequently requested area for additional training for managers. It is also the key area for success in the overall appraisal process. IBM employee opinion surveys show that employees who feel satisfied with the objective- and target-setting process are also the most satisfied with their overall appraisal rating when the review is complete.

In considering management-reporting relationships for the more senior specialist employees a significant factor is the manager's likely ability to conduct a realistic appraisal. The development, by the employee and the manager, of mutually acceptable objectives and measurements is essential. A frequently cited problem is the tendency for objectives to go out of date. Managers in many areas of IBM's business conduct interim reviews, typically quarterly, to update objectives and perhaps complete the assessment of finished tasks. Current pilot testing within IBM of online objective setting, maintained within the internal computer network, encourages such updates. Other modifications to IBM's appraisal system are currently under review with changes being pilot-tested. The changes are designed to aid the objective-setting process and clarify the roles of the employee and the manager. Changes will also enable more flexibility to encourage line management ownership of the process.

PERFORMANCE REVIEW

Twelve months after the objectives were prepared a formal review takes place. Prior to the review the employee will have received a form entitled 'Preparation for counselling'. This form encourages the employee to think about various aspects of the job and also about his or her own development. It is the employee's decision whether or not this form contributes to part of the discussion during the review.

Prior to the review the manager will have rated each of the objectives on a 1–5 scale, noting the results achieved relative to the previously agreed measurements. An overall rating, on the same 1–5 scale, is also made, bearing in mind the priorities. The manager prepares comments associated with each objective, notes overall comments about the year's performance and items for discussion and finally reviews the form with his or her own manager prior to the interview.

The rating scale for individual objectives and overall performance is

4 results met the requirements of the job
3 results met the requirements of the job and exceeded them in some areas
2 results consistently exceeded the requirements of the job in most areas
1 results far exceeded the requirements of the job in all areas.

Unsatisfactory performance

For objectives where the achievement was unsatisfactory a 5 rating is given. If the employee's overall performance during the year warrants only a 5 rating there is a different process which will have been invoked as soon as the deterioration was recognized. This procedure for 'unsatisfactory performance or conduct' is primarily concerned with analysing the reasons for the failure and actions needed to recover. It will usually involve setting new objectives, with well-defined targets and early review dates. The time scale must be appropriate to the time required to demonstrate results in that job and to the nature of the failure.

The performance review interview

The completion of performance reviews when due is regarded as very important, with over 95 per cent taking place within four weeks of the planned date. During the review the employee's perception of the year will be discussed as well as the manager's assessment. A list of actions will be developed for improvement of job performance or measurement and for employee development. The improvement plan will usually include actions by the manager. These might typically be in areas such as inter-departmental co-operation or training. The manager writes a short summary of the interview, to which the employee can add comments, prior to a further review by the manager's manager.

The performance review interview also results in a development plan for the employee and new objectives for the forthcoming period. These usually include challenging goals for the forthcoming period and the knowledge that there is a recognition and reward system to support their achievement.

RATING DISTRIBUTIONS

In constructing salary ranges and establishing the company's overall salary budget consideration has to be given to the likely rating distribution across the company. With a twenty-five-year history of ratings and analysis of factors such as the proportion of new hires, knowledge of forthcoming retirements, forecasts of promotions and the creation of new positions, a fairly accurate forecast can be made for the total 18,000 population.

Further analysis, to include corrections for the varying mix of experience and seniority, enables a more detailed forecast for major units such as a manufacturing plant or a large marketing unit of, say, 1,000 people. Tracking measurements, on a monthly basis, of actual rating distributions across groups of that size enables forecasted distributions to be achieved, without limiting managers' use of ratings at the individual level.

Salary increases, based on the expected rating distribution and increased timing, are forecast at budget time. Experience shows that about 15 per cent of forecasts are changed as a result of performance changes during the year, with about equal numbers going up and down.

PAY FOR PERFORMANCE

The *Employment with IBM* booklet (referred to at the beginning of this chapter) says 'Your individual job performance is the main factor that decides the amount of salary you will receive within the range of your job level'.

Although IBM does not publish salary ranges, individual employees can be told the current salary ceilings for their own job level. For a performer rated 1, that ceiling will be the maximum for that job level, while the ceiling for a performer rated 3 will be the midpoint of the range. Similarly the ceilings for performers rated 2 and 4 are at the first and third quartile in the range. If an employee is a new entrant or newly promoted to that job level, their salary will normally be within the bottom quartile of the range.

Higher performance ratings attract larger increases, taking the salary of performers rated 1 or 2 up beyond the midpoint and opening up a significant differential between those employees and performers rated 3 or 4. Over a period of several years the differential between a performer consistently rated 1 and someone consistently rated 4 might be as high as 35–40 per cent. They would, of course, both benefit from any upward shift of the salary range, although the company has no cost-of-living or general increases. The system not only rewards sustained high performance but also allows the outstanding up-and-coming employee to overtake the longer-established lower achiever.

A particular characteristic of the system is the effect of a change in performance. Employees with several years of performance at level 3 would be approaching the ceiling for performers rated 3, the midpoint of the range. They would receive a much larger than usual increase if their performance improved to a 1 or 2 rating. Sustained performance at that higher rating would result in larger increases than a performer rated 3, and a salary limited by the third quartile point or top of the range, rather than the midpoint. A deterioration in performance, following a number of higher performing years, results in smaller increases, until performance recovers or the ranges catch up.

The overall effect of the IBM merit-based system is seen in Figure 5.2.

Timing of increases

Salary increases are not awarded at a fixed point in each year and they are not settled across the company. Each manager decides when an individual's salary will be reviewed. The manager can thus adjust the timing to reflect both the time since the last increase and performance considerations. Typically a manager might bring forward a planned increase to reflect outstanding work or extend the interval between increases to give an employee the opportunity to recover from a bad patch.

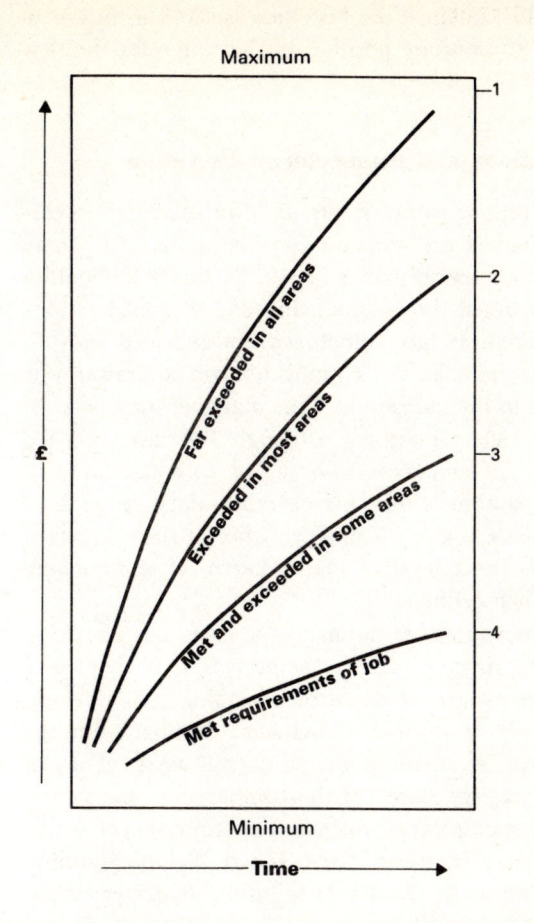

Figure 5.2 Employee progress through the salary range
Note: Curves represent movement of employee's salary, over time, giving proper pay for a particular category of performance.

The effect of promotion

An outstanding employee might be promoted to a more senior job level with two or three years of entering the current level, while another employee might have to wait ten years before promotion. Dependent on their performance history they might be at very different places in their current salary range when promoted. Employees who are promoted receive an increase related to the work done in the old job since the last increase and a top-up to bring them into an appropriate position in the range for the new job level.

Performance variations and management discretion

Managers have discretion, within limits, to vary increases to correct anomalies and reflect performance considerations which may not be containable in the performance rating. Particular difficulties which may have impacted the results achieved, or considerations of attitude and willingness, are sometimes not reflected fully in ratings. It may also be that the employee's last appraisal was several months prior to the increase and the manager may be able, with confidence, to reflect progress, although the last recorded rating is still valid. An employee who shows potential for promotion and has headroom within his current salary range may receive a larger increase than an employee who, in the opinion of the manager and the next level of management, is approaching his or her performance ceiling.

It is common in many areas for managers to carry out a ranking process from time to time, to satisfy themselves that they have equity in salaries across several departments doing similar work. Led by a second-level or third-level manager familiar with the work and the employee's contributions, an overall assessment can be made. This ranking snapshot can be compared to the actual salary position of those employees, to enable appropriate corrective adjustment when future increases are planned. Salary planning professionals in Personnel are available to advise managers when out-of-line actions are planned.

Exceptions

The information technology industry changes rapidly, employee's skills can become obsolete and reorganization is common. Following redeployment or retraining, an employee may hold a position which does not justify the current job level or rating. The company's practice, apart from providing all necessary training to enable the employee to get up to speed in a new role, is to retain the job level and rating for at least two years to enable a catch-up. This means that the employee will be given the advantage of increases appropriate to the old job level and rating during the catch-up period.

Trainees and some newly joined professional specialists may also have salaries which, in the short term, are not justified by their contribution. They will, however, be in line with their anticipated future role and the expectation that they will, on completion of their training or familiarization, move into the appropriate place in the normal ranges.

Incentive payments

Employees in sales and similar revenue-related jobs are paid commission on sales results achieved. They are also appraised and rated in the usual way against their other job objectives. Their total income will reflect achievement of other objectives, although heavily influenced by sales results.

Customer satisfaction share plan

An innovation in 1991 for IBM's UK employees is an additional payment, payable in 1992 in the form of IBM shares or cash, based on IBM customer satisfaction measurements. An independent survey is carried out twice each year to measure the satisfaction of information technology industry customers with their suppliers. IBM has set targets for its entire UK work-force to improve those satisfaction ratings, which, if achieved, will be payable on a percentage of salary basis, to all employees.

Awards

In addition to salary, about 10 per cent of IBM's employees each year receive cash awards. These awards range from informal awards of, say, £75, at the discretion of the immediate manager, to thousands of pounds for high-level achievements recognized at a corporate level. Awards recognize noteworthy contributions, usually outside the scope of the employee's normal job. Some awards are linked to specific programmes such as quality improvement or cost-saving suggestions, the development of patentable designs or achievement of professional recognition in a specialist field. Employees may also be awarded research funding or opportunity to pursue academic or research projects, in recognition of creative achievement.

Pay-performance linkage

IBM's merit pay system, while linked to the appraisal system, is not synchronized with it, and performance reviews are not regarded as personal pay negotiations. If, at performance appraisal time, employees want to discuss salary, or their next increase, the manager will defer the appraisal and instead discuss the pay concern. The concern could be triggered by salaries being quoted in job advertisements, or the employee's perception of market-place rates for similar work. Alternatively it could be a problem associated with some newly arrived employee whose salary is thought to be higher, or to additional job responsibilities which the employee feels warrant a higher job level. These are all issues outside the objectives and performance achievement discussion and best resolved prior to the performance review.

At IBM, such discussions are uncommon and the performance management process is seen as separate from, although related to, the pay system. Performance planning and review takes place ordinarily on an annual cycle. Pay increases are usually awarded approximately every twelve months, but only accidentally would that be at the same time in the year as the appraisal. The link is that the increase, when awarded, must be seen to be fair and reflect performance. When problems do arise, as stated earlier, they are likely to be due to poorly chosen objectives or measurements, rather than inaccurate assessment or an inappropriate salary increase.

THE SUCCESS OF IBM'S MERIT PAY SYSTEM

If an employer asks employees, even anonymously, whether their pay is satisfactory the answers are likely to be loaded. IBM's employees have been asked that question in surveys on a regular basis for more than twenty years. Their answers today are essentially no different from twenty years ago, with about 35 per cent expressing satisfaction and a further 30 per cent neither satisfied nor dissatisfied.

The key issue is recognition of good performance. Surveys show that pay satisfaction is higher among those who feel that their performance assessment has been fair, regardless of the rating. Satisfaction with performance ratings, measured in the 1990 employee opinion surveys, was high, with over 70 per cent satisfied that their last rating was accurate.

IBM is in a highly competitive industry where most of IBM's people have skills much sought after in the market-place. The ultimate test of IBM's personnel practices might therefore be the attrition rate. It is exceptionally low, at around 3 per cent per annum. Fewer than 2 per cent of professionals leave in any year.

SUMMARY OF IBM'S MERIT PAY EXPERIENCE

In any performance-linked pay system, the key issue must be the validity of the performance measurement. Defining objectives and agreeing ways to measure them, especially in creative professional job areas, is not easy. Joint involvement of the manager and the employee, frequently drawing on the experience of others, improves the process. In some cases as much as 40 per cent of the job objectives may be incomplete and measurable only in terms of indicators, rather than proven outcomes, when review time comes around. More frequent interim review of objectives to ensure currency can help with fine tuning of measurements and with constructive feedback.

Over time, and with the good will and co-operation of all those involved, the performance review process can be improved and tuned. Better objectives can be defined and improved indicators of performance identified. This can result, for the organization, in higher performance, and for the employee, increased job satisfaction and professional growth. The merit pay system enables some additional reward and recognition for those who are the most deserving.

REFERENCES

Maisonrouge, J. (1988) *Inside IBM*, London: Collins.
Rogers, B. and Shook, R. (1986) *The IBM Way*, New York: Harper & Row.
Watson, T. J. jnr and Petrie, R. (1990) *Father, Son and Co.*, New York: Bantam.

Chapter 6

The history of teachers' pay negotiations

Rene Saran

This chapter reflects on how the concept of performance-related pay has been viewed by teacher unions and their employers when salaries were negotiated in the Burnham Committee, and how the Interim Advisory Committee (IAC), set up under the Teachers' Pay and Conditions Act 1987, has viewed it.

One of the discoveries of researching Burnham negotiations for the period 1945–85 (Saran 1989) was that the salaries structure responded slowly to changes in the education system, to the educational needs of children and the resulting organizational and managerial requirements in the schools. The explanation which emerged is reminiscent of J. K. Galbraith's argument in *The Affluent Society* (1962) that events move faster than attitudes, so that the *conventional wisdom*, as he called it, was always well outdated by the time it was adopted. This meant that the ideas and actions of many individuals, groups and organizations were cast in the reactive rather than proactive mode.

No one would doubt the speed of change in the education scene in the last decade, and especially in the late 1980s. It is during this period that concepts like more flexible pay systems and performance-related pay have come to the fore, based on their claimed importance in helping to raise standards and improve the quality of the education service (DES 1983). The pursuit of quality is not the prerogative of any one party or government. For example, the Labour leader Neil Kinnock promised a new Education Standards Council, compulsory appraisal of teachers and the establishment of a General Teaching Council (*Observer* 2 December 1990: 2). Similarly, the prime minister, John Major, described education as 'top of my personal agenda', the main aim being 'to improve quality and standards in schools and elevate the status of teachers'

(*Observer* 10 February 1991: 3). Two months later Kenneth Clarke, secretary of state for education and science, was 'considering setting up a general teaching council', an idea which 'has the backing of the prime minister', and which 'is likely to be included in the Conservative Party . . . manifesto' (*Education* 12 April 1991: 292).

It seems highly likely that teachers and their unions will continue to be overwhelmed by many changes and that their workloads will leave little time for longer-term reflection to enable them to be proactive rather than merely reactive. As events are moving now it seems that by the mid-1990s the fragmentation of the schools system will result in local bargaining over pay and conditions of service for teachers.

Until April 1991 it seemed that legislation would provide for the establishment of national machinery to restore limited negotiating rights over pay and conditions, but unexpectedly the secretary of state replaced the first parliamentary Bill with a second one, under which a review body for teachers' pay and conditions has emerged instead. How important will a national review body be, given the cluster of other changes since the mid-1980s? By the mid-1990s possibly all that will be determined nationally will be the classroom teachers' standard scale and the pay spine covering headteachers' and deputy headteachers' salaries. The real place where major decisions on pay and conditions of service will be made might by then be the school or college, that is at the institutional level.

What, confronted with this new scenario of institutional control, of flexible pay structures and of pressure for performance-related pay, can this chapter contribute? How relevant is the history of teacher pay negotiations, or even of the four Interim Advisory Committee reports published between 1988 and 1991? What a review and analysis of the history can provide are insights into attitudes, into the conventional wisdoms of the past, which tend to linger on and therefore make up part of the policy-making environment in which decision-makers in the 1990s have to operate.

The next section will aim to convey such insights, gleaned from an in-depth study of Burnham salary negotiations. In the early 1980s these negotiations were still prominent on the political agenda but in the late 1980s they were already part of history, another sign of the speed of events. An analysis of the Teachers' Pay and Conditions Act 1987, and of changes brought by the

Education (No. 2) Act 1986 and the Education Reform Act 1988, provides the background for the advice given to the secretary of state by the Interim Advisory Committee in its four reports.

The IAC resulted from the 1987 Act which abolished the Burnham Committee and union and employer negotiating rights at national level, and instead imposed on school teachers a new salaries structure and a legally binding contract of employment. The third report of the IAC (1990) laid the basis for wider discretion and flexibility in the structure of teachers' pay. Thus the third section of this chapter includes an up-to-date summary of these reports. This in turn provides a basis for assessing and understanding what scope is already given for the introduction of performance-related pay and in pointing the direction in which events are likely to move, as the pay review body for school teachers starts its work.

Finally the fourth section of this chapter speculates about the future of teachers' pay and conditions, addressing issues such as these:

1 whether a national framework and pay structure will remain
2 what the implications are of the more permanent loss of bargaining rights at national level
3 whether through institutional decisions, either managerial or negotiated, pay flexibility and performance related pay for individual teachers are likely to become important features of teachers' conditions of work.

HISTORIC INSIGHTS

Butler's Education Act 1944 was enacted even before the Second World War had ended. In those days of national unity and coalition government an egalitarian spirit pervaded public life. The former divisive separation between the elementary and secondary school systems was no longer acceptable. The old Burnham Committee, set up in 1919, had negotiated the salaries of secondary school teachers in one committee and those of elementary teachers in another. The newly constituted Burnham Committee for schools covered both primary and secondary sectors, and speedily started work to ensure that the reformed education system was not marred by an outdated salaries structure. Under previous arrangements the salaries of secondary teachers – grammar school teachers in those days – were higher than those of elementary teachers, even in those rare instances when the latter were graduates. Introduction of the basic scale under the 1945 Burnham Report abolished these distinctions and even placed headteachers on the same basic scale. This scale can be likened to the main professional grade introduced in 1987, and renamed the standard scale in 1991. It was a scale with incremental points for all teachers and gave no flexibility of pay beyond certain arrangements, for example awarding extra increments on entry in recognition of pre-teaching experience.

In addition, there was what the Burnham negotiators called the superstructure, giving some recognition to the need for differentials. However, in 1945 such recognition was restricted to a small personal addition for graduate teachers, an allowance for a limited number of posts of special responsibility, and an addition for headteachers of schools with pupils over 15 years old.

Thus the 1945 Burnham Report unified rather than differentiated the pay of teachers, quite contrary to current government aims of devising flexible pay systems within which differentiated rewards can be given for individual performance.

In order to understand the lessons of Burnham it is important to recollect that the National Union of Teachers (NUT) then held the majority of seats on the Burnham Teachers' Panel. For a quarter of a century the NUT succeeded in maintaining the negotiating pattern set in 1944–5: the basic scale was negotiated first, followed by the superstructure. This tended to favour a relatively high basic scale. Inevitably there are always cost ceilings, and more on the basic scale meant less for differentials. This pattern suited the NUT membership, predominantly primary and female teachers, who gained most from the establishment of and increases in the basic scale. At the same time, unions representing the better qualified, mainly graduate teachers, at the time known as the Joint Four, as well as the local authority employers, constantly endeavoured to devote more of the available money to differentials. In this they were supported by the Ministry of Education (now the DES) which has always favoured a differentiating salaries structure.

The dominant position of the NUT is well illustrated by a detail from the 1944–5 negotiations. The structure of basic scale plus additions which was adopted demolished the proposals put forward by the local authority employers. Their plan would have offered advancement to all qualified teachers on merit. Their aim was to 'reward teaching ability and good work, and to attract graduates into schools other than grammar schools' (Saran 1989: 110). They called it an 'establishment plan' with three grades; grades II and III were to be for promoted teachers. The local authority representatives did not favour a graduate addition, because paper qualifications in their eyes were not necessarily an indication of performance as a good teacher (Saran 1989: 113). The local authorities thought the teachers would welcome their plan for a career pattern which encouraged high professional standards of performance. They were mistaken. The word *grade* turned out to be anathema to the Teachers' Panel: it involved grading teachers 'like grading eggs' and aroused immediate suspicion. Teachers clearly did not trust management with any discretion to reward merit; thus – in those days – there was no scope for performance-related pay (Saran 1989: 111). Suspicion of favouritism weighed heavily with the Teachers' Panel. The establishment plan offered no uniform objective basis for assessing a teacher's merit and worth for promotion. Each local authority would have made assessments in its own way.

Even by the 1970s, no acceptable solution had been found to the problems raised by the 1944 plan of the employers. By whom and how would teacher performance be assessed? It is an interesting comment on events that the suspicions aroused in 1945 have held sway for a very long time. As in 1944, it was in 1971 the Burnham Committee Management Panel's intention that teachers of merit should be given promotion simply as good teachers. Research by the Economist Intelligence Unit in 1970 had shown teacher frustration because promotion involved acceptance of administrative posts with fewer teaching duties. Hilsum and Start (1974), writing after the 1971 Burnham Report, confirmed that many teachers felt that Burnham arrangements denuded the classroom of good teachers, yet there was no evidence that the 1971 settlement had noticeably affected promotion patterns (Saran 1989: 120–1). The dilemma posed by this evidence remained unresolved. Teachers at one and the same time resented the correlation between promotion and administration, yet were suspicious of differential rewards based on quality of teaching performance.

Under the salaries structure introduced in 1987 one of the four criteria for the award of incentive allowances is 'outstanding performance as a classroom teacher'. Yet the general evidence suggests that they are rarely awarded for this reason. The compulsory introduction of appraisal for all teachers by the mid-1990s may change this, but the controversy over whether appraisal is to be developmental or linked to promotion and performance-related pay, or both, may be better understood if the 1945 outburst about 'grading teachers like grading eggs' is remembered.

The search for objective yardsticks – to ensure fairness in the distribution of any given cake and more particularly to justify salary differentials – underlies another aspect of the former Burnham arrangements which continues to underpin some administrative and managerial devices in the education system of the 1990s. Children on school registers are given age-weighted units from which the unit total for each school is calculated. The unit total of each school in turn determines the school group in which it is placed. Since 1991 six school groups have replaced the previous fourteen. The unit total system was introduced under the 1948 Burnham Report, extended in 1951 and 1956. It underpinned the developing careers structure by achieving particular levels of salaries and numbers of promoted posts in different types and sizes of school. With amendments made since and changes to the age-weights, this remains the case under the *School Teachers' Pay and Conditions Document* (DES 1990) which has replaced the Burnham Report.

Using an age-weighted pupil count was considered an objective method for the allocation of resources. So often the value assumptions underlying quantitative methods remain hidden. A more accurate description of the age-weighted pupil count is to see it as a non-arbitrary instrument. Over many years the Burnham Committee battled over the primary/secondary differential, a result of the unit total system, because the larger a school and the older its pupils, the higher the school group, resulting in higher pay for headteachers and deputy heads and more and better-paid promoted posts. Unions like the NUT, strong in its primary membership, tried repeatedly to reduce the primary-secondary differential.

What is interesting here in terms of the conventional wisdom is that age-weighting as such was not challenged; criticism was directed instead at the differential values attached to children of statutory school age. But, it might well be asked, why should more resources *per capita* be given to older pupils? Saran (1989: 117–18) found the explanation lay in widely accepted value assumptions concerning advanced work in schools and colleges. Higher value was given to advanced levels of work, undertaken by older and brighter children in schools, or by students taking higher level academic, rather than vocational courses in colleges. Specialist academic knowledge is not taught to younger children, and teaching early years pupils was often viewed as an extension of the parental role. Similarly, the differential staffing and resources for grammar compared with modern schools which resulted from age-weighting were justified in terms of higher levels of work. In the 1940s the secretary of the employers' panel of the Burnham Committee implicitly revealed his awareness of some of the hidden values. He argued that such differentiation would be rejected only by 'strange beings [who thought] the head of a kindergarten should get the same salary as a university professor', or who saw the work of a teacher of infants on a par with that of a grammar school teacher (Saran 1989: 118).

Gradually, in the 1980s, the importance of vocational education came to be recognized, and the low staying on rate post–16 caused widespread concern. John Major, soon after becoming prime minister, stated that he wanted 'much more choice, and better training for all young people... more vocational options in schools of equal rigour and repute to the academic courses' (*Observer* 10 February 1991: 3) so that more pupils would stay on after the age of 16. The secretary of state for education and science ten days later added his voice. It is the level of qualification that counts, 'not whether it is academic or vocational'. The message must be repeated 'over and over again until it gets across!' (*DES News* 58/91, 20 February 1991). Given the origins of the age-weighting device, anchored as it was in traditional academic values, perhaps its use in LMS (local management of schools) formula funding and in current pay arrangements for teachers merits critical scrutiny.

To return to the lessons from Burnham history, the shortage of certain subject teachers – notably in mathematics and science – was an issue in the 1950s, and of course later, which the ministry raised with the Burnham Committee. This was one of the pressures leading the local authority employers to develop proposals for a career structure which consolidated the trend towards clear differentials based on the unit total system. The grammar school teacher unions had exerted similar pressure on the employers, incensed that not even all the permitted 'promoted' posts of special responsibility were being used by local education authorities. The 1956 Burnham Report thus moved strongly in favour of pay differentials, but was accepted by the Teachers' Panel, NUT dominated at that time, only after the employers had agreed to raise the top level of the basic scale.

Similarly in 1970 – by which time under the Remuneration of Teachers Act 1965 the DES was represented directly on the Burnham Management Panel – both central government and local authorities pressed for a change in salaries structure, arguing that the career structure of 1956 no longer met the needs of schools. Again the shortage of mathematics and science teachers was pressing. The minority unions on the Teachers' Panel (Joint Four, National Association of Schoolmasters and National Association of Head Teachers) were concerned about lack of adequate career prospects. By 1970 the Assistant Masters Association and the NAS favoured consolidated scales which became the basis of the Management Panel's scheme. But as in 1956, so in 1971, the NUT opposed the employers' structural proposals. This time the deadlock in negotiations led to arbitration under the Remuneration of Teachers Act 1965 and as a result consolidated scales were introduced.

A feature of the 1971 negotiations was that the period of educational expansion was drawing to a close and the earlier salaries structure was too rigid in the changed circumstances. The Treasury and Cabinet promised larger sums of money if used for restructuring. The employers sought restructuring for various reasons:

1 Education officers around the country were suggesting that staffing of schools was generally a major problem, that there was a lack of staffing stability, and that this pointed to the need for a clear career structure.
2 The fact that recruitment publicity was by the existing structure prevented from stating the salary for the post gave teaching a bad image.
3 Consolidated scales as proposed could be used to differentiate levels of responsibility and the incremental structure would reward experience, unlike the one-time allowance under the 1956 system.
4 Using the 1956 allowances in order to attract shortage subject teachers was very unpopular in staffrooms.
5 There were problems in attracting young and able staff into schools because the bottom end of the basic scale compared unfavourably with further education salaries.

The negotiating difficulties in the Burnham Committee to secure structural change were compounded in the 1980s. By then demographic trends were resulting in spectacular falls of school rolls, first in primary, then in secondary schools. This coincided with an ageing profile of the teaching profession following closure of many colleges of education and a fall in recruitment of young teachers. Younger teachers were demanding promotion but many older colleagues were nowhere near retirement age. All this played havoc with teachers' career and promotion opportunities, leading to the setting up by the Burnham Committee of a joint working party to review the salaries structure. Burnham always needed to be subjected to explicit pressure before addressing the difficult issues of structure. All too often the Management Panel was dominated by worries about finance and global sums of money, while the Teachers' Panel concentrated on the traditional claims based on cost of living and comparability with other professions, which tended to result in flat-rate or percentage increases across the board and, in the former case, a reduction in differentials.

Apart from reduced opportunities for promotion, other chestnuts reared their heads. The DES again pressed for differential scales for mathematics and science teachers, as these were still in short supply. Both unions and local authority employers resisted this demand on the familiar grounds that such an arrangement would generate bad feeling in staffrooms. There were also doubts over the market mechanism providing a solution: Alexander, who as secretary of the local authorities' negotiating panel dominated Burnham for some thirty years, always argued that the answer to shortage lay on the supply side. However, evidence showed that shortage subject teachers benefited from accelerated promotion compared with other teachers and were sometimes recruited above scale 1. Furthermore, the unwillingness of teacher unions to accept special reward for excellence as a classroom teacher meant that some shortage subject teachers were syphoned off into administrative posts which earned them higher pay.

A newer feature of the 1980s was criticism of the country's post-16 provision (Briault and Smith 1980; Macfarlane 1981). Both reports drew critical attention to the age-weighting and salaries system.

Some progress was made by the joint working party, but as always there arose a host of difficulties in reaching agreement. By this time the government was placing emphasis on improved quality through improving teacher performance (DES 1983). As structural change is always expensive, Treasury and DES support was essential and by 1984 the Burnham Management Panel was prepared to draft a scheme under which teacher appraisal might be linked to a new salaries structure, to make reform acceptable to the secretary of state before he went cap-in-hand to the Treasury and Cabinet. The proposed linkage between teacher assessment and pay resulted in the NUT representatives walking out of the joint working party.

Another attempt by the Burnham Management Panel to facilitate agreement through negotiation involved seeking DES approval for legislation to create one forum to negotiate both salaries and conditions of service. This would have facilitated trade-off bargaining widely practised in other fields of employment. Initially the DES supported this endeavour and Mark Carlisle as secretary of state opened discussions on the issue. The unions were not supportive and there was some procrastination. Then, in 1981, Carlisle was succeeded by Sir Keith Joseph and DES support for legislation was withdrawn. Sir Keith argued to the local authority representatives that he remained unconvinced that the Burnham set-up prevented trade-off bargaining. The local authority employers had their doubts and were left to put this to the test; there followed the period of industrial action of the mid–1980s which ended with Kenneth Baker, who succeeded Sir Keith in 1986, sweeping away the Burnham Committee and imposing his own salaries structure and contract of employment. Seven years had passed during which negotiations had failed to produce a new salaries structure and an agreed contract of employment. The Advisory, Conciliation and Arbitration Service (ACAS) had become involved to try to achieve a negotiated settlement, but Baker found the resulting proposals unacceptable. He argued that the proposed maximum of the standard scale was too high and that there should be five, not merely two, incentive allowances. Once again the secretary of state believed in sharper differentials than the Burnham Committee was prepared to accept.

It is Baker's 1987 salaries structure which still prevails in 1991, although the Interim Advisory Committee recommendations, and especially those contained in its third report (IAC 1990) which were accepted by the secretary of state, have introduced greater flexibility. Table 6.1 shows for 1945, 1956, 1971 and 1974 the salary arrangements for all school teachers and describes the differentials in operation.

Table 6.1 Major Burnham settlements: the salaries structure

All schoolteachers	Differentials
1945 Basic scale	• Personal additions, extra qualifications • Posts of special responsibility • Headteachers: addition for each unit of 100 pupils and of 30 pupils over 15 years
1956 Basic scale	Career structure based on unit total system: graded posts; heads of dept; deputy heads; heads
1971 Five consolidated scales	Career structure based on unit total system: Promotion to higher scales. Separate incremental scales for deputies (1971) (heads 1965)
1974 Four consolidated scales	Career structure as above, but scale for senior teachers added to hierarchy (1972)

Source: Saran (1989: 100)

PAY FLEXIBILITY AND THE IAC

The four reports of the Independent Advisory Committee were published between 1988 and 1991. These will be examined against the backcloth of government policy for the public services and for pay flexibility in particular. Pay flexibility is a precondition for the introduction of performance-related pay. An extension of the use of performance-related pay increases differentials on the basis of individual performance. It was noted in the previous section that the DES and often the local authorities favoured increasing differentials.

While performance-related pay is only one method of achieving sharper differentials, it is the method that has topped the policy agenda. The first school to introduce performance-related pay for the whole teaching staff was Kemnal Manor Boys School in Kent (*Education Guardian* 14 May 1991: 23); their system involves the setting of personal targets, the achievement of which could entitle a teacher to a bonus of between £500 and £1,500. The head at another school (Dorridge Junior School in Solihull) had accepted a five-year 'fixed-term contract with performance-related pay', which promises 10 per cent (about £3,000) over the going rate for a Group 3 school 'if he performs satisfactorily' in relation to a checklist of thirty-two requirements involving an 'agenda any head might set himself' (*Education Guardian* 14 May 1991: 23).

Clearly the pay structures for school teachers had changed to permit the above arrangements to be made at these two schools. The changes in question resulted in particular from the recommendations for greater flexibility of the third IAC report which are outlined later in this chapter. For some time the government's explicit policy statements have favoured more flexible pay systems in the public sector.

Since much of the funding for public services comes from the centre, the government's declared policy has been an important pressure for changing pay structures. In his autumn statement in 1990 the chancellor of the exchequer said that government money would be withheld if future pay settlements failed to incorporate 'further flexibility and differentiation' (Trinder 1991: 9). Within a few months John Major revealed

> that he is pushing his performance related pay reforms for public sector workers through the Whitehall machinery at breakneck speed, in order to offer a 'Citizen's Charter' in mid-summer. . . . Although the latest blueprint for quality avoids pay deductions for shoddy work, it envisages free tickets for passengers suffering chronically late trains and raises the prospect of teachers, train drivers, dustmen and civil servants all being given additional pay only on the basis of performance and public satisfaction. In effect, part of a pay settlement would be set aside each year for bonuses.
>
> (*Guardian* 10 May 1991: 1)

However flexible pay structures may be, two preconditions for the implementation of performance-related pay are decentralized decision-making structures and a system of staff appraisal. Higher pay for persons exercising a particular function, for example, headteachers and deputy heads as managers of institutions, can be specified in a national pay structure. But whether a particular manager in a given school should be placed, on performance criteria, at a point in the pay spine higher or lower than another manager ostensibly doing the same job in another similar school cannot be decided nationally. Furthermore, if performance-related pay differentiation is to have a chance of being accepted and seen to be fair as between colleagues working together at the same institution, then the system of appraisal of performance has also to be accepted as fair. This raises all the debatable points about whether and how performance in a caring profession like teaching can be assessed, qualitatively let alone quantitatively, since productivity is such an elusive concept when a service like education is compared with the output of manufacturing industry. There is the further problem about appraisal for development, often described as 'teacher friendly', or appraisal for purposes of awarding merit pay, the direct or 'indirect' linkage to pay.

Leaving these debates aside, decentralization of decision-making and teacher appraisal were provided for in the legislative package of the late 1980s. The Education (No. 2) Act 1986 required the reconstitutions of school governing bodies and conferred on them wider responsibilities. The same Act empowered the secretary of state to make regulations requiring local authorities and schools to establish a system of staff appraisal. The Teachers' Pay and Conditions Act 1987 permits the secretary of state to make different pay awards for different areas of the country. Thus it laid the legal basis for the fragmentation of pay settlements or, put differently, for regional variation and flexibilities in pay structures. As it happens the reports of the IAC recommended against regional variations.

Under the Education Reform Act 1988 the powers of local education authorities were further weakened and that of school governing bodies extended by the delegation of budgets under LMS and by the opting-out arrangements. The governors of grant-maintained schools and the governors of county schools with delegated budgets – all schools, including small primary and special schools, are to become LMS schools – have also acquired from the LEA the employment powers hitherto exercised by governors only in the case of voluntary aided schools. Pay, appointment and dismissal – as regulated by law – have been devolved on governors, although in county schools the LEA has remained the employer, retaining employer responsibilities but stripped of the usual concurrent powers. To sum up, the various government measures have aimed to subject public services to the discipline of the market as part of wider government policy to give consumers more choice and to curb the power of producers, particularly the power of organized labour in trade unions.

When the IAC was appointed by Kenneth Baker in 1987, his new imposed pay structure was already in place. It replaced the consolidated scales of the 1971 settlement with a single scale for main professional grade (MPG) teachers – from January 1991 called the standard scale – and created a system of incentive allowances (IAs), as well as spot salaries for deputies and heads. Teachers previously on scales above scale 1 were assimilated into the new system: scale 2 teachers were transferred to a higher salary point in the standard scale than scale 1 teachers; those on scales 3, 4 and the senior teacher scale received B, D and E incentive allowances respectively. The IAC inherited this structure, and initially the IA system gave little flexibility because, except for A and C allowances, all the available higher ones were absorbed by the assimilation process from the old to the new structure. In its first report the IAC (1988:2) stated that the percentage of the salaries bill for flexible allocation would need to be increased over time. Because of the secretary of state's specified cost ceiling of £300 million the IAC recommended for 1988 the same percentage increase for all scale and salary points, but included some differential increases for IAs.

Since it is the secretary of state who sets out the committee's brief year by year, the committee will also have been influenced by the explicit government aim that no major changes in the pay structure were envisaged for 1988–9 (IAC 1988: 6). The letter from the secretary of state to the IAC made explicit his four objectives which the committee was to take into account in its recommendations on pay and conditions: adequate recruitment, retention, motivation and quality of teachers (IAC 1988). Recruitment, retention and motivation of the teacher force preoccupied the IAC throughout the four years.

The second report drew attention to the representations of the National Employers' Organization (NEO), suggesting that the spot salaries for headteachers and deputy heads should be replaced by salary ranges, with guidelines setting out criteria for determining the pay point of individual heads and deputies (IAC 1989: 9). The impact of the introduction of local management of schools (LMS) on the work of headteachers was given as a reason by the NEO for wishing to differentiate the pay rewards on the basis of performance. This was a clear pointer to the coming of performance-related pay, at least for the top managers in schools. An important comment on differentials in the salaries structure was made at this stage: the standard scale, it was argued, should form the greater proportion of the salary earned by IA holders. The conclusion drawn was that unless the standard scale was adequately resourced, expansion of the IA system would have limited effect. On this assumption, in contrast to DES views at the time, the IAC suggested that the increase in the number of IAs in the next few years should provide allowance for two-thirds of teachers on the standard scale: the DES figure was 50 per cent (IAC 1989: 32). While the IAC was clearly constrained by cost limitations imposed by government, it nevertheless tried to exert pressure for more resources to achieve the secretary of state's declared aims.

Before analysing the third IAC report, which, of the four produced, was by far the most important for performance-related pay, it is useful to study some figures (Table 6.2) drawn from IAC reports, press cuttings and DES circulars. These figures show trends over the four years and demonstrate beyond doubt that differentials have become steeper, even though it remains true that the greater proportion of salary earned by standard scale teachers comes from their basic pay. It is particularly striking that in 1991 IAs were raised by 30 per cent; furthermore, using detailed figures, not in Table 6.2, of increased money values for each year in pay points and IAs, it can be shown that, whereas the standard scale increased by 38.2 per cent between 1988 and 1991 (when fully implemented), the number of incentive allowances increased by 54 per cent over the same period. It was calculated that, by December 1991, almost 50 per cent of primary and 70 per cent of secondary school teachers would hold an IA (*DES News* 32/91 31 January 1991: section on IAs). The money value of the A allowances over the four years rose by 141 per cent, of Bs and Cs by 95 per cent

Table 6.2 Increase in pay and incentive allowances 1988–91

	Percentage	increase	when	fully
		implemented		
	1988	1989	1990	1991
Standard scale	4.2	6.0	8.3	9.5
Deputy heads	4.2	7.5	10.4	12.75
Headteachers	4.2	7.5	10.4	12.75
Incentive allowances				
A	60.0			
B	20.0			
C	20.0	7.0	17.0	30.0
D	6.7			
E	4.8			

each, of Ds by 73 per cent and of Es by 70 per cent. Lastly, it is interesting to know that in 1991, when the proposals were fully implemented, teachers at the top of the standard scale holding an E allowance received 30 per cent of their total pay from the value of the IA; those on Ds, 23 per cent, on Cs 18 per cent, on Bs 10 per cent, and finally those on As only 6.4 per cent.

Given the growing importance of the IA system, it should be noted that when the relevant body (in most cases the governors) award an allowance (no teacher may hold more than one simultaneously), at least one of the four listed criteria must be fulfilled (DES 1990: 7, para 27). The teacher concerned must

1 undertake responsibilities beyond those common to the majority of teachers
2 have demonstrated outstanding ability as a classroom teacher
3 be employed to teach subjects in which there is a shortage of teachers
4 be employed in a post which is difficult to fill.

The first two of these criteria relate to the performance by individual teachers and could thus be seen as part of a performance-related pay system. The last two are more to do with market conditions relating to availability of particular specialisms or skills. It is not surprising that the demonstration of 'outstanding ability as a classroom teacher' has not frequently been cited as a reason for awarding IAs; the IAC and others have commented on non-use of this criterion. Yet it is the use of this criterion which would be important for any extension of performance-related pay for classroom teachers. Teacher unions have always accepted that undertaking responsibilities beyond those falling to all classroom teachers should be given recognition by way of extra pay, so the setting out of special responsibilities in job descriptions of IA holders has become common practice. Acceptance of differential rewards for performance as an excellent classroom teacher has always been problematical because of suspicions about unfairness. As confidence grows in appraisal systems this may change.

An outline of the important pay flexibilities recommended by the third report of the IAC (1990) follows. The main aim was to extend the range of discretion exercised by local education authorities (LEAs) and governing bodies in accordance with the dominant market ideology of the government. The discretion given is twofold: over the salaries of headteachers and deputy heads on the one hand and over pay for classroom teachers on the other.

For heads and deputy heads the former fourteen school groups and their spot salaries were in January 1991 replaced by six school groups and a 49-point pay spine (51-point spine from December 1991). Each school group, determined as before by the number and ages of pupils on roll, is placed against a given range on the pay spine (DES 1990: Annex E). It should be noted that the payspine range is not an incremental scale for heads and deputy heads. Each relevant body, usually the governing body, has discretion to determine the particular spine point on which its head and deputy is paid; this may be reviewed, but there is no automatic entitlement to moving up the spine. Salaries of existing head teachers and deputy heads were assimilated into the new pay spine on the basis of their old school group. As in the case of incentive allowances, the IAC laid down several criteria to which the relevant body shall have regard when exercising its discretion, although these need not be seen as exclusive:

1 the responsibilities of the post
2 the social, economic and cultural background of the pupils attending the school
3 the difficulty in filling the post
4 whether the head or deputy has demonstrated 'sustained exceptional levels of performance'.

The last of the four listed criteria is particularly relevant to performance related pay. It was reformulated in the fourth report, following comments that defining its meaning was difficult. The new formulation refers to 'sustained overall performance by the head teacher or deputy head teacher which appreciably exceeds that normally expected from the holders of such posts' (IAC 1991: 38, para 5.41).

For classroom teachers incremental enhancement was introduced, enabling the relevant body to award to individual teachers a supplement of four specified amounts, subject to certain constraints: no supplement is to exceed the next scale point, nor to take the teacher's salary above the top of the standard scale; supplements are subject to review each September, which could provide the basis for linking review to appraisal. In this case the IAC set out no criteria for the award of supplements; relevant bodies should award them 'according to local circumstances' (IAC

1991: 36, para 5.30). Incremental enhancement was seen as providing pay flexibility for teachers not yet at the top of the standard scale.

To provide flexibility for teachers already on the maximum, the third IAC report suggested that LEAs be empowered from January 1991 to establish a local extended scale, raising the standard scale maximum by not more than £2,000. The award of additional increments to individual teachers on such a local extended scale was placed in the hands of the relevant body. Under the fourth report the ceiling was raised to £3,000, and the terminology changed from 'local extended scale' to 'discretionary scale points'. Furthermore, from September 1991 it is for each relevant body to decide not merely on the award of discretionary scale points but whether to create such pay points above the maximum of the standard scale (IAC 1991: 37, paras 5.32–5.33). Advice was offered by the IAC about how discretionary scale points might be used. The fourth report argued that the award of IAs was usually based on a combination of the four listed criteria, and 'seldom on the second criterion alone', that of outstanding classroom teaching. The report's recommendation was that 'discretionary scale points should be awarded to teachers against the criterion of the performance of the teacher across all aspects of his or her professional activity, but with particular attention being given to classroom teaching' (IAC 1991: 37, para 5.35). It will be interesting to see whether, when appraisal is fully in place, good classroom teaching will eventually, after fifty years – 1945 to 1995 – be given recognition in terms of performance related pay.

To sum up, by September 1991 the IAC's recommendations, accepted by the DES, and enacted under regulations, will enable relevant bodies to exercise discretion within the national pay structure by means of:

1 the award of incentive allowances
2 incremental enhancement
3 the award of discretionary scale points beyond the maximum for headteachers and deputy heads, placing them on the appropriate salary point within the range of the pay spine for the given school group.

The fact that flexibility is now an in-built part of the pay structure in itself does not mean that performance-related pay will spread rapidly. School governing bodies will be managing very tight budgets; giving more to some means less for others. Furthermore, a high proportion of teachers' total remuneration will continue to depend on the level of the standard scale. It is possible that the trend of a rising proportion of the pay bill put into differentials, continues. However, to achieve the aims of the pay system, that is to recruit, retain and motivate teachers in adequate numbers and of adequate quality, it is essential to offer to teachers not earning the higher levels of salary adequate pay on entry and in the early stages of their careers. The traditional trade union claims based on cost of living and comparability will retain their importance to ensure adequate basic pay for teachers. Motivation is affected by teacher morale. The IAC has repeatedly noted that unfavourable pay levels and pay comparability affect morale adversely (IAC 1990: 22, para 3.48). Performance-related pay as part of a flexible pay system is an inadequate tool, at least in achieving the aim of recruitment; its role in retention and motivation is likely to be much more significant.

A heavy responsibility rests on governing bodies to develop clear criteria whenever the available discretions over pay are exercised. There is no compulsion to use them. Indeed, 'in education in the UK . . . the early indications are that they are very under used at present and not just because of budget constraints' (Trinder 1991: 12). The National Employers' Organization (NEO) saw the new flexibilities as 'key features of the national framework which has to respond to issues such as changes to staffing structures in schools and difficulties of recruitment and retention'. But the NEO expressed concern about the fact that the document (DES 1990) showed a 'lack of criteria' for the exercise of the new discretions; they argued that this lack increased 'the need for LEAs to give advice' and to monitor the use of the wide ranging discretionary powers now available (LACSAB 1991: 3). The *Employers' Commentary on Salary Provisions* (LACSAB 1991) provides a detailed account of the new arrangements, and of the interrelationships between the different salary provisions. It stresses the importance of governors making their criteria crystal clear so that fairness is seen to be done:

> decisions of LMS schools should be subject to the same tests of reasonableness which would be applied to decisions by LEAs. LEAs are respondents to claims for equal pay and will want to bear this in mind in giving advice to governing bodies.
>
> (LACSAB 1991: 23)

A PAY REVIEW BODY FOR TEACHERS

Most public services are labour intensive and, given the size of the teacher force, teacher pay is big business. One example of this is that the education sector would have accounted for half the estimated total cost in 1990 of restoring to public sector employees their 1981 relative pay levels (Brown and Rowthorn 1990: 19). In central and local government services in the UK the number of employees in education – approximately 1.4 million – outstrips the next largest group, in the National Health Service (NHS) – approximately 1.2 million (Trinder 1991: Table 1). School teachers in England and Wales number around 400,000: this is the group with which this chapter deals.

Trends for public sector pay show 'a pattern of prolonged falls in relative pay, and sometimes absolute pay too, followed by large, expensive "catching up" awards' (Trinder 1990: 1). Peaks in teacher pay have occurred after several years of restraint and have usually coincided with general elections. In 1987–8 teachers were given a 'catching up' award of 16.8 per cent. But by 1991 the whole of the gain had been wiped out: 1990–1 was the second year running in which teacher pay was lower than private sector pay, and the pay rises for that year were below the rate of inflation, for 'the first time ... since 1982–83' (Trinder 1990: 2).

Such a cyclical pay pattern is not conducive to stable industrial relations. The number of teacher working days lost between 1985 and 1987 was 910,000 (IAC 1988: 1, para 3). By the mid-1980s it was generally recognized that the Burnham machinery was in dire need of reform (Saran 1988: ch. 2). It was at the end of those years of industrial dispute in the schools that Kenneth Baker, secretary of state, enacted the Teachers' Pay and Conditions Act 1987, under which unions and employers lost their bargaining rights at national level. Burnham was not reformed: it was simply abolished.

The advisory committee set up under the 1987 Act was called the *Interim* Advisory Committee because the legislation provided for the restoration of negotiating rights within two years. In the event parliament extended the time limit and the IAC operated for four years. There was a first round of consultations about DES proposals for future negotiating machinery (DES 1987), but this Green Paper received a universally unfavourable response and was eventually withdrawn. What was clear was that the suggested powers to be retained by the secretary of state would have been considerably greater than under the former Burnham system. During 1989 and 1990, while John MacGregor was secretary of state, discussions between the DES, teacher unions and employers were resumed and the government's proposals for new negotiating machinery were announced in July 1990. It fell to Kenneth Clarke, on succeeding John MacGregor as secretary of state in November 1990, to introduce the School Teachers' Pay and Conditions Bill during his first month of office. It provided for the restoration of limited national negotiating rights for employers and teacher unions. The main features of the Bill were

1. no government presence at the negotiating table
2. agreements to be recommendations to the secretary of state
3. a separate sub-committee for headteachers and deputy heads
4. a firm deadline for the completion of negotiations, failing which there would be reference to an advisory committee
5. reserve powers for the government and, as a last resort, the ability to impose its own settlement
6. certain government pledges about total costs
7. changes in pay and conditions to be implemented through a statutory instrument
8. provision for withdrawal from national arrangements and determination of teacher pay and conditions locally by LEAs or the governing bodies of grant-maintained schools.

(*DES News* 372/90 16 November 1990)

However, this first Bill was withdrawn in favour of a second one (School Teachers' Pay and Conditions (No. 2) Bill) which provided for the setting up of a pay review body for teachers. The secretary of state announced the review body in April 1991, adding that he expected in return 'an agreement not to strike over pay and conditions'. Immediately the NUT 'demanded a return of negotiating rights' and the NAS/UWT, by contrast, commented 'this is a very promising day for the teaching profession' but added that 'it is most unfair to demand that we give up our ability to influence events by surrendering the right to take action' (*Guardian* 18 April 1991: 20). During the Second Reading debate shortly afterwards, the secretary of state stated that 'five of the six teachers' trade unions support the notion of a review body', and that 'opposition within the NUT is more muted than some of its militants would wish' (*Guardian* 30 April 1991: 4).

Review bodies have existed for some time in some of the other public services, for example for doctors and nurses in the NHS. In announcing the government's change of policy to the House of Commons, the secretary of state explained that the government hitherto had not favoured a review body for teachers because of the 'emphasis teacher unions had placed on their ability to take industrial action'. However, the situation changed substantially:

> Teachers have worked with great professional commitment on the implementation of the 1988 reforms. The recommendations of the interim advisory committee... have produced a more progressive and flexible salary structure.... The public and the vast majority of teachers do not want to see any return to industrial action affecting the education of pupils... I am confident that the public will welcome the Government's acknowledgement of the professional status of teachers, and our offer to them of the review body status reserved to certain key non-striking professions.
>
> (*Hansard* 17 April 1991: col. 433)

What, then, are the differences between the IAC and the new pay review body? Many features are similar: the secretary of state is the person to refer to the review body matters relating to conditions of employment of school teachers; the review body is required to invite submission of evidence and representations from employers, unions and governors of grant-maintained schools, unless the last mentioned have requested to be exempted from national pay and conditions; implementation of pay and conditions will be by statutory order, but before making an order the secretary of state is to consult relevant bodies.

The secretary of state has power to amend the review body's recommendation or even to make alternative provisions. One point that was raised in the Second Reading debate was whether the powers the Bill will confer are excessive. But, on behalf of the government, Kenneth Clarke undertook 'to implement the Review Body's recommendations unless there are clear and compelling reasons to the contrary' (*DES News* 124/91 17 April 1991). He also praised the work of the IAC, 'which had indeed produced a welcome improvement, especially in local flexibility in settling teachers' pay'. Distinguishing the review body from the IAC the secretary of state said:

> The difference between the new review body and the interim advisory committee ... is that the new body will not work within any predetermined financial remit. It will be enjoined to have regard to affordability and the need to recruit and retain ... but there will be no predetermined financial remit. Also the body will be appointed by the Prime Minister and report to him. He will give effect to its recommendations unless, as we have always said with all review bodies, there are clear and compelling reasons for not doing so.
> (*Hansard* 17 April 1991: col. 437)

Kenneth Clarke also attached importance to 'allowing schools the scope to tailor pay to their own needs in the light of local labour markets'. The IAC had already conferred on schools 'the freedom to choose from a wide menu of options within the national framework' and he expected the review body to build on that approach. Grant-maintained schools 'will be able to make their own arrangements if they want to go further' (*Hansard* 17 April 1991: col. 434).

An assessment of the merits of pay review bodies might require consideration of the following advantages:

1 the promise of industrial peace, partly by diminishing or eliminating the difficulties that arose in negotiations through the multi-union situation which made the reaching of agreement on structural changes practically impossible
2 the possible reduction in pay cycles: review bodies might act as a counterweight to short-term governmental pressures.

As for the disadvantages, these include

1 doubts about the independence of review bodies, although the history of the Burnham Committee shows that public sector bargaining and arbitration were also constrained by government
2 the loss of bargaining rights at national level, which weakens unions and employers.

Beyond this one might well ask how relevant a review body will be, given that many decisions about pay and conditions are likely to be made at local level. The government is encouraging more schools to opt for grant-maintained status; their governors will have the right to be totally exempt from the national system and to negotiate directly at institutional level the pay and conditions of their teachers. While schools in the LEA-maintained sector will not be empowered to claim exemption from statutory pay and conditions orders, under LMS their governors will be able to make full use of discretions granted within the national framework.

Maybe, then, it will fall to the review body to extend the permitted flexibilities which have been established so recently that we do not know yet how they will work. Maybe the review body will in addition make recommendations on the levels of a national standard scale, on lower and upper limits for the award of incentive allowances, and on the pay spine for headteachers and deputy heads. Despite its commitment to the fragmentation of national pay structures and the undermining of union power, perhaps the government will in the end favour maintenance of such a national framework alongside local flexibilities because it will facilitate retaining overall control of the pay bill for teachers. The government's commitment to a review body rather than to the restoration of negotiating rights is understandable as long as a national framework for pay is retained. While unions and local authorities can make their representations, their power remains curtailed. Consultation, the right to be heard, is very different from the right to negotiate.

Loss of negotiating rights at national level in combination with fragmentation of decision centres will have profound effects on the way teacher unions operate. They will need to develop negotiating skills locally, and especially at institutional level. The Assistant Masters and Mistresses Association (AMMA) had 'already negotiated several local deals with CTCs [city technology colleges] on salaries and conditions' (*Education* 12 April 1991: 292). The more abrasive NAS/UWT was reported to be adjusting its strategies to the 'emerging reality of school-based "negotiations" and increased governors' powers'. The union would be fighting individual redundancy bids and promised its members at its annual conference to 'tear into [governors] who awarded huge pay rises to heads' (*Education* 12 April 1991: 297). There have already been press reports of governors doing precisely this, but so far these cases are the exception.

The industrial relations implications of using pay flexibilities to introduce performance-related pay in schools are considerable. Much has been written about participative styles of school management as the preferred model in terms of sustaining teacher morale and professional commitment, so important for constructing a school development plan in which all staff share ownership of its content. It is at least arguable that teamwork produces better quality education for children than a hierarchical style of management. Performance related pay is an individualistic concept. Can it also be tailored to reward team performance? In the NHS, when a team performs a successful operation or when a patient is cared for in an intensive care unit, who can tell how much of the success is attributable to the doctor, the nurse or even to those who maintain essential equipment? It may be that such questions do not plague ministers who have acclaimed pay flexibility and performance-related pay, but they will surely preoccupy many a governing body and the headteachers who have to advise governors how their school can best deliver a high-quality service to pupils and parents.

One of the first warnings about the extension of performance-related pay to schools is to recognize that individual differentiation in reward for people working as a team necessitates clarity of purpose as to what the payments are rewarding. This is as true for the headteacher or deputy head as it is for classroom teachers. So governors who decide to use the pay flexibilities which became available in 1991 need to develop clear policies if undesirable side-effects are to be avoided.

REFERENCES

Briault, E. and Smith, F. (1980) *Falling Rolls in Secondary Schools*, Parts 1 and 2, Slough: National Foundation for Educational Research.
Brown, W. and Rowthorn, B. (1990) *A Public Service Pay Policy*, London: Fabian Society.
DES (1983) *Teaching Quality*, Cmnd 8836, London: HMSO.
—— (1987) *Teachers' Pay and Conditions: A Consultative Document*, Cm 238, London: HMSO.
—— (1990) *School Teachers' Pay and Conditions Document 1990*, London: HMSO.
Economist Intelligence Unit (1970) *The Remuneration of Young Teachers, Effect on Recruitment and Wastage*, for ATCDE, London: *The Economist*.
Galbraith, J. K. (1962) *The Affluent Society*, Harmondsworth: Penguin (in association with Hamish Hamilton, original publishers, 1958).
Hilsum, S. and Start, K. B. (1974) *Promotion and Careers in Teaching*, Slough: National Foundation for Educational Research.
IAC (1988) *Report of the Interim Advisory Committee on School Teachers' Pay and Conditions*, Cm 363, London: HMSO.
—— (1989) *Second Report of the Interim Advisory Committee on School Teachers' Pay and Conditions*, Cm 625, London: HMSO.

—— (1990) *Third Report of the Interim Advisory Committee on School Teachers' Pay and Conditions*, Cm 973, London: HMSO.
—— (1991) *Fourth Report of the Interim Advisory Committee on School Teachers' Pay and Conditions*, Cm 1415, London: HMSO.
LACSAB (1991) *Employers' Commentary on Salary Provisions*, London: Local Authorities Conditions of Service Advisory Board.
Macfarlane Report (1981) *Education for 16–19 Year Olds*, London: Department of Education and Science.
Saran, R. (1988) Schoolteachers' pay and conditions of employment in England and Wales, in R. Saran, and J. Sheldrake, (eds) *Public Sector Bargaining in the 1980s*, Aldershot: Gower.
—— (1989) *The Politics behind Burnham*, 2nd edn, Sheffield: Centre for Education Management and Administration, Sheffield City Polytechnic.
Trinder, C. (1990) *Teachers' Pay*, London: Public Finance Foundation.
—— (1991) Monitoring pay flexibility in the public sector, seminar paper at Public Finance Foundation (CIPFA), 14 February, London: Public Finance Foundation.

Chapter 7

Teachers' pay and personal professional development

Alan Marr

The professional context for teachers is rapidly becoming more complex as the timetable for implementing the changes enshrined in the Education Reform Act 1988 unfolds. The legislation has provided both a potential and an impetus for increased variability and flexibility of contract, conditions of service and levels of pay which are now only just beginning to be realized. School governors are becoming increasingly aware of the new options that are available to them, and at the same time are steadily more critical of the residual powers and authority that remain the responsibility of LEAs, now themselves ambivalent about their future roles and functions. It appears as if everything is in a state of flux. Instability and uncertainty are the new watchwords for a system where opportunities are created by the new autonomy, as responsibilities, powers and potential are realigned and begin to dawn.

Although the cumulative impact and effect of the policy changes is filtering into media reports and the professional literature alike, there is still little understanding of the ways in which teachers' professionalism is changing and being redefined, as the tasks they undertake in their daily working lives are reshaped under the aegis of the legislation.

Since 1988 during the operation of the Interim Advisory Committee on Teachers' Pay, a range of measures has been introduced and deployed which offers employers some degree of flexibility in regard to the assessment of teachers' salaries (IAC 1991). However, there is still very little recognition of the differential impact the changes are having on LEAs or individual schools, let alone on the teachers themselves.

If the new funding arrangements for schools are beginning to have a differential impact upon provision, either because of formula funding or the option of grant-maintained status, this can only be exacerbated in the years ahead by the increased drive for a greater differentiation of the profession itself, through performance-related pay schemes particularly. The problem is that there is no evidence whatever that the actual performance of teachers has been either influenced directly by salary levels, or improved in those schools where this type of scheme has been in operation, notably in the USA.

The model for performance-related pay schemes in this country is perhaps inevitably derived from those of industry and commerce. Following acute prompting by the government, the greatest advocates are the private management consultants who have often worked in those spheres. Unfortunately the model that is becoming commonly used has two features which should be viewed with some scepticism: first, it assumes an empirical relationship between selected criteria and the quality of performance which does not exist, and second it assumes that the tasks involved to reach performance levels are qualitatively equal. The problem is that these schemes then tend to ignore the interrelationships that exist between the activities and performance of numbers of teachers, and do little to differentiate management objectives from educational objectives.

What is acknowledged by all parties to the debate about performance-related pay, is that a change in the professional culture is required if the ambitions for the improvement in the quality of the service are to be met. But this professional culture is distinctly difficult to identify and describe. There is, for instance, still an overwhelming tendency to treat teachers as an undifferentiated mass. This is a key feature even among those with responsibility for decisions about conditions of service and salary levels. In a sense this is perhaps inevitable since the job is usually spoken of as a profession, despite the number of organizational and administrative dimensions which fit uncomfortably with that definition, and point towards a series of dilemmas that has remained inherent and unresolved in the system for many years.

Indeed, it could be argued that it would be remarkable if the cultural change that is anticipated, expected or asked for, particularly by politicians, had taken place so quickly and smoothly, even among administrators and LEA officers at the heart of the decision-making process, let alone among teachers, who have traditionally been on the periphery of power and influence, and been denied access to good information. These assumptions mistake the nature of the professional culture and mistake the ways in which cultural changes occur.

What appears to have been forgotten or ignored, even by members of the IAC in their attempts to introduce the government-sponsored differentiation scheme among teachers, is the strength and influence of claims for a common purpose which frequently accompanies discussions about the idea of being a teacher. What is absent from the political debate is the realization that all personnel involved in the machinery of the system inadvertently subscribe to a common, all-embracing heritage which embodies a legacy assuming agreement and uniformity, only at the level of rhetoric. For, in practice, teachers are widely diverse, and fiercely protective and defensive of their idiosyncrasy and individuality. In short, they often assume common aims and values outside the classroom, which in their conduct is undermined, modified and transformed.

Goals can be met in a diversity of ways that are invariably almost indiscernible, and often barely conscious. It is this which complicates the processes of teaching and reduces our understanding of what actually takes place. Possibly the greatest question for those with responsibility for establishing conditions of service and levels of pay which are founded upon assessments of performance is how the targets, goals or criteria reflect qualitative differences in the ways in which they might be reached.

One of the major issues facing policy-makers is the continuation of their practice considering questions in isolation. Modern management needs to recognize the importance of the links between the professional and personal circumstances of teachers' lives, and then create new practices which reflect the ways in which this relationship shapes and influences performance. So far this dimension has always been ignored, and it still remains the mystery it has always been. However, it is these links which also shape individual and collective responses to change. All teachers weave the questions of curriculum initiative, career trajectory, working conditions, levels of pay and institutional and organizational politics into a colourful fabric that is then further imbued with the tones of their personal concerns, values and beliefs. It is this which shapes ideas about professional identity, and heavily influences responses to calls – or demands – for change.

At one level the legislation would appear to offer employers opportunities to undermine or modify, if not yet abandon entirely, national agreements and create personal contracts. This will inevitably become a more pronounced feature of the profession in the years to come, especially if the present momentum for performance related pay is maintained. The question it raises concerns the basis on which this differentiation is to be conducted. It could, for instance, stem from appraisal procedures, if these were to incorporate information which could be provided by a coherent and detailed task analysis. Some LEAs have already chosen to bypass that route, in order to speed up the introduction process, and have developed schemes which pay teachers on a performance-related basis. Assessments about effectiveness are made against often general, if not superficial, criteria which are only at best questionably indicative of quality.

It is not, for instance, the same task to increase levels of pupil attendance at any two schools. Nor should it be assumed that the process requires similar levels of professional expertise, or even similar skills. If pupil attendance can be seen to improve, then the reasons why it might have done so and the effects this has on the quality of education may still either remain hidden, or be non-existent. Many inner urban schools have been criticized for poor levels of attendance among pupils. The easy way to improve the figures would be for schools with those problems to take recalcitrant and regular truants off roll. That would not be any indication of an improvement in the quality of work done, although it then might have the effect of changing the pupil–teacher ratio. In any case in those schools which still have their budgets controlled by LEAs, reducing the roll would probably lead to a demand for a decrease in the number of staff, and this might adversely affect the curriculum that was offered.

The measurement of performance against pre-specified objectives is more and more a feature of modern schooling in this country, but it is a methodology which is inherently flawed, irrespective of the assumptions that are made about the selection of the objectives themselves. It is preordinately a methodology which screens out the important, if not crucial, recognition of unintended consequences and influences of action, and in this way cannot be presumed to be more than indicative of change. The results tell us very little about why situations change, or indeed what has actually happened. Objectives can be met, but the reasons why they have been fulfilled will remain a mystery. In these circumstances there will be no basis for establishing a coherent and relevant programme of professional development, and no new basis for the development of teachers' career trajectories which could claim to be any less irrational or unreasonable than that which affects teachers at present.

If a greater differentiation of the teaching profession is seen as desirable and as a way of improving performance, then the way ahead would be better served through a task analysis. The problem is that we are a very long way from even establishing the benchmarks for that because of the complexity of the job itself.

TEACHING AND TEACHER IDENTITY

There is widespread disquiet and unease in the profession over teacher identity: exactly what teachers should be like and what they should do. In constructing their identities, individuals are attempting to marry a series of very disparate elements: curriculum, pedagogy, home life and career are knitted together. How teachers then describe themselves should be seen as indivisible from their actions, hopes, fears and values, although policy-makers tend to treat them as an undifferentiated conglomerate mass. It is this which is having serious consequences for school managers, administrators and the individuals alike. Policy-makers tend to consider issues in some isolation, but, for the individuals, questions are not experienced as separate concerns disassociated from their personal lives. Professionalism is being redefined, but from within, by the individual teacher, and on an *ad-hoc* basis.

It is reasonable to assume that certain gross characteristics of context, such as the political complexion of an LEA, or resourcing levels and spending priorities for instance, provide both boundaries and constraints upon the work and lives of teachers, but these exigencies are not predictive in any straightforward way of teachers' attitudes, expectations, practices and performance. Teachers are individually appearing to construct their context according to their own biographical agendas which are created from the nexus of their concerns, values and aspirations.

The problem for those people advocating the development of schemes for performance-related pay is that they will need to know far more about the culture of the profession, if the criteria chosen to indicate changes in effectiveness are to be genuinely believable. The advocates too need to be far more explicit about what they wish the new culture to be, if the option of assessing pay against performance is to continue to be conducted on a voluntary basis. The experience of the Royal Borough of Kensington and Chelsea, for instance, is interesting in this respect, since only about half of those eligible have accepted the offer to have pay assessed against performance indicators, and for widely differing reasons.

Structurally stratifying factors such as *age* or *length of service* in the profession, take on a variety of different meanings for each teacher. The implications of such factors are very much dependent upon the personal circumstances of the individual. How these questions are then discussed also changes, even within the context of single accounts by individuals, depending upon their concerns at any particular moment, and what the focus of the interviewer's questions might be. *Age*, for example, can be an irrelevance for some people, and an impediment to others. It can be attributed as a factor at some times during professional service, and less so, or not at all, at others.

These changes of emphasis and importance have been a feature of personal accounts which have been overlooked or ignored by the so-called 'life-cycle' analyses of teachers' identities, and the nature of age-related attitudes has certainly not been explored.

If teachers are looked at in terms of how they choose to explain themselves, and how they personally create specific categories as identity markers, it is evident that identity becomes an unstable concept: a site for struggle, rather than a property or a given dimension. It becomes an explanatory device which is used to justify action, and explain or make sense of what is happening, albeit in terms of conduct, career, values or personal circumstances. What is certain is that teachers' identities are in a considerable state of flux, crisis and disarray, and this ought to be of concern to those with responsibility for the organization and administration of the service.

As the calls for change accelerate and job descriptions and workloads increase the pressure and the sense of responsibility that each teacher experiences, so they increasingly begin to question the basis on which these calls are apparently being made. Levels of expectation are placed in new perspectives as priorities are realigned and reordered. Whether these are seen as reasonable or not then depends upon how teachers can accommodate the work, and whether they can discover alternative ways and means of undertaking existing commitments and exercising responsibilities. Short cuts become almost professionally institutionalized; an inevitability and endemic at all levels. Furthermore, as they are increasingly seen as being necessary, so values such as commitment become threatened, identity becomes more unstable, and morale declines.

TEACHER MORALE

Many teachers and commentators have been reporting low morale in the profession for some time now, and particularly since the professional action taken in 1985–6. At that time the designated 1,265 hours was a considerable source of complaint among staff, but since then teachers have realized that, if they are to undertake their work with any degree of professionalism, they will have to work far longer. In any case working to the designated time was seen as a way of making their lives more difficult. What has replaced the grievances about designated time is the massive concern about the denial of negotiating rights and the setting of the overall sum available to the service for salary increases even before IAC considerations.

One reason given for the low level of morale has been low pay and increases below the publicized levels of inflation. Yet the problem is that teachers' identity, performance, morale and salary levels have a more complex relationship than is often apparently presupposed. Perceptions about salary levels cannot be presumed to be reflected in poor performance, and there is no evidence which can suggest that pay has ever been the solitary influential factor which determines performance in any simple way. However, this is a relationship which is apparently taken for granted by many people with responsibility for salary levels and the amounts of annual increases.

What is more indicative of morale is the sense of alienation from the perceived values and practices of their schools, LEAs and government. Those with the most serious concern could no longer reconcile their identities with the job, and were planning or had taken early retirement. The level of alienation that exists among those of whatever age who have left the profession in recent years is high, and appears to reflect a serious mismatch in perceptions of the educational values implicit in the recent legislative proposals for change. It is also ironic that this mismatch in values is ignored by much of the government advertising which is attempting to lure qualified people back into the service, or attract people into professional training. Much of this advertising is viewed by people as harking back to more traditional values which no longer appear to apply to the task of teaching.

Teachers who have taken early retirement had often experienced long periods of illness, usually diagnosed as stress related, and others in this group reported frequent and regular absences from work because of the increase in the level of pressure. Some industrial management studies have suggested that attendance at work is often conditioned by and related to the level of responsibility embodied in the tasks undertaken. Boredom, it seems, drives people to stay away, but in schools the causes of absence may be markedly different, and founded upon a totally dissimilar basis.

Frequent absences are taken when morale is low, whether this is caused by either professional or personal circumstances, and is irrespective of responsibilities, longevity in the service or salary levels. The key professional features are:

1 a disillusionment with a management style which appears to be inappropriate for a profession, and particularly one which presumes sharply defined lines of accountability, limits the flow of information, and tends to take decisions on an executive principle, rather than through discussion and consultation.
2 limited access to management or where access is severely conditioned by hierarchy
3 little influence upon decisions, particularly those directly concerned with timetables, cover for absent colleagues, the allocation of resources, spending priorities and designation of in-service training (INSET)
4 when lesson content and pedagogy are predetermined more by executive action, and when the interpretation of content is seen as unproblematic
5 preparation becoming less thorough, especially when lessons are resource-based
6 marking is completed less frequently, not kept up-to-date, and undertaken in a short-hand fashion
7 when there has been internal reorganization under the auspices of institutional development and individuals have been either overlooked or other appointments have been made which are seen as controversial in some way
8 when requests for INSET have been turned down, either

because funding is not available, or when differences in perceptions of need have been cited as the reason
9 when institutional priorities have overridden personal needs
10 when attendance at meetings becomes infrequent and irregular, irrespective of when they are timed to take place
11 when communication is seen as being dominated by written information and instruction, and occurs in the absence of opportunities for discussion and consultation.

Many teachers claim that they want to get out, or that they feel trapped and alienated. These teachers report a pervasive sense of bewilderment and acute frustration at a system that they see as unsympathetic to their needs, not recognizing or rewarding their virtues and not helping with their sense of a future career trajectory. One of the most frequently used expressions which summarizes this aspect of low morale is 'What's the point, my face doesn't fit'.

There are a significant number of teachers who make these claims, and they constitute an important disaffected underclass who nevertheless promulgate a back-to-basics philosophy, founded upon a stated desire to concentrate on classroom activity, as if it was in some special way immune and insulated from much of what is happening to the curriculum in schools. It is as if they wish to create some haven of comfort, and make a vestigial demonstration that their skills and personal values remain intact. It is, however, often a pretence, a mask for thwarted ambition and confusion about their sense of career and the future.

There is widespread suspicion of a credibility gap between the rhetoric of school or LEA managers and politicians who make encouraging noises about hard work and creativity, and the reality, which is felt to derive from a covert agenda. This is most commonly presumed to be based upon

1 personality, or personal dislike and disapproval
2 perceptions about supposed pedagogy
3 union activity
4 a close association or identification with miscreant pupils who are more generally disapproved of within the school
5 lack of status attached to subject specialism as a result of the greater definition and specification of the curriculum.

Other, usually older, teachers conveyed their sense of low morale through the use of golden-age accounts of their professional service. These accounts convey a sense of spoiled identity, and concern a profession that had changed for the worse. Colleagues were portrayed as being dramatically different from those of earlier times, or were described as having changed to further their careers. Some were perceived to have abandoned important ideals, values and interests. These stories often contained apocryphal accounts of individual children, or concerned notorious groups, and the descriptions were meant to be shocking. Very often in these accounts the past was juxtaposed with present conditions as a form of critique, and noticeably was meant to lend credibility to the idea that standards of behaviour and pupil attainment were now much lower. Ironically too, there was apparently also a greater acceptance and tolerance of precisely the kind of dictatorial management style that was cited as a cause for complaint and regret in the current situation.

A marked feature of the golden-age accounts was the way in which they tended to contradict the criticisms that were being made, and the reasons why individuals were disaffected and wanted to get out. Demoralization can be attributed to a combination of factors, such as additional responsibilities, often without extra pay, and incurred through statutory obligation or even because of reappointment during internal reorganization. Senior staff, particularly, now often have unrealistically complex job descriptions, and have seemingly little chance of fulfilling the objectives or requirements that are designated and specified. This feature has important consequences, both for the individuals concerned, and their colleagues.

1 Longer-term planning is often subverted and misaligned as managers resort to a crisis management model of operation, often because of the changes that are made during the implementation stages of assessment procedures and the composition of the national curriculum, and as their understanding of LMS develops.
2 Performance criteria become more generalized instead of becoming more specific as the constraints on work are recognized and understood.
3 Staff outside the management hierarchy bear a greater workload to compensate for the increase in management tasks: this causes frustration and resentment, largely because it emphasizes the

real lack of any professional accountability procedures or mechanism which can be invoked.
4 Accountability procedures are being increasingly removed from the control of those teachers who operate outside of management circles. If line management models are to predominate in the future, as they may, then schools and LEAs need to develop procedures which can ensure that senior staff become professionally accountable. It appears that it is unlikely that staff will accept the justification of accountability solely through the procedures which will be invoked to establish senior colleagues' salaries. In any case, the actual levels of salary, and the reasons for awarding them, may never become known, and therefore the accountability factor will also remain confidential.

Staff outside the management level have little redress if there is cause to question senior colleagues' performance. The problem is that the performance of individual teachers is extremely difficult to isolate given the interrelationship of tasks and functions that are shared and held in common, despite the attempts to differentiate responsibilities.

More than half the teachers want to deny at least some part of the identity of teacher. This has been commented upon in research (Ball and Goodson 1985; Sikes *et al.* 1985), but what remains unexplored is its prevalance and diversity. One of the most important features of this characteristic is the denial of social contact with other teachers. The claim was that teachers out of school were often boring, talked shop and were generally dull. Teachers often want to embrace the role, but wanted to shed the identity. In a sense this explains the increase in professionalism and also accounts for the apparently low level of morale, although the contrasting of role and identity does appear to be contradictory, if not paradoxical.

Teachers are working longer hours, out of necessity, and making difficult personal decisions which affect their conduct and practice, but they see this demand as being eminently produced through the insistence of policy-makers and managers. They are committed to hard work, but are distinctly uncomfortable with the ways in which it is solicited from them. They are particularly concerned by the way in which the responsibility allowance scheme is organized, structured and operated, because it is an instrumental factor determining their ambivalence over identity and role which is manifested in their poor level of morale.

A significant proportion of teachers espouse denials of vocation, claiming that they were treating the work more and more as a job. Their real lives and identities were to be found elsewhere: in leisure pursuits, in their families, in their religious beliefs and practice, in their community involvement or their political activity. What was said to be increasingly important for the majority were the so-called quality-of-life factors, especially evident in discussions concerning changing posts. The traditional reasons why teachers moved, such as career development or enhancement, no longer have the importance they had in the past. Current expectations about mobility centre on ambitions concerned with life-style rather than career opportunities. However, entry into the profession is still largely dependent upon the traditional claims and values associated with vocational aptitude.

As the service increasingly embraces managerialism, so the likelihood that morale will be affected increases, especially for those teachers who espouse values clearly based upon professional democracy and accountability. Modern conditions of service are seen as unappetizing because they are felt to be distinctly unlike those which have been traditionally culturally legitimized, and which still form the bedrock of values for many in the service. Diversity of opinion and a certain scepticism may not be new features among teachers, but could point to an erosion of the traditional iconographies of the profession which saw a virtue in vocation, care, dedication and personal investment. Similarly the new identities which are being offered by employers and policy-makers could be increasingly difficult to believe in and reconcile.

TEACHERS AND THE IDEA OF CAREER

In recent years there has been an increased emphasis on in-service training as a way to improving both the quality of teaching and the management of schools. Attendance on courses has always been seen as a positive component of the search for professional enhancement and achievement. Promotion has nevertheless very often been the product of dubious, if not irrational processes which have little logic, and do nothing to develop a coherent concept of the educational career. Career stories are typically told as journeys through time. They are assembled to fit discrete events into a plausible, if not rational or coherent trajectory. The story is now much more difficult to tell as teachers at all levels report a diminishing sense of agency and control over their working lives as their responsibilities increased disproportionately to their powers to choose and decide for themselves.

Policies which have perhaps always affected career prospects, such as who receives allowances, what INSET is on offer and which activities are noticed and approved, now increasingly appear to be pragmatic at best, and capricious at worst, especially for those at the foot of the professional ladder. Recent entrants into the service and those teachers who had not gained promotion are affected by these features most because the traditional virtues of vocation, dedication, care and classroom practice no longer appear to hold the same credibility for those who are now making appointments, even though there is still a powerful and influential rhetoric in place which says that they do count.

In the past INSET was always seen as a key which unlocked the doors to promotion. Teachers went on courses to improve their skills and make themselves appear more credible applicants. However, it has generally been the case that promotion preceded an understanding of the job. Now the situation is dramatically different. More and more schools are appointing people to posts through internal reorganizations, made under the auspices of institutional development plans (IDPs). As a consequence promotion can now be said to be the key to access to INSET.

The circumstances have been reversed. INSET is far more readily available to those in post, and the question arises as to the nature of the criteria on which new appointments are being based. The most pronounced feature of this growing trend is the development of a new underclass of disenfranchised classroom teachers, who have failed to make any advancement up the promotion ladder, and as a consequence are being denied access to INSET, which is more and more likely to be organized by LEAs in response to their perceptions of priorities and needs.

In the primary sector these teachers are predominantly women because of the disproportionate ratio of men to women. They may well be mothers who have the major responsibility for the welfare of their children, even if their partners are themselves teachers. In a sense they are victims both of a system which denies them opportunities and of relationships which are still eminently sexist. The problem is that many see themselves in the traditional role of second breadwinner, and may be relatively content with the situation. In some southern LEAs for instance, over 80 per cent of teachers in primary schools are married women with families. They teach, but their priorities lie with their families. They are seen as being difficult to motivate, and have little sense of career because their incomes are supplementary to those of their husbands. Yet elsewhere in Britain there are significant numbers of primary teachers who are victims of the paucity of allowances available.

Primary headteachers bear the brunt of the problem that there are now in their schools far more responsibilities than there are available allowances. This means that they have to offer additional moneys for limited periods of time, usually a year, and have difficulty attracting applicants for the posts even if they advertise. Consequently more posts are now shuffled around existing staff. The problem is that many eschew applying because the amount of money available is incommensurate with what they see as the additional workload, and would involve considerable disruption to their personal lives. The greatest difficulties surround appointments for assessment and evaluation posts, although this is considered to be a crucial aspect of future responsibilities. In general, the policy of appointing internally and for limited periods of time is undermining the quality of work, and seriously disrupting the sense of career that teachers have.

In secondary schools the situation is different. There have been more allowances available to secondary schools because they are bigger. If comparisons are made between the two sectors, a post that warrants a D allowance in a secondary school, will usually be offered as an A or B allowance in a primary school on the assumption that the more children on roll, the more complex and demanding the job. The question is whether this remains a reasonable proposition. It is not just that allowances are attributed on the basis of numbers, because older children are considered notionally to cost more as well.

There is nothing in the Education Reform Act 1988 which offers schools or LEAs the incentive or powers to question the proportion of money that is allocated to each sector. The formulas which exist mirror the traditional practices which maintain existing assumptions and beliefs. It is not uncommon for a 10-year-old child to be worth one-third of the amount for a 16-year-old, or an 11-year-old to be worth about a quarter of the amount of an 18-year-old.

Without any future revision, this feature will exacerbate still further the difficulties under which primary schools already operate. The basis of formula funding constitutes the forgotten debate of education. It is one which primary headteachers in particular would seem justified in reopening.

Internal reorganizations have resulted in the appointment of disproportionately more men to senior posts in secondary schools than would appear to be warranted. Many reappointments are made on the basis that headteachers wish to retain staff who work in shortage subject areas, and these are overwhelmingly held by male teachers. However, the problem is that the new job descriptions are often so complex that delivery is unlikely. What is suffering is the classroom teaching in the very shortage subjects that headteachers wish to maintain and protect. If schools continue with this expediency then they will be undermining the very feature on which at least part of their public credibility rests; at the same time they will be seriously restricting opportunities for women teachers who are already heavily outnumbered in the echelons of management in the secondary sector.

The creation of in-service days has done nothing to alleviate the problems associated with INSET, partly because the quality of much of the work is questionable, and partly because many schools now use at least some of the time available for administration and the moderation of external examinations. In some authorities it is difficult to see how the additional money is distributed, how it is used and how the work undertaken is justified. The DES is supposed to be monitoring the situation but the results have never been published.

The extent to which in-service days contribute to professional development is uncertain, although teachers report that they are grateful for the time in which to catch up. Even if examination moderation is professionally useful, it is not INSET. When in-service days were first introduced they were publicized as an important contribution to professional development, but now, because of the ways in which schools choose to use them, those claims cannot be justified. Staff may apparently have some statutory rights to INSET, but executive discretion is often undermining them; the people who are suffering most are those very people who have no chance of access to other INSET which is provided to those in post.

The current use of these days highlights a problem which schools will have to solve in the future: how are they to align perceptions of institutional need with those of personal professional development? At present disproportionate amounts of INSET budgets are being spent for management training. Deputy heads appear to be doing quite well because many LEAs and schools recognize that there is an acute need for senior staff to train, but very little is being spent on developing classroom practice. Teachers are being offered new professional identities which emphasize activities and conduct outside as well as inside the classroom and the school, but these identities are no less problematic than the old models, even for those people who find it difficult to abandon them.

The *reflective practitioner*, the *self-actualizing professional* and the *extended professional* are labels that are becoming increasingly common, but they pose questions for teachers as much as any others ever did. Whether this crisis of identity and career is really a new phenomenon, or one that surrounds new labels is difficult to resolve. There has always been a preoccupation with the nature and adequacy of the self which may reflect teaching's continued status as a semi-profession, in which claims to professionalism revolve around investment of the self in the occupational sphere.

What is clear is the considerable unease among teachers about the restricted range of culturally endorsed identities available to them now. This suggests that if working conditions and professional development were really to be accommodated with the personal needs of the individual, policy-makers would have to contemplate a much more diverse range of needs, aspirations, interests and identities than they do at present.

In a sense, the differentation of the profession would appear to be an initiative which should cater for this need. The problem is that it is being pursued in a context of policy incoherence and increasingly pronounced power differentials. The gap between the managers and the managed is increasing rapidly, communication is deteriorating, and many individuals are being left stranded.

What is being offered does not match the diversity that is being claimed. Policy does not reconcile personal need with institutional goals, and makes it difficult for teachers to ascribe rationality to the notion of career. So far, the signs suggest that the introduction of performance-related pay will do little to alleviate the schisms that already exist between those in the classroom and those who manage the system, since it offers no potential for a reconciliation of a career which is founded upon good classroom practice with one founded upon good management practice.

REFERENCES

Ball, S. J. and Goodson, I. F. (eds) (1985) *Teachers' Lives and Careers*, Sussex: Falmer Press.

IAC (1991) *Fourth Report of the Interim Advisory Committee on School Teachers' Pay and Conditions*, Cm 1415, London: HMSO.

Sikes, P., Measor, L. and Woods, P. (1985) *Teachers' Careers, Crises and Continuities*, Sussex: Falmer Press.

Chapter 8

School teacher appraisal
For monetary reward, or professional development, or both?

John Heywood

The thesis of this chapter is that whatever arguments are advanced for performance-related pay for teachers, a biennial system of developmental appraisal is not the instrument to deliver this.

TEACHER APPRAISAL IN THE 1980s

While there had been many examples of formal annual interviews between headteachers and members of their staffs, there were no LEA wide schemes and certainly no national systems of appraisal in practice in the early 1980s. The secretary of state for education and science at that time, Sir Keith Joseph, is the person credited with bringing appraisal into the national forefront when, having visited some states of the USA, he suggested that a system of teacher appraisal would be an effective way of weeding out weak, incompetent teachers and relating pay directly to performance. Speaking in 1985 in the House of Commons, he said: 'During the period of contraction that lies ahead, I believe that a solution is most likely to be found by way of reforms which link higher pay to higher quality performance in the classroom and in the management of schools.' In fairness to Sir Keith and essentially due to the work of the National Union of Teachers, he in due course changed his mind about the purposes of appraisal and issued a joint statement with the NUT later in 1985 which pointed the way towards a developmental model of appraisal.

> I have come to realise under the influence of my advisers and other bodies such as the NUT, that the value of appraisal is far more in relation to career development, inservice training and promotion and is only indirectly linked with pay.

This was summarized in *The Times Educational Supplement* (27 July 1985) under the headline 'Sir Keith drops merit pay.'

In the same year the DES funded a research project on appraisal, carried out by a group from Suffolk LEA under the direction of Duncan Graham, then Suffolk CEO and later chairman and chief executive of the National Curriculum Council. Their study explored four main areas associated with appraisal: commerce, industry and public services; overseas appraisal systems; school systems in England and Wales; research publications and current literature. The results of their research were published in a seminal document, *Those Having Torches* (Suffolk 1985); we shall return to this document from time to time, particularly in the matter of merit pay. It was this research which turned out to be influential when, in 1986, at a time of serious unrest in industrial relationships within the education service, the ACAS agreement on appraisal was signed. This was particularly significant since this was the one area of agreement reached between the DES, the employers and the teacher unions and occurred at a time when stalemate had been reached in negotiations about salaries and other conditions of service issues. Subsequently negotiating rights were removed. This agreement established the principles upon which a system of teacher appraisal might be based. The nature and purpose of teacher appraisal was described as follows.

> The working group understands appraisal not as a series of perfunctory periodic events but as a continuous and systematic process intended to help individual teachers with their professional development and career planning and to help ensure that the in-service training and deployment of teachers matches the complementary needs of individual teachers and the schools. An appraisal system will take into account the following matters:
>
> 1 Planning the induction of Entry Grade teachers and assessing their fitness to transfer to Main Professional Grade [MPG].
>
>   (This is historically interesting because the distinction between Entry Grade teachers and MPG teachers was never established and reflects the deadlocked negotiations about conditions of service at that time.) However, the other matters remain pertinent:
>
> 2 Planning the participation of individual teachers in inservice training.

3 Helping individual teachers, headteachers and their employers to see when a new or modified assignment would help the professional development of individual teachers and improve their career prospects.
4 Identifying the potential of teachers for career development with an eye to their being helped by appropriate inservice training.
5 Recognition of teachers experiencing performance difficulty, the purpose being to provide help through appropriate guidance, counselling and training. Disciplinary procedures would remain quite separate but might need to draw on relevant information from the appraisal records.
6 Staff Appointments Procedures: the relevant elements of appraisal should be available to better inform those charged with providing references.

> It will be seen that what the working group has in mind is a positive process, intended to raise the quality of education in schools by providing teachers with better job satisfaction, more appropriate inservice training and better planned career development based upon more informed decisions.
>
> (DES 1986)

Other than a reference to career development which may, although not necessarily, imply advancement in pecuniary terms, it will be noted that there is no reference at all to pay.

The nettle of the relationship between appraisal and teachers experiencing performance difficulty was grasped; indeed the recognition that an appraisal system would better inform reference writing is clear. There is nothing within the principles to imply cosiness or lack of rigour. The ACAS report (DES 1986) went on to recommend the setting up of a pilot project in order to develop practical programmes including training arrangements for introducing procedures and methods and to develop and design, test and refine appraisal documentation. It was suggested that a group of between six and eight LEAs, selected to give good geographical balance, would best form this pilot and that a range of schools – from small to large, of all phases and including aided schools – would give a sound foundation for future appraisal work. In order to direct and monitor the project, a National Steering Group (NSG) consisting of representatives of the unions, officers of the

DES and representatives of the LEAs would be set up. This group would be responsible for reporting and disseminating the results of the project and ensure that what was developed would be replicated throughout England and Wales.

In due course, after some preliminary meetings, the NSG was set up, with Duncan Graham as chairman. The National Development Centre for School Management Training, under its director, Ray Bolam, and under the project leadership of Agnes McMahon, won the contract for co-ordinating the work in the six pilot authorities. The Cambridge Institute of Education, under its director, Howard Bradley, was awarded the contract for the monitoring and evaluation of the pilot study. Because of the breakdown in industrial relations and the withdrawal of teachers' negotiating rights, the National Union of Schoolmasters Union of Women Teachers (NAS/UWT) and NUT, with some considerable regret, withdrew from membership of the NSG. NUT returned in January 1988 and NAS/UWT rejoined the NSG for the final two crucial residential meetings of the group in June and July 1989. The remarkable fact about the NSG report, which was sent to the secretary of state in July 1989, was that complete consensus was reached among all six teacher unions, representatives of the employers and, indeed, representatives of the DES. 'We are firmly of the view that the aims and purposes of the national appraisal should be as set out in the passage from the ACAS report' (DES 1989). That consensus was undoubtedly due to the consistent approach to appraisal which saw it as developing teachers rather than judging teachers although some confusion was caused at the time when the secretary of state published the report, when he also published a hurriedly assembled report from Her Majesty's Inspectorate (HMI) on appraisal which included the statement: 'Essentially, however, appraisal is about the judgement of performance' (HMI 1989). This was not the case so far as the pilot authorities were concerned where appraisal was essentially a two-way process looking forward rather than looking backward. Responsibilities rested upon both appraisee and appraiser. It is this judgement of performance which lies at the nub of the problem in linking performance-related pay with appraisal. Appraisal certainly can be used as a system of judging performance in order to allocate reward in terms of merit pay and promotion but this was never the intention of school teacher appraisal as outlined in the ACAS agreement and subsequent NSG report.

At the same time as the NSG report was submitted to the secretary of state, the *Report on the Evaluation of the School Teacher Appraisal Pilot Study*, produced by the Cambridge Institute of Education (1989) was also submitted although interestingly, when the NSG and HMI reports were published and sent to the fifty-one consultee groups, this evaluation was not included. The evaluation suggests that the aims of appraisal as outlined in the ACAS agreement had clearly been achieved within the pilot study. Appraisal had been an instrument for professional development. It was a two-way process in which the appraisees could suggest ways in which they could be helped by their line managers and ways in which the school system could be improved. The model set outcomes before records. The process was not just another way of carrying out a tick/cross assessment. Thus the main lesson of the pilot study was that the professional developmental model of teacher appraisal actually worked. Although it demands time, energy and training, not only in terms of awareness raising but also in skills coaching, it was a model which produced improvement in teaching performance. The importance of implementation following reasonably soon after the training so that the skills were not lost was another important lesson.

The benefits of this model were seen in terms of process outcomes and product outcomes. Among the process outcomes, that is the benefits from actually taking part, the opportunity to reflect and have time to discuss work in a non-threatening atmosphere was greatly appreciated, as was the recognition given to teachers. This was often articulated in words such as 'This was the first time that anybody was prepared to sit down with me and for two hours or so share with me a professional dialogue about my particular work'. The evaluation also pointed to increased motivation and confidence among the appraisees and a clearer understanding of what was expected of them. Appraisees indicated a greater sense of feeling part of the school. Appraisal was found to get close to people, to celebrate success. It was a means of offering support and help to *all* teachers and moved them towards the attainment of potential, thus offering greater job satisfaction.

So far as the product outcomes were concerned, for the individual there was the opportunity to develop skills and to link needs with in-service training. Individuals could experiment with style. A number of teachers were helped by organizational change which had come out of the appraisal dialogue. Undoubtedly career development was helped not only by opportunities for in-service training being provided but also, for example, by negotiation of a change of role in order to widen the experience of the appraisee. For the school, the benefits which were reported included improved relationships arising from greater collegiality, a clarification of aims and the linking between appraisal outcomes and school development planning. The school also gained from an increased knowledge of the individuals within the staff. Most crucially, learning opportunities for pupils were improved in a significant number of cases, often as a result of changes in the management and support of the learning process. The system helped to clarify responsibilities and priorities and gave the opportunity for improved communication and exchange of ideas within a more supportive environment.

Thus the benefits of a developmental system of appraisal had been clearly demonstrated. It is the contrast between the developmental and judgemental models of appraisal which lie at the nub of the problem of the direct linking of appraisal with pay. Indeed, the conflict between the two groups of purposes within appraisal is felt to be irreconcilable and there is much evidence within industrial practice to support this position. *Personnel Management Fact Sheet 3* (March 1988), for example, explains that

> one of the most frequent causes of failure or dissatisfaction in a performance appraisal schemes is the fact that it seeks to fulfil many different and/or conflicting requirements at once. The most common difficulty arises from marrying up a system which is primarily aimed at providing information for salary review with a system which is intended to improve current performance.

So far as teacher appraisal is concerned, this is best explained by quoting from the response of the NUT to questions posed by the secretary of state for education and science:

> Systems designed to improve performance which are therefore future orientated, depend upon ensuring that the appraisee is able to be as frank and open as possible during the appraisal process. This is hardly likely to be the case if his or her level of salary, promotion, or indeed job security depends on the outcome of the appraisal process. Only in an atmosphere of trust and openness will serious discussion take place of an appraisee's dissatisfaction with an area of his or her work, of limitations in

the circumstances in which he or she works or of weaknesses he or she identifies in the management. Such discussion is essential if targets for future action are to be agreed and hence improvements in organisational performance – in the case of schools teaching and learning – brought about.

(NUT 1989)

Let us now explore in greater depth some of the important components within an appraisal process in order to see any effects which the direct linking of appraisal to pay would have on benefits revealed in the pilot study. The element of self-appraisal was shown to be a vital component in the whole process. Teachers needed training in this element because of a tendency to be too self-critical and start with the negative aspects of their work rather than their positive achievements. Again frankness in answering questions would be discouraged if there were to be a direct link with pay. The following questions formed part of a suggested format for a self-appraisal/interview preparation form.

1 During the past academic year, what parts of your job have given you greatest satisfaction? How could those be used to best advantage?
2 What parts of your job have given you least satisfaction? Is there something that could be done to overcome this?
3 Were there any problems or difficulties which prevented you achieving something you intended or hoped to? Are they still a cause for concern? If so, could they be eliminated?
4 To help improve your performance in your job, what changes in the school organization would be beneficial? What additional things might be done by your headteacher, your head of department, you, anyone else?

The answer to such questions are likely to improve the management process within a school as a whole, providing that they can be answered freely and without restraint. However, if salary is foremost in the minds of appraisee and appraiser, it is unlikely that the appraisees will suggest shortcomings on the part of management lest such professional criticism should work against them.

Central to the appraisal process is classroom observation. The working assumptions for classroom observation are based on the fact that teachers spend most of their time teaching! Most are competent and want to increase their effectiveness. This is to be achieved through professional development, thus enhancing the quality of children's learning. 'The one undisputed requirement of good education is good teaching and performance in the classroom lies at the heart of the teacher's professional skill and of the standards of learning achieved'. (HMI 1985). It was classroom observation which caused among teachers in the pilot the greatest apprehension beforehand: in many cases, teachers had not been observed formally in the classroom since their year of probation.

The approach to classroom observation which worked most positively was when the observer met the appraisee beforehand in order to agree the focus of the observation, which might for the first observation be general but for the second become more specific. The appraisee will play a large part in setting the agenda rather than the appraiser, which would convey a sense of inspection such that the teacher would feel threatened. Key to the success of an observation is agreement on the major purpose which is to support and assist teachers in their teaching, that is to say looking *with* the teacher rather than looking *at* the teacher. It is important to agree the criteria to structure the observation and the methodology to be used, for example where to sit or whether to get involved in the lesson. The observer will collect data from the observation and use these as the basis for analysis of what has taken place. The feedback needs to be confidential to the teachers, giving them the opportunity to compare what actually happened with what they thought or hoped had happened. If this should be thought to be too cosy, experience in the pilot showed that appraisees expected more than a pat on the back. They expected discussion about, for example, why they used a particular method. Observation is valuable for the observer and often as much is to be gained for the appraiser as the appraisee. It should be recognized that all observation is partial. We all go in to observe with our own prejudices but it helps if one tries to put on a different pair of spectacles and go in endeavouring to defer judgement, with 'clean eyes', as it were. Thus classroom observation is another example of a shared experience, a two-way process and surely not the means of determining, by means of just two or at most three observations biennially, a teachers' pay packet. Indeed, there is a strong argument for peer observation to be used on occasions to provide data for an appraisal discussion.

Target setting or action points will arise from the appraisal interview and form part of an appraisal statement. Targets should be S M A R T:

- Specific   avoiding ambiguity by keeping simple
- Manageable   no more than four targets, short-term and long-term
- Achieveable   there must be a likelihood of success and the criteria for success agreed
- Realistic   they need to relate to the individual teacher's experience and expertise
- Time-constrained   a stated time period concentrates the mind.

If the achievement of the targets is going to be a main criterion for the allocation of merit pay in the appraisal process, then there is much greater likelihood of safe targets being set. Often the achievement of targets will depend upon the support of the line manager or some other member of the senior management team. If such support is not forthcoming the appraisee should surely not be penalized. Appraisers should be able to achieve the vast majority of their targets given a commitment from themselves and the support of others. The resourcing of schools is such that it is highly unlikely that funding will be available in order to reflect the achieving of so many targets. Inevitably, this will result in disappointment and disillusion.

In the summer of 1989 a new secretary of state was appointed to replace Kenneth Baker. John MacGregor took over to find the NSG report on his desk. In his first major speech on education he stated that he wished to extend the period of consultation on the NSG report until April 1990 before deciding how to introduce regulations (MacGregor 1989). During the period of consultation, a conference was organized in London by the NUT at which Alan Howarth, MP, parliamentary under-secretary of state at the DES, addressed the issue of the link between appraisal and pay. He acknowledged teachers' concern about the relationship of appraisal to the award of incentive allowances and promotion. He said the government did not envisage the creation of any direct or automatic link between these decisions and appraisal but the government believed that it was legitimate for appraisal to be taken into account along with other relevant factors.

In July 1990 MacGregor decided to introduce appraisal but on a voluntary basis, the decision lying in the hands of LEAs or, in the case of voluntary-aided and grant-maintained schools, the governors. However, events overtook this decision and the election of a new prime minister and the subsequent Cabinet reshuffle saw Kenneth Clarke installed as secretary of state for education and science. He very quickly saw the opportunity of linking compulsory appraisal for all teachers with the raising of standards and gave notice of his intention to introduce regulations making appraisal compulsory for all, the phasing-in to be completed by the end of the academic year 1994–5. Although there were grave misgivings with regard to his resourcing, there was, in general, approval on the part of most teachers of his almost complete adoption of the NSG model, bearing in mind that inevitably the Education Reform Act 1988 had meant that there was the need to ensure that governors had an appropriate role in the appraisal process.

Clearly governors have a part to play in the matter of appraisal but not as appraisers. This view was supported by the then secretary of state, John MacGregor, when he wrote on 31 October 1989, to the teachers' side of the NSG as follows: 'I am clear that appraisal should be a professional process carried out by staff who are competent and trained for the purpose, with the aim of improving the quality of teaching'. However, governors need to understand the appraisal process, to be aware that it is happening. It is reasonable that Chairs, if they so wish, should be informed as to the targets which teachers have agreed. The achievement of these targets may well have resource implications and the NSG report suggested that:

> Proposals for action deriving from appraisal should be reported to the governing body of the school if they require an executive decision by that body or if they relate to the use of resources for which the governing body has specific direct responsibility.
> (DES 1989)

Governors will certainly contribute to the appraisal process of headteachers by providing information. Questions to be asked and information to be sought will, of course, need to have been agreed initially between the appraisers and the appraisee headteacher. So far as linking appraisal with pay was concerned, in the secretary of state's paper to the Interim Advisory Committee, which was meeting in late 1990 in order to advise him about teachers' pay and conditions of service, he wrote: 'In advising the relevant body on decisions about the *promotion* of teachers, or about the use of their discretion in relation to pay, headteachers may take account of any relevant information deriving from appraisal along with other factors'. (The 'relevant body' means, within the teachers' pay and conditions document, the governors if the school has a delegated budget or is grant maintained, otherwise it is the LEA.) This indirect link has always been accepted, certainly by SHA members, inasmuch as it would be quite unreasonable to expect a headteacher to 'unknow' what was contained within an individual teacher's appraisal statement. However, the fact that appraisal statements of teachers do not reach governors, except in the case of headteachers where the Chair sees the appraisal statement, removes any direct link between appraisal and pay.

The second and third reports of the Interim Advisory Committee (IAC 1989; 1990) on *Teachers' Pay and Conditions* refer to teacher appraisal on both occasions under the section associated with quality, one of the key objectives which the committee was asked to address, alongside recruitment, retention and motivation of teachers.

> School teacher appraisal is also important in the context of teacher quality. Appraisal should help LEAs to plan teachers professional development, including in-service training and should help teachers to clarify their objectives and enhance their performance.
>
> (IAC 1989)

The 1990 report states:

> The teacher unions and teachers, including heads and deputies, to whom we spoke during our school visits, expressed disappointment at the Secretary of State's decision [to delay the introduction of appraisal]. In their view it had been taken on resource grounds and because ministers felt that the NSG report had placed insufficient emphasis on linking appraisal performance with levels of remuneration. It was argued strongly to us that appraisal is not an appropriate tool for determining pay and should be used solely for its more generally accepted purpose of helping with professional development of individual teachers . . . We are clear that appraisal is a vital tool for the managers of schools as it is for managers in other occupations. It enables individual teachers to explore ways of improving their pro-

fessional skills and, in consequence, enhancing their contribution to the quality of work in the school.

(IAC 1990)

In its fourth report, the IAC (1991) devotes a whole chapter to appraisal. It goes further than in its previous reports in suggesting some link between appraisal and pay. However, it qualifies its statements as follows:

> We certainly do not envisage an automatic or precise relationship between appraisal and pay. But it seems to us that information about appraisal could properly be taken into account, along with other evidence, in taking decisions on whether to award discretionary payments. Indeed, it would be unfair to teachers to discount it, and we are pleased to see this is acknowledged in the Government's plans. But it would be better if information were taken into account overtly rather than covertly when considering performance for pay purposes.
>
> (IAC 1991)

Nevertheless, elsewhere in the report, the committee returns to what it sees as the main purpose of appraisal, namely:

> more importantly it [appraisal] also provides for the systematic assessment of performance and the targeting of any necessary support and training to promote professional development and to remedy defects.
>
> (IAC 1991)

In 1990 a report by the School Management Task Force was published entitled *Developing School Management: The Way Forward* (DES 1990). The Task Force, members of which did not come solely from the education service but which included a senior member of the Training and Development Department of Marks and Spencer plc, produced a report emphasizing management development as a school-based activity supported by LEAs. In dealing with appraisal, we read 'Every teacher deserves the opportunity for regular review of their professional and career development'. There is no suggestion at all of the desirability of linking teacher appraisal with pay.

In its response to the question posed by the secretary of state as part of his consultation in 1989, namely how appraisal should feed into decisions about career progression including the award of incentive allowances, SHA stated 'The direct linking of appraisal with possible monetary reward will discourage the very openness and honesty which the NSG model encourages'. (SHA 1990). This was brought home to me in my own personal appraisal. As school teacher appraisal co-ordinator for Cambridgeshire, I reported to the assistant chief education officer. As part of my appraisal, I provided him, in advance of the interview, with my own detailed self-review in which I put alongside my job description my own views as to my successes and failures throughout the year. He, being used to a local authority performance management scheme, was staggered at the openness with which I revealed the ways in which I had failed to achieve my targets and neglected certain areas within my job description. Because I knew that my salary would not be in any way affected by my frankness, I was able to share with him the ways in which I felt that I needed additional support within my job in the best interest of the education service. I could have done a perfectly good public relations exercise in my self-review which I believe would have convinced my line manager of the many successes achieved if there had been additional money at the end of the process. What is certain is that this would have been inevitably something of a 'con' job and would in no way have helped me, my line manager or the authority.

In *Those Having Torches* (Suffolk 1985), addressing the issue of merit pay for teachers, is the statement:

> we have concluded that the necessary conditions for success do not exist in England and Wales. Teachers manifestly believe their base salaries to be low, some believe their working conditions to be poor; the criteria for determining the factual base for assessing a) their classroom performance and b) their total contribution to the school community as a whole are largely undeveloped and in any case exceedingly difficult to construct. In these circumstances, the introduction of merit pay for a sceptical and organized teaching force might, we suspect, be self defeating.
>
> (Suffolk 1985)

Since that time, we have seen the development of a handful of City technology colleges where teachers may have different conditions of service and pay and indeed may operate in working conditions which are vastly superior to those which obtain in the vast majority of the nation's schools. Funding might be such that merit pay could be available for all teachers and so circumstances are very different. This may well be the case also in grant-maintained schools which again have considerably enhanced funding but funding is not the only issue.

Reference is also made in *Those Having Torches* (Suffolk 1985) to research in the USA where, although it is concluded often in reports on public education that the performance of the teaching profession would be enhanced by the award of merit pay, the vast majority of merit pay schemes have been set aside as unworkable and the few remaining are under continuous review and modification.

Merit pay involves assessment, that is to say grading people on a scale of performance. Those of us involved in training in teacher appraisal constantly need to stress the difference between a system of appraisal and a system of assessment. The report also makes the point that merit bonuses need to be substantial in order to be effective. Funding for education is such that merit bonuses will inevitably be limited in number: this is a likely cause of friction within a school staff which relies very much by the nature of its job on collegiality, working together openly as a profession in order to serve the best interests of the children.

A lack of funding can also lead to frustration on the part of employees. I am aware, for example, that members of HMI operate within an appraisal process which assesses them on a scale of points and, in theory, rewards accordingly. Because funding is inadequate, even though inspectors may qualify through their points score for particular bonus payments, such payments have to be reduced because there are limited funds. The situation is different in commerce where, for example, the cost of a bank's merit payments to its staff can be passed on directly to the customer.

Some further practical arguments against linking a system of appraisal with pay need consideration. The 1990 pay award, based on the recommendations of the Interim Advisory Committee, is dealt with in Chapters 6 and 12 in this book. It must, however, be clear that this pay award, introducing local scales, incremental enhancements and new discretions, was revolutionary and we have yet to see its full impact. Indeed, its impact so far is severely limited because of the lack of funding provided nationally and therefore unavailable locally to implement the many flexibilities. Although the recent DES Regulations conveniently ignores self-appraisal, this most valuable component, certainly as revealed in the Cambridge Institute of Education (1989) evaluation of the pilot study, will still figure pre-eminently within a teacher appraisal system, serving as the basis for the discussion between the appraisee and the appraiser. Again, openness and honesty are of paramount importance. The appraiser will normally be the direct-line manager of the appraisee; only in the smallest primary schools will this mean that the head teacher is the sole appraiser in the school. The NSG report recommended that, because of the responsibilities and workload associated with the role of appraiser, no appraiser should be involved in the appraisal of more than four appraisees in any appraisal cycle. Thus in secondary schools for example, the appraisers will consist of heads of department, heads of year and deputy heads as well as head teachers. Within the larger primary schools, appraising will be undertaken not only by head teachers and deputy heads but also by heads of section or key stage co-ordinators. Appraisal for each individual will occur every second year and certainly within a larger school, the appraisal cycle could be stretched over a two-year period in order to minimize disruption to the children's learning. Thus, for example, one-sixth of a staff complement of 100 teachers might be appraised in any one term. There will therefore be a mismatch both in timing and in intention within the processes of appraisal and pay awards. Pay will be tied to the structures and requirements of the school, its curriculum and its unique objectives as opposed to the individual teacher. To quote from *Managing the 1990 Pay Award* (SHA 1990), which has done so much to explain the intricacies of the 1990 Pay Award

> Undoubtedly a properly managed appraisal system which has the understanding and support of staff and which identifies good practice, will inform careful, thoughtful decisions about allocating staff budgets, if such extras are available. Surely, however, it will never be a strict assessment process where graded marks are allocated for jobs or performance and a pay rise directly results. (There is an argument here, that given the high quality of teaching in many schools, there will have to be a massive increase in the budget to allow for all the pay enhancements that would ensue!)
>
> (SHA 1990)

The first moves towards performance-related pay for the teaching sector in a number of LEAs have centred upon headteachers.

Within these LEAs there was initially a move to link directly a system of headteacher appraisal to pay. Cambridgeshire, Kensington and Chelsea, and Westminster have sought so to do. Undoubtedly, we shall see the development of alternative appraisal schemes which link headteachers' appraisals and the achievement of their goals to pay. It must be obvious that difficulties lie ahead in this area. As a former headteacher with fifteen years experience of headship, the extent to which any achievement of my goals lay within my individual powers rather than through the combined efforts of myself, deputy heads, heads of year and heads of department, and indeed the teaching and ancillary staff as a whole, was never clear to me. To return to the School Management Task Force report (DES 1989)

> School management requires a team approach with the head reliant on the specialist expertise of colleagues. Heads should integrate their personal development plans within the work of the school for the same principle must be seen to apply to all. The implementation of headteacher appraisal will have a key part to play in this process.
>
> (DES 1989)

The situation is further exacerbated at a time when governors are more severely restricted than ever before within their school budgets. Governing bodies will be hard pressed to decide between performance management payments for teachers and heads if it means a reduction in the number of, say, assistants for children with special needs. The longer-term funding of the superannuation implications is a further complicating factor. However, these are issues more associated with merit pay than appraisal.

It is my firm belief that if there is to be a system of performance-related pay, then the instrument for it must operate distinctly from the appraisal process. Indeed the move to link appraisal and pay in Britain has lost momentum in industry and commerce recently. As a result of the teaching of Dr William Deming, who first took the 'quality' message to Japan in the 1950s, there is a clear move to separate appraisal from pay. Peter R. Scholtes (1987), elaborating on Deming's teachings on performance appraisal, writes:

> Using performance of any kind as a basis for reward of any kind, is a flat-out catastrophic mistake. It is a sure road to demoralizing your workforce. Employees' income becomes

dependent on capricious factors well beyond their ability to influence. Just don't do it.

Base your organization's salaries, wages and bonuses on other things:

- Market rate: What would it cost to hire someone on the open market at this employee's current level of capability?
- Accumulation of skills: Pay an employee for having acquired potential or flexibility.
- Accumulation of responsibility: Pay an employee for having acquired a depth of contribution to a greater number of processes and for exercising influence over a large number of employees.
- Seniority: Recognizing that with years in the company comes an expanded sense of how and through whom many things can be made to happen; more contacts and networks; more business savvy and clout.
- Prosperity: Sharing in the welfare of the entire organization (not just one division, product or operation). This should not be given preferentially to certain groups or individuals.

To use performance evaluation to direct a system of monetary rewards will have the opposite effect: concern for monetary rewards will inevitably contaminate the feedback and evaluation system. The whole activity becomes a charade.

(Scholtes 1987)

A number of UK companies have recently founded the British Deming Association, believing that his approach can transform British industry in the way that he transformed Japanese industry beginning thirty or so years ago. Among these companies are Birds Eye Walls, Iveco Ford Truck, Hewlett Packard, British Telecom Research Laboratories, Hardy Spicer, Texas Instruments, Plessey Business Systems, Hoechst Celanese Plastics and Mars Confectionery, all of whom are committed to producing quality. They think first about who their customers are and then they study the processes they have for satisfying those customers, since it is customers who are the only ones 'qualified' to give feedback. Since the main customers of the teaching profession are pupils, it may well be useful to gain feedback from them but I hesitate to suggest that this should be a basis for allocation of pay.

It is becoming increasingly old-fashioned for organizations which want their people to achieve to assess their performance one against the other. Such a technique is regarded not only as divisive but also as counter-productive. In fact, there is a growing body of organizations firmly against traditional techniques of individual performance ratings although the suggested virtues of such schemes will continue to be peddled by those organizations who have built up empires on the mystique of job evaluation and performance management.

Deming's arguments on performance appraisal are summarized as follows by the British Deming Association's Appraisal Research Group:

- Ranking individuals on the basis of performance is fundamentally unsound because, with few exceptions, apparent differences in performance mainly result from variation inherent in the system. Linking merit pay to such ranking only makes matters worse.
- Individual and departmental targets and objectives, which are often built into performance appraisal, are nearly always destructive of customer-focused teamwork within or between departments.
- Reliance on pay as a motivator destroys pride in work and individual creativity.

I return to the seminal work *Those Having Torches* (Suffolk 1985) to draw attention to the concept of corporate excellence:

> Under this system, a whole school staff, professional and non-professional, is rewarded when the school achieves its annual objectives. Although the various problems associated with merit pay schemes remain, they are perhaps less sharp than when the focus is on the individual rather than the group.
>
> (Suffolk 1985)

Such an approach of collegiality within a school, informing its relationships with its pupils, parents, governors and LEA, is far more likely to encourage excellence than an assessment which is based on competitiveness where every teacher fights for as great a share of limited funding as can be achieved by whatever means.

I conclude by quoting, as an example of the positive approach to teacher appraisal, Pauline Perry, formerly HM Chief Inspector, Teacher Training. At a BEMAS conference she stated:

Assuming responsibility for the level of one's own performance seems to me to be at the heart of what is meant by being professional: that is, one is motivated at least as much by internal standards and personal commitment as by the demands of the rule book or the pay packet, or even the requirements of one's superiors.

The prime purpose of an education service appraisal scheme must be to enhance and develop the professional skills of the people in the service. The biggest resource in education is people. Appraisal is one way of ensuring that people are encouraged and supported to give of their best. This objective can be achieved only if there is openness, honesty and trust between appraisee and appraiser. Systems of merit pay, if linked to appraisal, will throttle the benefits of a professional developmental process of appraisal.

NOTE

The British Deming Association is at 2 Castle Street, Salisbury, SP1 1B.

REFERENCES

Cambridge Institute of Education (1989) *Report on the Evaluation of the School Teacher Appraisal Pilot Study*, Cambridge Institute of Education.

DES (1986) *ACAS Report of the Appraisal and Training Working Group*, London: DES.

—— (1989) *School Teacher Appraisal: A National Framework*, Report of the National Steering Group on the School Teacher Appraisal Pilot Study, London: DES.

—— (1990) *Developing School Management: The Way Forward* London: HMSO.

HMI (1985) *Education Observed 3: Good Teachers*, London: HMSO.

—— (1989) *A Report: Developments in the Appraisal of Teachers*, 299/89, London: HMSO.

IAC (1989) *Second Report of the Interim Advisory Committee on School Teachers' Pay and Conditions*, Cm 625, London: HMSO.

—— (1990) *Third Report of the Interim Advisory Committee on School Teachers' Pay and Conditions*, Cm 973, London: HMSO.

—— (1991) *Fourth Report of the Interim Advisory Committee on School Teachers' Pay and Conditions*, Cm 1415, London: HMSO.

MacGregor, J. (1989) Speech to Secondary Heads' Association East of England Conference, 2 October.

NUT (1989) *Teacher Appraisal: The NUT's Views and the Questions Posed by the Secretary of State*, London: National Union of Teachers.

Scholtes, P. R. (1987) *An Elaboration on Deming's Teachings on Performance Appraisal*, P. R. Scholtes, PO Box 5445, Madison, WI 53705.
SHA (1990) *Managing the 1990 Pay Award*, Secondary Heads' Association, J. Weeks, 130 Regent Road, Leicester, LE1 7PG.
Suffolk Education Department (1985) *Those Having Torches... Teacher Appraisal: A Study*, Ipswich: Suffolk County Council.

Chapter 9

Performance management and performance-related pay in an education department

David Cracknell

As pressure has grown for all public services to demonstrate that they are accountable and that they offer good value for money, so has a more explicit interest emerged in the performance of individual staff. Judging performance in public services is a complex exercise and has always posed particular challenges (Carley 1988). Nevertheless, performance management, which Fowler (1990) argues is quite distinct from previous managerial tools like management by objectives, has been adopted in local government as part of its response to managing radical changes in major services like education. A helpful working definition of systematic performance management with local government is 'an integrated set of planning and review procedures which cascade down the organization to provide a link between each individual and the overall strategy of the organization' (Rogers 1990). Performance-related pay has been seen by many local authorities as an important element in effective performance management and a growing number now operate a performance-related pay scheme. Arguably this helps to sharpen the focus for managers.

For local government, performance-related pay is an individualized system of payment linking all of the reward of employees to their performance in the job and commonly uses rating scales or comparison of achievements against objectives (LACSAB 1989), a definition which may be of wider value. Performance-related pay is distinct from group incentive schemes, profit-sharing and market pay supplements. It is easy to confuse performance-related pay with merit pay systems which have operated in local government since the 1950s. It is less subjective and does not focus on behavioural and personality issues; it has a clear association with performance objectives.

At best performance-related pay has played a part in enabling local authorities to improve their strategic management and the quality of their services; at worst it has been a painful and expensive experience (Brading and Wright 1990; LACSAB 1990b; Spence 1990; Wills 1988). Industrial models have been available to local authorities, IBM, John Lewis, Nissan, Alliance & Leicester, Legal & General, and Hanson, but the transfer of business methods and technology to public service has been far from straightforward. Problems in transferring business tools to public services are not unique to performance-related pay. Pascale (1990) argues that one of the important tasks of managers is to reconcile the strategy, structure and reward systems of their organization. He calls this *fit* and it may be that a lack of fit is what left local government managers frustrated after unsuccessful efforts to introduce performance-related pay.

EXPERIENCE IN EDUCATION DEPARTMENTS

A short survey of senior officers in education departments in England, Wales and Northern Ireland, which I undertook in December 1990, identified a number where performance-related pay schemes of different kinds had been introduced. The majority of the thirty-three LEAs which replied had not introduced schemes; among those where schemes were in operation, some applied only to senior or chief education officers (see Table 9.1).

Cambridgeshire has a long experience of performance management and performance-related pay; many of the LEAs which have followed that example and become involved over the last two or three years are in southern England where recruitment problems have been most severe. There was evidence to suggest that many of the schemes were related directly or indirectly to systems based on the Hay-MSL approach.

THE EAST SUSSEX APPROACH TO PERFORMANCE-RELATED PAY

Experience of introducing performance-related pay has demonstrated the importance of developing a scheme which is tailored to the specific needs of the business or organization concerned (Brading and Wright 1990). There is therefore no single package to be taken from the shelf. Until LACSAB became active in this field and published guidance from 1989, the main sources of advice

Table 9.1 Summary of responses to postal inquiry of education departments

LEA	Date introduced	Comment
Bexley	1988	
Bromley	1989	
Cambridgeshire	1984	
Cheshire	1989	Chief officer only
East Sussex	1988	
Gloucestershire	1989	
Harrow	1989	
Norfolk	1990	
Northamptonshire	1989	
Sheffield	1988	JNC officers only
Solihull	1990	Officers on PO grade only
Somerset	1989	CEO-PEOs in 1991
Hertfordshire	–	Under consideration
Northumberland	–	Chief officer scheme
Nottinghamshire	–	Under active consideration
Suffolk	–	Considered but deferred

to local authorities setting out on the path to performance-related pay were consultants with experience of business schemes and the pioneers among county and district councils. When the county management team of chief officers in East Sussex decided in April 1986 to seek committee approval to pursue performance management, they did so in a climate of general national interest but with little readily available outside experience upon which to draw. It was agreed that consultants should undertake a feasibility study (completed in 1987); they were also asked to support the initial process of job evaluation for senior managers. Performance-related pay was introduced for approximately ninety chief officers, deputies and senior managers across all council departments in April 1988; their performance was assessed against targets in 1989, 1990 and 1991. During 1989 work was undertaken to extend the scheme to approximately 280 middle managers across all departments. Job evaluations were handled by four panels of senior managers chaired by deputies. Performance-related pay was extended to middle managers in April 1990, with the first assessment of performance completed by April 1991.

The schemes for senior and middle managers differ in some details, such as car-leasing arrangements, but essentially they both operate as follows:

1 The emphasis is on performance management; performance-related pay is seen as subordinate and complementary.
2 The focal event of the performance management process is the annual review day in April, which gives county councillors a first opportunity to review the previous year's performance for each service or department, based on the chief officer's commentary.
3 This commentary and an associated business plan incorporate a statement of service objectives for two to three years which reflects county-wide objectives and, in the education department, have been built up during an annual planning cycle involving staff throughout the department.
4 In January each year a period is set aside especially for departmental planning during which service objectives are worked up into more detailed targets and performance indicators within and across all of the major sections and teams in the department.
5 These targets form the basis for individual targets and performance assessment.
6 The focal event of the performance management process for the individual is a performance management interview which takes place in February or March with each person's manager; there are also short briefing and updating sessions when changes in circumstances and agreed targets can be recorded during the year.
7 The interview gives an opportunity to review individual performance and set a reward for the past year, establish targets for the next year and agree a development plan for the individual manager.
8 The interview is structured around a set of simple forms and is initiated by the individual who makes an initial assessment of performance and drafts the targets. The outcomes are moderated by the manager's manager and the process is kept under general review by the chief executive and the county personnel officer.
9 Managers are asked to select one of four performance ratings and an appropriate performance pay reward (see Table 9.2).

Table 9.2 East Sussex performance rating and reward scale

Performance rating	Within scale	Scale maximum
Exceptional	3 or 4 increments	8–10% lump sum
Good	2 increments	5–7% lump sum
Satisfactory	1 increment	NIL
Unsatisfactory	No increment	NIL

10 The pay scales in 1990, for example, provide for six increments (of approximately £500 to £1,000) on each of the four senior and five middle manager bands which have all been developed locally following surveys of other local authorities and national scales.
11 Review and flexible interpretation are seen to be essential features of the scheme: 'The process should not become unwieldy but be sufficiently light and well focused to allow an open review so that we can improve what we are doing and how we are doing it.' (ESCC 1989).

It is difficult to separate the impact of performance-related pay from other initiatives in which the county council and the education department have been engaged over the last four to five years. An emphasis on better communications, on service quality and on being more responsive to customer needs have been associated with a general extension of delegated management and the introduction of service-level agreements between departments. In 1988-9 there was a distinct feeling of 'innovation overload' in East Sussex. Performance management has, however, been consistent with the thrust of these other initiatives, reinforcing a more systematic approach to managing change and sharpening the focus of activity. In retrospect, the various changes in management style and structure now look more coherent and performance management is welcomed by most managers. The performance-related pay element in these developments has, however, been more contentious.

THE EAST SUSSEX EXPERIENCE OF PERFORMANCE-RELATED PAY

The responses from senior and middle managers in the East Sussex Education Department to a questionnaire on performance management and performance-related pay in July 1990 illustrate the issues which have emerged.

First, most managers had been enthusiastic in 1987 although several were less happy about performance-related pay. One manager was strongly opposed to it from the outset 'Money will buy no more hard work from me'. Performance management was seen by most as a valuable complement to service planning, helping to focus on priorities, reducing over-ambitious targets, and defending staff to some extent against the unplanned accretion of tasks. It brought managers together to produce better communications and more thinking time. Performance management set the work of individuals within the wider context of what the county council and the rest of the department were trying to achieve. In some cases the practice had not quite matched the theory with priorities being overwhelmed by the 'morass of day-to-day work'. Looking back over the experience of performance management and performance-related pay in East Sussex, most of these managers continued fully to support the initiative but recognized that it needed 'constant care to preserve the right atmosphere'. An initial opponent of performance-related pay was dissatisfied on a personal basis and convinced even more of its demotivating effects; these views were echoed by another manager.

Second, although it was too early to come to a clear judgement, there were signs that performance management was helping to improve services by staff being prepared for change, responding to customer needs and using performance indicators. Performance management was seen to be as much about style as technique and effective services depended upon a whole range of management actions. Improvements to services had come with better cross-departmental understanding but there was still a danger of the performance management process being marginal to the continuing challenge of day-to-day management.

Third, generally the introduction of performance-related pay into the education department was not seen to have improved staff motivation, recruitment and retention. Some felt that it had positively harmed motivation through specific decisions about job evaluation and ratings for senior managers and unresolved reservations of principle from middle managers and NALGO. Performance management still attracted a great deal of support but for some, 'performance-related pay is a side issue which potentially distorts the whole performance management process'.

Fourth, performance management interviews were generally seen to have great value. They made it easier to see key success factors, to set priorities and stick to them. They enhanced morale, informed personal development and through praise and positive criticism helped to motivate. For some it corrected an over-pessimistic self-evaluation. Managers identified a number of ways in which the interviews could be improved:

1 the need for managers to give sufficient time to preparation and the interview itself
2 more honesty in setting criteria and in assessing outcomes
3 the timetable for the process to be set well in advance
4 more training in interviewing and counselling
5 the need for more emphasis on interim discussions to ensure that the decisions reached in the annual interviews were vigorously acted upon.

Fifth, most dissatisfaction was felt about the arrangements to decide performance-related pay ratings for individual senior managers. There was a perceived failure to moderate the first year's ratings across departments; although most managers saw the second year as much improved, there was concern about delay in informing managers, returning forms and securing comparability across departments. Although the terms used in the rating were defined for managers there was unease about the category *satisfactory*, which was felt not to match adequately a performance which was on target.

Finally, the education department had used for some years an annual management development interview for senior staff which the performance management interview incorporated. Some newly appointed managers, without this background of experience in East Sussex, were happy with the staff development element in the interview. Most other managers, however, could see little or no evidence in 1990 that there were tangible improvements in staff development following the introduction of performance management. It may be too early to judge since a new formal management development programme became available to senior managers only in 1990. However, there was a feeling that staff development was taking a lower priority as the department's focus switched to performance and that staff were not aware of training opportunities or receiving the development they needed.

East Sussex reached the stage in 1990 where it was considering whether it should modify its performance management arrangements and, in particular, if and how it should extend performance-related pay to other categories of staff. It was already evident that different approaches to job evaluation might be needed, in particular for those staff who did not see themselves as primarily general managers but offering a professional or advisory service. It may be that different frameworks for performance-related pay ratings and rewards are appropriate within one organization.

LEARNING FROM THE PERFORMANCE-RELATED PAY EXPERIENCE

The *Handbook on Performance Related Pay* (LACSAB 1990a) offers helpful and practical advice but it is not for the faint-hearted: 'While many organizations believe that PRP helps to clarify the intentions of management and motivate staff, some have found it inappropriate or hard to get right'. A majority of performance-related pay schemes are perceived to have failed, to have lost their focus on performance so that the wage bill is inflated without securing any benefits. Some local authorities like Coventry have recently abandoned performance-related pay schemes and others like Suffolk have, after careful investigation, not introduced the scheme. This should not come as a surprise since 'The history of performance appraisal has, in some local authorities, been an unproductive one, with a life cycle ... of only two to three years, during which time a scheme is designed, never fully implemented and supported and gradually withers away as a result of direct opposition, or of simple neglect, or because it did not produce the performance results anticipated' (Rogers 1990). For an organization which is heavily committed to performance management and performance-related pay, the message is not necessarily that it too should withdraw but that the lessons of experience should be rigorously applied.

We need to be sure why we want performance-related pay

It is not always clear how performance-related pay is intended to promote quality improvements in a public service operating within a democratic framework. Account must be taken of the political dimension of local government. Performance-related pay is primarily about individual and organizational performance but some schemes have been introduced to improve recruitment and retention. East Sussex, in a competitive market for staff, was undoubtedly influenced in its early interest in performance-related pay by recruitment worries. Anyway, it is misleading to draw a sharp distinction between performance and recruitment/retention: the one depends heavily on the other, especially in public service.

However, improved performance expressed in service terms must be regularly reinforced as the primary driving force for performance-related pay if it is to retain its edge as an effective tool of management.

We need to be clear about every job in the organization

Job evaluation in East Sussex was a difficult but productive exercise. A growing number of local authorities are moving towards Hay-MSL-type job evaluation systems and have had to come to terms with the investment in time and training which these require to be effective. Performance management and associated planning arrangements to set shared objectives across the department have helped to build a better understanding about the complementary nature of managers' jobs.

We need to get better at defining performance

It has been recognized (Brady and Wright 1990) that defining and communicating an objective assessment of performance is one of the most difficult aspects of performance-related pay. Loose or muddled thinking about performance is readily exposed as performance-related pay sharpens issues and highlights inconsistencies. Increments in one local authority are awarded to chief officers for 'corporate endeavour' which is not defined and in another these are awarded on a basis which has no explicit linkage to an appraisal system. In East Sussex the department has worked hard to involve managers in setting more precise but manageable service and individual objectives and to identify linked performance indicators. Good and convincing performance indicators are elusive in many areas of work in an education department. Members were involved in East Sussex but schools, colleges and other clients had not been drawn in systematically to help set performance criteria. These are likely to be important disciplines for performance-related pay in the future.

We need to defend stability in the organization and continuity of purpose

Performance-related pay can tempt managers to set targets and reward achievement where change is occurring and not sufficiently in areas of essential business maintenance. Indeed some appraisal systems linked to performance-related pay explicitly focus on a limited area of marginal change. Performance is rarely just about managing new initiatives: it is important that performance in the rest of our work is not allowed to go by default. *Short-termism* has been used to describe attitudes in industry (Kinder 1990) which have led to an unhealthy weakening of strategic objectives by succumbing to short-term pay-offs. Such attitudes are not unknown in local government and can be encouraged by performance-related pay if the focus is too narrow. Relating performance-related pay to a three to five year vision ought not to dismay us.

We need to continue to emphasize non-financial recognition

Some managers believe that it is inappropriate and ineffective to use marginal changes in pay as a reward or recognition for good performance, believing it to be demotivating. This scepticism is healthy if it leads to reappraisal and to the evolution of more effective approaches to performance management but it risks degenerating into damaging cynicism. The search for more and different forms of recognition and reward, particularly the kind that make it easier for individuals to do their job, must be extended. The introduction of performance-related pay should not be seen as an excuse for assuming that this continuous search need no longer preoccupy the effective manager.

We need a scheme that operates fairly and openly

Equity and justice are not, in the East Sussex experience, matters requiring vague assurances and they are continually relevant in the operation of performance-related pay. Staff want to know that they will be treated equitably across the organization, that equal opportunities criteria will be rigorously applied and that the administrative machine will not be allowed to grind on with scant attention to individual needs.

> But perhaps the most problematic area is the degree of inaccuracy which may be exhibited by appraisers when making evaluations and rating performance. Inaccurate assessments naturally create feelings of injustice and quickly lead to a deterioration in the perceived value of the scheme... there is ample evidence

that appraisers consistently make errors when rating performance (Rogers 1990).

East Sussex experience demonstrates how difficult it is to resist being secretive about some aspect or other of a performance-related pay system. It also shows that performance-related pay will not, in itself, resolve long-standing problems of grading and comparability.

We need to minimize the divisive potential of performance-related pay

Having made considerable efforts to reduce historical divisions and to weaken hierarchies, it was galling for senior managers in the education department to be faced with a performance-related pay scheme which was to be introduced, no doubt for good reasons, on a phased basis from senior management downwards. There was also some concern that the emphasis on the individual would undermine team unity but so far this has not been apparent. Typically, the full involvement of trade unions has not been given great emphasis in introducing performance-related pay. In the longer term this may well weaken its chances of success.

We need to maintain a strong staff development focus in performance-related pay

A significant weakness of the performance management scheme operating in the East Sussex Education Department is that it failed until 1990 to give sufficient priority to implementing the development plans which it was intended should form an integral part of the process. This is ironic given that the roots of the present performance management system lay in a management development process and that East Sussex successfully pioneered school-focused staff development. Performance management will succeed or fail in the eyes of some managers to the extent to which it integrates organizational objectives and staff development needs.

We need to communicate better and train more

If managers and staff at all levels are to be committed to performance management and performance-related pay, the former will need to be given more senior management attention. East Sussex operated *team briefing* and the department had reviewed its internal and external communications. All these channels need to be fully exploited to sustain the impetus for making effective use of performance management. Training for performance-related pay was better for middle managers in East Sussex than for senior managers but there is a clear need for continuing preparation of individuals and teams of staff if the process is to be effectively embedded in the management of the department.

We need to see performance-related pay in its wider context

This chapter began with a reference to sharpening the focus of the work of managers: a visual metaphor which highlights the contribution that performance management and performance-related pay have made to management thinking. Periodically, managers need stimulation to see things from another perspective. Performance management has certainly helped to do that in local authorities like East Sussex. However, performance-related pay seems to some managers in education departments to be a dispensable subset of performance management. Linking pay to performance has the advantage of showing that the organization really recognizes good performance and sees performance generally as important but it runs the risk of creating unnecessary tensions. 'Pay is important and must be got right but it is a means to the end of improved performance not an end in itself' (LACSAB 1990a). Performance-related pay may be, for some organizations, a valuable step along the road to making performance management stick but it is by no means evident that it is a necessary step. That conclusion is relevant to appraisal systems in schools and colleges as well as in local government departments. It is also clear from experience in education departments that the introduction of performance-related pay is successful when part of a wider drive for cultural change. Performance-related pay may therefore be useful as the thin end of a bigger wedge but if it is to survive and not be swept away in another wave of managerial ephemera, it has to be demonstrated that it contributes to internal consistency and that it reflects the shared purpose of the people who work in the organization.

REFERENCES

Brading, E. and Wright, V. (1990) Performance related pay, Factsheet 30, *Personnel Management* June.

Carley, M. (1988) *Performance Monitoring in a Professional Public Service*, London: Policy Studies Institute.

East Sussex County Council (1989) *Performance Management: Guidance Notes*, Brighton: East Sussex County Council.

Fowler, A. (1990) Performance management: the MBO of the '90s? *Personnel Management* July: 47–51.

Kinder, J. R. (1990) Short-termism as a recurrent British theme, *Financial Times* 7 August: 16.

LACSAB (1989) *Performance Related Pay: An Update*, LACSAB Research Paper no 1, London: Local Authorities Conditions of Service Advisory Board.

—— (1990a), *Handbook on Performance Related Pay* Report no 2, London: Local Authorities Conditions of Service Advisory Board.

—— (1990b), *Performance Related Pay in Practice: Case Studies from Local Government*, Report no 3, London: Local Authorities Conditions of Service Advisory Board.

Pascale, R. T. (1990) *Managing on the Edge*, London: Viking.

Rogers, S. (1990) *Performance Management in Local Government*, London: Longman.

Spence, P. (1990) Performance management, *Local Government Employment* February: 14–15.

Wills, J. (1988) Linking pay with performance, *Local Government Chronicle* 20 May: 17–18.

Chapter 10

Experience in schools
Case study I Kemnal Manor School for Boys

John Atkins

THE SCHOOL

How often in the past has the performance of a member of staff been judged by staffroom gossip, subjective comment or innuendo? This scenario is all too familiar to experienced headteachers and deputy heads. My firmly held belief is that there is a more structured and equitable way of assessing a teacher's performance. This can be done through appraisal, with a voluntary teacher-elected element of increased salary linked to performance.

The scheme outlined below is one that is working well at Kemnal Manor School, a boys' school with a rising roll from Year 7. There are 720 boys aged 11 to 18 on roll and the teaching staff complement is 45. It is a single-site school in pleasant, well-kept buildings, some of which are listed; it is surrounded by its own playing fields. I took up the post of headteacher in January 1990.

All teaching staff are appraised and in addition have opted voluntarily for the performance-related pay element. It has been developed within the existing LEA resource allocation for the school. It has been accomplished by first, the willingness of the staff to embrace change through a comprehensive programme of middle-management training conducted by external consultants, second, a reorganization of directed time, and third, an audit of the administrative tasks undertaken by teachers, which has led to these tasks being hived off to a new support division within the school.

INTRODUCING APPRAISAL AND PERFORMANCE-RELATED PAY

Appraisal and performance-related pay cannot be viewed as additions to existing structures. They form the bedrock of a new school culture and ethos which regards the curriculum as central, the pupils as the most important people, and the teaching staff as the most important resource. My strongly held belief is that the curriculum should be the central focus of any school; the curriculum is more than just a collection of subjects:

> The curriculum of the school is larger than the subjects or even the areas of knowledge and experience it offers. It also includes the school's ethos, its code of conduct, the values and achievements celebrated in its public life, and the nature of relationships embodied in its informal life.
>
> (O'Hear and White 1991: 8)

The new ethos required in schools, necessitated by recent government legislation, involves a cutting edge accountability, where teachers' potential must be maximized through appropriate appraisal policies, if a quality education is to be delivered in the classroom. In simple terms then, appraisal is an inherent part of successful curriculum delivery.

Appraisal should be inextricably linked to the school development plan, school aims, pupil entitlement, rigour in the classroom and accountability. The increasingly competitive market which exists within education in the 1990s makes this necessary. There are many models of appraisal. The following case study which outlines the Kemnal Manor model does not involve a paper-chase and takes approximately 4.5 hours of a manager's time per year. It is important to note that the right balance must be struck between maximizing the potential of appraisal within a realistic time framework, the flow of documentation, and supporting the school development plan without removing teaching staff from the classroom. The Kemnal Manor model has been developed to operate successfully within existing resource allocations (see Table 10.1).

Table 10.1 Kemnal Manor use of time for appraisal and performance-related pay interviews and observations per annum

	Appraiser	Appraisee
Initial meeting	1 hour	1 hour
Discussion prior to classroom observation	10 mins	10 mins
Classroom observation	1 hour	—
Debriefing on classroom observation	30 mins	30 mins
Collection of information	1 hour	—
Appraisal interview	1 hour	1 hour
Total	4 hrs 40 mins	2 hrs 40 mins

1 The time for both appraiser and appraisee is found within directed time.
2 Appraisal linked to performance-related pay is a whole-school policy agreed by the staff and an integral part of the school development plan. This model requires no additional staffing.
3 Each new member of staff, whatever their position, completes a staff development questionnaire as a one-off to be used as a point of reference for their first initial meeting.

STAFF DEVELOPMENT QUESTIONNAIRE

Following the drawing up of an initial school development plan in January 1990, I needed to know what was happening in the classroom, what type of curricular experience was being offered to our pupils and the standard of teaching within the school. I also wanted to establish and link individual career development to the newly instituted, yearly faculty targets, and to the school development plan. In order to achieve this, an action plan was formulated.

First, I met each member of staff informally during the spring and summer terms of 1990. Each interview lasted one hour and the time was used by me to gain a perception of the school from the point of view of the teaching staff. The interviews clarified my own views of the strengths and weaknesses of the school which complemented and supplemented documentary evidence. These interviews were carried out against a background where staff development interviews had not been the norm, INSET had been staff driven, since a school development plan had not yet been established, and lesson observation had not been on the agenda. Every member of staff was then given a staff development questionnaire to complete.

Objectives of the questionnaire

1 to assist staff in identifying their own personal priorities for professional development
2 to help staff reflect on their present post in a more systematic way and help them in future career decisions
3 to see how personal job satisfaction could be increased
4 to help the school and appropriate line-managers decide future staff development needs
5 to create a positive atmosphere of review and in doing so enhance the effectiveness of all members of staff.

The questionnaire was divided into five main areas and there were questions under the following headings.

Present position

1 In the context of your present job description which aspects give you most satisfaction and why?
2 Which aspects of your job description give you most concern and least satisfaction? Try to define reasons for this.
3 Are there any aspects of your job description in which you feel you need more training and support?

Life in the classroom

Which aspects of your teaching do you

- enjoy?
- dislike?
- find difficult?
- find interesting and challenging?
- need to develop?
- Any other comments?

Future professional development

1 Do you feel that your present post is preparing you for future responsibilities? If so, in what ways?
2 If not, do you want it to? Please specify areas of responsibility for which you would like preparation.
3 Where do you see yourself in three years' time?

4 In what ways can the school help you to reach any future ambition?
5 Can the senior management team support you in any way?
6 Can your faculty support you in any way?
7 Other ways?

Personal development

1 Do you wish to study further? If so, specify in which areas.
2 Which courses have you attended in the last twelve months?
3 Are there any gaps in your experience which you would like to address as part of your own staff development?

Own targets for the next twelve months

Please list your own targets for development over the next twelve months. You may list as many as you like but try to list realistic targets and where possible outline the INSET and support you would need to meet these targets.

STAFF DEVELOPMENT INTERVIEW AND CLASSROOM OBSERVATION

The completed staff development questionnaire was given to me a week in advance of the staff development interview. At the end of the interview, which was teacher led, we had an agreed set of targets for that teacher for the next twelve months. They all involved elements of personal development, faculty targets and the school development plan. Without exception they were curriculum focused. Details of agreed areas of INSET and support were also noted. The agreed targets and INSET requirements formed the final page of the document, which was signed by both the teacher and myself. Copies were forwarded to the appropriate line-managers and the INSET co-ordinator.

Running parallel with this was a programme of classroom observation. The staff agreed the criteria for an effective lesson and the sheet was headed with the following quotation.

> Where pupils understand the teacher's objectives for a lesson, and know why they are doing what they are doing, they are able to participate more intelligently.
>
> (HMI 1985)

A checklist for classroom observation acted as the framework for judging the effectiveness of each lesson and notes were taken using the following headings:

1 timing: of the lesson and arrival of pupils and staff
2 lesson content
3 materials used
4 relationships and communication
5 pupil learning
6 marking and records
7 environmental factors.

It is important to note that the criteria for an effective lesson were discussed and agreed during the last academic year by the teaching staff. However, this is not enough to ensure quality, as different interpretations could be placed on the criteria. Triangulation of lesson observation was the solution to this possible problem. Thus, if heads of faculty were to observe the staff in their faculties teach they would initially carry out the exercise with a deputy head. The result of their schedules would be compared. Before any member of staff is observed there is a ten-minute discussion with the teacher, so that the outline lesson plan and focus can be explained. Within two days of the lesson observation there is a half-hour debriefing. During the academic year every member of staff is observed three times: first, by the headteacher as part of the appraisal process, second by a deputy head as part of the faculty review, and third, by the head of faculty as part of our monitoring procedures. All schemes of work are written to a common format, and these are used as a framework for the lesson observation.

To monitor our delivery of a quality education in the classroom and ensure that the new curricular plans are indeed improving the education for the boys, we bought in external evaluators at inspectorate level to monitor the effectiveness of our classroom delivery. In addition, at a parents' evening, parents completed a short and simple questionnaire which asked for their perceptions of the quality of teaching, the setting of homework, the marking of books, the reporting procedures and home-school communications. The questionnaire results were both positive and constructive. Thus the quality of classroom delivery is monitored by teaching staff at different levels, external evaluators and parents.

The staff development interviews, coupled with the classroom observation, gave a clear indication of the learning experience and the quality of teaching, and led to changes in the culture of the school. Teaching staff became more accountable and their contribution to the school was valued. This has led, in turn, to improved morale: there is now a realization that parents and pupils are our customers, with the right to the delivery of a quality education.

SCHOOL MANAGER

It is necessary to outline the thinking behind two factors: the appointment of a school manager on performance-related pay, and my own performance-related pay. These put the introduction of our appraisal programme in context.

Teachers at all levels in the profession carry out administrative tasks that take them out of the classroom. Many of these tasks detract from the main purpose of teaching, the delivery of a meaningful educational experience in the classroom. It is not cost-effective to have teaching staff carrying out administrative tasks which could equally well be carried out by support staff. This argument gains more credence when one looks at the administrative duties that senior managers carry out. In June 1990 I discussed with the governors the possibility of appointing a school manager as a non-teaching post but as a member of the senior management team and on performance-related pay. They were fully supportive of this initiative and an appointment was made from January 1991.

The post has broadly five key accountabilities:

1 financial management
2 school premises and environment
3 administration: school office systems and procedures
4 marketing and fund raising
5 support to personnel recruitment procedures.

At the same time, to reaffirm my commitment to the new culture, the governing body supported a move to link my salary to performance and I signed a new contract for January 1991.

The governors quite rightly wanted my performance-related pay scheme to have both positive and negative aspects. The governing body is under an obligation to pay the headteacher's salary at a certain level on the pay spine: it can be moved up the pay spine but not down. To overcome this problem I was bought into the scheme by being moved up the pay spine two points above my substantive salary. All credible appraisal systems are led by the person being appraised. It was up to me, within the framework of the professional duties of a headteacher, to set appropriate objectives. The broad headings are

1 the curriculum: the learning experience
2 staffing
3 appraisal and staff development
4 pupil support
5 beyond the school boundary
6 resource management.

The number of objectives under each heading varied, and are dependent on the stage of development of the school and will of course vary from year to year, depending on the progress of the school development plan. Each of the headings was then given a percentage rating of importance for the review period. Each objective is graded on a five point scale ranging from 1 (unacceptable) to 5 (outstanding). My starting-point was point 3.

At the end of each term I meet with the chair or vice-chair of governors and the chief schools' officer to see if there should be any changes to the objectives due to changing circumstances. At the annual review some of the objectives are graded statistically, some subjectively and others externally evaluated by the chief inspector. A final calculation is completed and salary adjusted accordingly. If I move further up the pay spine by scoring 4 or above, this new salary figure is regarded as point 3 for the next year's exercise. Each point on the 1–5 scale represents two points on the pay spine. The negative aspect of the exercise is that if I were graded at level 2 or below, my salary would decrease to the substantive level and the governors would seek my resignation. In my view, this can only be right.

My first appraisal/performance-related pay interview took place in October. It drew on evidence from two inspectorate visits over the previous twelve months, three full day visits from the chief inspector, and numerous governor visits to the school. In addition, statistical information was supplied. The chief inspector provided a short report on the objectives which were to be externally evaluated, and both the chief inspector and I answered questions/queries and points of clarification from the appraisal committee. The chief inspector and I then withdrew for the appraisal committee (chairman/vice-chairman of governors under the guidance of the chief schools' officer) to discuss and award performance scores on the key accountabilities (professional duties) of a headteacher. In summary, I know this was the right path to follow. There is now written documentation on my ability as a headteacher, gained through a rigorous system of appraisal, based on 'hard evidence' against a range of criteria and this performance has been recognised financially.

APPRAISAL AND PERFORMANCE-RELATED PAY FOR TEACHING STAFF

Both my and the school manager's appraisal and performance-related pay puts further development of appraisal and performance-related pay for the teaching staff in context.

The *Fourth Report of the Interim Advisory Committee on School Teacher's Pay and Conditions* (IAC 1991) includes a good deal of flexibility for the payment of teachers' salaries. I incorporated a similar high degree of flexibility in my own document, which had governors' approval. These flexibilities are as follows:

1 The headteacher, with governors' approval, can give any member of staff on the top of the standard scale, with or without an incentive allowance, discretionary scale points, to a maximum of £3,000. The criteria for such payments would include the performance of a teacher across all aspects of his/her professional activities with particular attention to classroom teaching.
2 The headteacher, with governors' approval, can move existing staff not on the top of the standard scale, up the standard scale by incremental progression.
3 The headteacher can with governors' approval introduce incremental enhancements.

I then offered staff on the top of standard scale voluntary performance-related pay which, if achieved, would be £500, £1,000 or £1,500, paid retrospectively as a lump sum at the end of the appraisal cycle. This addition to salary would be temporary. Staff who were not on the top of standard scale have the choice of the way funds are allocated as far as their performance-related pay is concerned. They can either opt for permanent movement up the standard scale or take a lump sum incremental enhancement which would be temporary and paid retrospectively at the end of the appraisal cycle.

The way extra money is available is clear to all staff. There are no negotiations behind closed doors. Access to extra funds is solely by linking pay to performance through the method of appraisal. This prevents staff asking for more money on an *ad-hoc* individual basis, with no clearly identified reasons. If headteachers follow this reactive policy, it would inevitably lead to discontent in the staff-room, at a time when maintaining and improving morale is so important.

At the first staff meeting of the summer term 1991, staff were introduced to both the pay policy and the policy on appraisal. There is a very fine dividing line between our system of staff development and appraisal. For the first year, appraisal of all staff was to be carried out, exceptionally, by me. From the second year, the task has been devolved after appropriate training to line managers. At the first appraisal interview staff made two decisions: first, whether to link their appraisal to pay, and second, whether to have their line manager appraise them. On the linking of pay and appraisal there was 100 per cent take-up.

The appraisal cycle

The appraisal procedure is as follows.

1 Initial meeting: one hour
This sets the scene for the appraisal cycle and will
- consider the teacher's job description
- agree the scope and focus of appraisal
- agree methods of collection of other data
- agree the focus of classroom observation
- agree performance indicators.
2 Discussion prior to classroom observation: ten minutes
3 Classroom observation: one hour
4 Debriefing on classroom observation within two days: thirty minutes
5 Collection of information: one hour
The information collected will differ according to the position of responsibility. However, for all teachers I wish to see the following: class register, mark book, lesson plans, schemes of

work, homework records and samples of pupils' work. If the teachers is also a tutor, I look at pupil daybooks.

For teachers with management responsibility, I focus in addition on their particular area of management, again drawn up from the job description in consultation with the teachers concerned.

6 Appraisal interview: one hour

The objectives are to identify successes, identify areas to be developed and training needs and agree targets for action.

The appraisal cycle for each member of staff takes place over an academic year. All staff new to the school complete a staff development questionnaire as a prerequisite to appraisal. It is important to note that appraisal is focused on the individual, and that the appraisee contributes to the school development plan.

During the initial meeting, the previous year's successes are recorded, and areas needing further development are noted. It could be argued that performance-related pay undermines the concept of appraisal as staff might be unwilling to reveal their weaknesses. In practice this has not been the case. First, performance-related pay builds on an established programme of staff development in which the staff have confidence. Second, individuals identify areas needing development, and INSET can then be provided. Third, the setting of targets is teacher-led within the framework of their job description and the school development plan. A culture of openness, honesty and support reduces the likelihood of teachers trying to cover up areas of potential weakness. The thorough nature of the appraisal process means that problems would be uncovered anyway.

The job description for every member of staff is divided into discrete areas, and performance indicators agreed to judge their success. The targets, also supported by performance indicators, may or may not overlap with areas identified by the job description. To gain an overall picture of a teacher's contribution to the school, there are sections on extra-curricular activities, classroom observation and data to be collected. There is also a space for any additional information the teacher may wish to add during the interview. At the end of the year, a joint statement of appraiser and appraisee is drawn up and depending on the individual's success in meeting targets the classroom observation and an agreed range of other quantifiable aspects, pay is allocated accordingly.

It is important to bear in mind, however, that not all performance indicators are quantifiable. It is again a balance between what is measurable and what is important. As Eric Bolton then senior chief inspector of HMI, has stated: 'The measurable shouldn't drive out the significant'. This tension cannot easily be resolved.

There are two questions that now need addressing. First, where does the money come from to pay performance-related pay? Second, what is the parental view of the scheme? The funds for performance-related pay are mainly allocated from the budget head *income generation* and the parents, without exception, have been supportive of the move. They are reassured by the fact that their sons will have an education where standards are under the spotlight and all staff are openly accountable for their classroom practice. When combined with my own performance-related pay, it adds a cutting edge to education which has been lacking in the past.

SUMMARY

Appraisal ensures that the possible contribution of each member of staff to the school is maximized; that the success of teachers is recognized, praised and rewarded; and that weaknesses are identified at an early stage and appropriate support given. Of course, human nature being what it is, there is always a danger that a minority of staff may interpret the process as unfair. It is up to the senior management team of schools to inculcate a positive and trusting climate where these feelings are at least reduced, and at best eradicated. This minor criticism is outweighed by far by the positive aspects of the process.

If as a profession we are to meet the expectations of parents and pupils by providing the quality education to which they are entitled, then appraisal is a way of monitoring this delivery. The quick identification of weak classroom teachers afforded by the opportunity of professional appraisal enables appropriate action to be initiated in the best interests of the pupils.

The new climate has led to a more structured system of accountability both within and outside of the classroom. There is a sharp focus on learning in the classroom as this is the central responsibility of all teachers. Appraisal and performance-related pay cannot be viewed in isolation but as a much wider agenda for change, which in turn is based on the premise that all teachers are classroom practitioners. This is the one strand that runs through the appraisal process: the ability to deliver the curriculum in the classroom. This overall philosophy has been enhanced by

1 a planned programme of review, monitoring and evaluation
2 the translation of all whole school and faculty policies into practice to enable classroom practice to be enhanced
3 a comprehensive staff development policy as an integral part of both the school development plan and recruitment and retention package.

Appraisal and performance-related pay are part of a much wider change in school culture and ethos. All newly appointed staff are offered performance-related pay linked to appraisal and all have accepted. The new culture has attracted young, forward thinking teachers. They come to Kemnal Manor not to earn their reward for long service but to be given a personal development programme. Career development is planned, and all staff share in a common vision of their school and its priorities. Appraisal must be a positive way forward for the 1990s, and performance-related pay another indicator to be used in quality assurance.

REFERENCES

HMI (1985) *Education Observed 3: Good Teachers*, London: HMSO
IAC (1991) *Fourth Report of the Interim Advisory Committee on School Teachers' Pay and Conditions*, Cm 1415, London: HMSO
O'Hear, P. and White, J. (1991) A national curriculum for all: laying the foundations for success, London: Institute of Public Policy Research, *Education and Training Paper 6*, June.

Chapter 11

Experience in schools
Case study II City Technology College, Kingshurst

Valerie Bragg

THE COLLEGE

I was appointed in September 1987 and provided with what must be every headteacher's dream: the opportunity to create from a blank sheet of paper. The college was to receive 180 11-year-old students every year and gradually build up to its full complement. Students were expected to continue in education or training to the age of 18, so it was planned that there would be a very large post-16 cohort. Since those early days slight modifications have taken place, with the result that we recruited our first post-16 intake in September 1990 and the college will increase in size to approximately 1,450 students with about 500 of post-16 age.

The first part of the college was a refurbishment of an old 1950s school, catering for 500 students. The second phase was a new design, built for another 500, and the third phase a refurbishment of the old school for the final 450. There were plenty of opportunities to be imaginative and to create an environment that was stimulating, interesting and different. The emphasis was on large open spaces, resource rooms, small work areas where students work unsupervised and social areas for students to sit and relax or work in groups.

The ambience we created has a corporate identity, with careful use of lighting to create low lights in corridors and an individual atmosphere in each room, using different furniture lay-outs, a variety of shaped furniture in hexagons and triangles, and varying colour schemes. The rooms are flexible with virtually no fixtures so they can be easily rearranged to suit the style of learning taking place.

STAFFING STRUCTURE

I believe that all teachers are managers, managing the classroom environment and managing people. In fact the students themselves are managers, managing their own learning. Teaching staff are very talented, and should have freedom, flexibility and plenty of scope. Everybody needs to have the opportunity to take responsibility and to become involved in their own enthusiasms. One of the problems in education is that in order to gain promotion to senior management, teachers are generally forced to make a decision to leave the classroom and cease being a head of department to become an administrative deputy. In many ways this loses good teachers and can provide them with rather mundane jobs. We felt that we had the opportunity to allow some of the administrative jobs to be carried out by support staff and thus enable us to create new roles.

Form tutor

In many schools in addition to heads of department, pastoral posts are created to look after the welfare of students. I decided we would have neither curricular nor pastoral heads and that the foundation, so far as looking after the welfare of the student, was the form tutor, who sees the students daily and regularly liaises directly with parents.

Area manager

I decided to develop a flat, less hierarchical structure and to incorporate deputy heads, heads of department and heads of year positions together, so creating *area managers*, who are responsible for curricular areas, administrative tasks and oversight of the pastoral welfare of students. Initially there were four area managers; now there are six. Their roles have changed considerably over the years. Other staff are responsible to the area managers, who hold area meetings, which incorporate members of staff from widely differing disciplines. Since opening, although the roles of area managers have changed and grown, they have acted as managers, delegating many of their responsibilities.

APPRAISAL

By August of each year the college will have decided on its aims and objectives for the forthcoming year. After my own appraisal and objective-setting, I appraise the area managers. This is part of their career development and is very much an annual report of the previous year and a time to discuss the future. After this appraisal all targets and objectives for the forthcoming year are agreed. Then area managers agree the targets and objectives with staff within their areas, and thus set their aims for the year. During the year one very important role of area managers and all staff is quality assurance, one aspect of which involves appraisal. The college appraisal system is seen very much as a development process for staff to help them personally, in their career or the future. It is designed to add job satisfaction and assist achievement as it will develop a member of staff and enable him or her to have more responsibility or opportunities for career advancement. It should also help staff plan for the future and consider their strengths and weaknesses. Staff discuss their appraisal with the area manager, the principal or the director of administration and finance. This is not a 'one-off': it occurs in several stages, both informal and formal. It is also felt important that before the final appraisal staff have time for preparation. All information is kept on file as a record.

As the year draws to a close, we summarize the achievements of all the staff in the college and obtain comments from the area managers on the performance of staff.

SALARY STRUCTURE

The college was to operate a longer than normal day and have very high expectations of staff and students. It was clear that a slightly different format for paying staff would be beneficial or indeed necessary. For too long teaching has not been looked on as a very prestigious profession, and support staff in many establishments are poorly paid. We wanted to reward staff with a salary more commensurate with their value. As the college would be totally autonomous and would manage its own budget, there was considerable freedom to offer an imaginative salary structure to all.

The national salary structure means that teachers are normally provided with a cost-of-living increase and also an annual increment each year dependent on the number of years' service. This does not really reflect the amount of hard work and effort many teachers put into the occupation nor are they rewarded for real flair or commitment.

Our salary scales are laid out in a very different fashion from the state sector and do not have any incentive allowances. These scales start at a minimum and rise to a maximum which in many cases is very high. This system provides the opportunity for outstanding staff, or a member of staff who has an outstandingly good year, to be given the equivalent of two, three or four increments. There is freedom and flexibility for these rises, and an overlap between the scales so that it is possible for someone on a qualified teacher scale to be getting more than a senior teacher with five years' experience.

If staff have a less good year, the rise is small and may be equal to the annual cost-of-living increase. At the end of the year staff appraisals occur and provide an opportunity for staff to discuss their own personal development, training needs and future career. There is a link between appraisal and their salary, but it is not the overriding factor as appraisal should be constructive and provide some action points.

Bonus payment

In addition to the annual salary increase there may also be a bonus, which is a one-off payment not related to the annual salary and is not pensionable. It is paid as a lump sum in July and reflects the year's efforts and success. Staff set targets and objectives in September and success with these is reflected in their bonus. Much is expected of staff at the college: it is anticipated that they will all achieve high standards in order to receive the annual salary increase. However, for outstanding achievement, the one-off bonus payment in July is given only to those staff who have achieved over and above their normal job. The use of the bonus can be varied, for example for an outstanding teacher whose commitment has been far beyond the call of duty, for tremendous contribution to the life of the college or to taking on extra responsibilities during the year. It provides a fair way of rewarding effort and talent.

The funding of the college is worked out on a per capita basis with extra grants for training, for example. When the college was small there were many expenses, which would have to be met regardless of its size. As we grow, the cost of organizing and managing the college should become proportionately cheaper. It is anticipated that when the college is fully operational both the salary and the bonus will be obtained from the normal annual running cost. The salary structure for the annual salary is contained within our recurrent budget; at present, however, because the college has been small we have been very fortunate in obtaining the bonus from one of our sponsors. The procedure will probably be modified and adapted further, but it seems to have worked well and has provided an excellent opportunity to reward staff and show appreciation.

Non-teaching staff

Support staff have been rewarded on a similar basis: they can also receive a bonus payment and their annual salary is performance related. Salaries are determined individually, reflecting not only the local market conditions, but also the pay and benefits policy applied to the teaching staff.

Pay and benefits policy

In arriving at the teaching staff's salary the governors will take into account the following.

1 market sector comparisons
2 additional directed time which the teaching staff are expected to work
3 additional in-service training days provided for teaching staff
4 the management structure which operates at the college
5 provision of a structure which allows for career progression
6 a facility within the structure for continued excellence in teaching to be rewarded
7 it is acknowledged by the governors that the staff of the college have a variety of roles and responsibilities not directly related to their teaching speciality.

The salary scale will provide for four levels for teaching staff.

1 *Probationers* Those teachers who are undergoing their probationary year prior to full qualification.

2 *Teachers* Those teachers who have satisfactorily completed their probationary year but have less than five years' service as a qualified teacher.
3 *Senior teachers* Those teachers with more than five years' service as a qualified teacher.
4 *Senior teachers with special responsibilities* The structure of the college is such that certain staff have specified college-wide duties which are in addition to the normal responsibilities they would undertake.

Salary scales operating at the college from 1 April 1991 are shown in Table 11.1.

Table 11.1 Salary scales at the City Technology College, Kingshurst

Teaching Staff	Minimum £ pa
Probationer	10,750
Teachers	12,381
Senior teachers	18,500
Senior teachers with special responsibility	21,000

Note: These scales will be reviewed by the governors on an annual basis. Movement for salaries above the minimum levels will be subject to annual review by the principal.

The scheme produced will enable the annual review of basic salaries to take account of changes in job size. These may have occurred for many reasons, such as government legislation, or because of new initiatives and developments that have taken place. Pay and benefits are based on an individual contract and not collective negotiation. This leads to differentiated pay based on performance. In coming to their conclusions, the governors considered the market sector for making comparisons. They identified the relevant area, and established what position in the market they were going to target. The governors looked at both the independent and maintained sectors.

The governors felt that the system must provide freedom so the college can recruit the best staff or appoint for specific purposes. There were constraints as, although the college is an independent school, it is still classified by the DES, and indeed funded by them, as a maintained school. Obviously, the Kingshurst salary structure should take account of the maintained sector scales. The freedom that the college enjoys is reflected by the fact that there are no set number of allowances that can be given. In the maintained sector a school may be provided with a certain number of allowances and once used, there is very little freedom for additions.

Many of the responsibilities and roles given to staff are large and varied but there is plenty of flexibility for rotation or the altering of roles. The governors have taken account of the importance of the process of salary determination being operated with an appropriate degree of flexibility while at the same time they have provided a strategy that would be advantageous to staff for career prospects or promotion. The governors will review the strategy periodically and will take due account of staff consultation.

Chapter 12

Performance-related pay for teachers in the 1990s

Harry Tomlinson

In the 1990s performance-related pay is beginning to be used openly in the teaching profession, although initially it was used mainly for headteachers and deputy heads. Only the occasional maintained school in 1991 has had the courage to reward teachers for the quality of their work, though increasingly in city technology colleges and grant-maintained schools this is evolving rather more quickly. Teachers have been unhappy for some time that promotion, at least in theory, has come only for moving out of the classroom. The main purpose for the introduction of the senior teacher allowance and the later scale A allowance was to reward good classroom teachers. The teacher unions have bitterly resisted any attempt to pay more for high-quality teaching, and so teaching quality has not improved sufficiently. In the 1990s this cannot be accepted any longer. The climate has begun to change but it is important for the teacher unions to work to ensure that the new payment systems, which will be implemented, genuinely reward excellence in teaching. This process will help gain the confidence of the public, and ensure that teachers achieve the higher pay that they deserve for the very demanding, complex work they do. Many of the proposals which appear in this chapter relate to headteachers, but this information, together with that in the final appraisal document, will provide the basis for paying for performance.

THIRD REPORT OF THE INTERIM ADVISORY COMMITTEE (IAC)

All the teacher unions, except the Professional Association of Teachers (PAT), argued according to the Third Report (IAC

1990) that allowances 'should be used to reward only responsibility, and not performance' (para 1.12). The National Steering Group (NSG) on teacher appraisal had supported the IAC view that appraisal clearly had the potential to strengthen and develop the quality of both teaching and management in schools in ways which would lead to better education for the pupils. The IAC note that teachers felt that the then decision not to proceed with appraisal had been taken

> 'on resource grounds and because Ministers felt that the NSG report had placed insufficient emphasis on linking appraised performance with levels of remuneration. It was argued strongly that appraisal is not an appropriate tool for determining pay, and should be used solely for its more generally accepted purpose of helping the professional development of teachers'.
>
> (para 3.62)

There is an assumption that there is some other means of determining pay which is more suitable.

The IAC judged that LEAs and governing bodies needed sufficient flexibility to reward responsibility and high performance. The secretary of state had asked the committee to consider what further increases in the number of incentive allowances was required because of 'the need to reward excellence in teaching' (para 4.29). In the schools visited the IAC found:

> few, if any, allowances were being awarded for outstanding classroom performance, at least overtly, despite the Government's stated view on the introduction of the new pay structure that this should be the primary purpose of the A allowance.
>
> (para 4.33)

The assumption that headteachers knew who were the better teachers seemed realistic. The present system of promotion to responsibility allowance does incorporate, if somewhat indirectly and artificially, judgements about classroom performance, together with an insecurely based consideration of whether a teacher can lead a department. There is often little evidence on which to base an analysis of potential leadership skills. Indeed references may very often concentrate on this, even though the evidence of classroom performance on which they are based is somewhat thin.

FOURTH REPORT OF THE INTERIM ADVISORY COMMITTEE

By the time of the Fourth Report (IAC 1991) there were some signs that the IAC was becoming irritated that better teachers were not being rewarded:

> We are convinced of the need for a framework for pay that will direct greater rewards to better teachers, and we are conscious that this, our last year of operation, is our final opportunity to complete the evolutionary changes we began four years ago.
>
> (IAC 1991: viii)

The next paragraph makes a reasonably strong link between this and appraisal:

> We regard appraisal as an important element in achieving the highest possible standards of teaching and learning, and in defining and identifying high quality teachers.
>
> (IAC 1991: ix)

PAT now 'strongly supported the use of the A allowance to reward exceptional classroom performance, for which clear criteria were needed' (para 2.13). Teaching can be evaluated. There are techniques such as microteaching, interpersonal process recall and interaction analysis which can be adapted to provide some rigour to this process. HMI has developed models for analysing the quality of classroom performance. One might argue that a profession which cannot recognize excellence in the central activity of its work is hardly a profession.

The annual report for 1988–9 of the senior chief inspector of schools (*Standards in Education*) was quoted:

> there are serious problems of low and under achievement; of poor teaching; and inadequate provision. It is particularly troubling that in schools some 30% . . . of what HMI saw was judged poor or very poor.

Such poor performance should be acknowledged. We need appraisers who have a sufficiently healthy realism to avoid the professional cowardice which fails to make judgements similar to those of HMI. When teachers will have the professional courage to recognize this, and can learn to avoid the defensive reaction which characterizes many responses then the search for improvement will be taken seriously.

There are many good reasons for high-quality teaching including 'good leadership from the head teacher to set the ethos of the school, and a strong senior management team with clear objectives, and which knows the strengths and weaknesses of each of the teachers in the school' (para 3.3). Quality is therefore essential and it needs to be recognized and rewarded financially, as well as in other ways.

Pay continues to be a key factor in determining morale. 'Teachers told us that although their starting salaries had been comparable with those of their contemporaries who graduated with them, in a very few years the salary gap had widened' (para 3.44).

Perhaps this raises the issue of teacher career. The Second Report of the House of Commons Education, Science and Arts Committee, Session 1989–90, on *The Supply of Teachers for the 1990s* (DES 1990), concentrated on this issue, particularly in the chapter on 'Career prospects and pay'. They noted that the criteria for the award of incentive allowances under the new system were

1 responsibilities beyond those common to the majority of teachers
2 outstanding ability as a classroom teacher
3 subjects in which there is a shortage of teachers
4 post which is difficult to fill.

Their major concern was the lack of salary rewards for the teacher who wishes to remain in the classroom rather than taking on administrative or managerial function. It is not clear if the additional money is simply for surviving. Mid-career teachers

> need encouragement if they are to consider teaching as a satisfying job in which new challenges and financial rewards await them throughout their career even if they decide to remain in the classroom.
>
> (DES 1990: para 42)

It recommended that 'a greater proportion of resources should be devoted to improving pay prospects for the mid-career teacher'.

A close reading suggests that they failed to tackle the issue of what the additional incentive allowances for mid-career teachers should be for. The question of the relationship of career to vocation, promotion and professionalism remains unclear. Most teachers regard themselves as professional, but it is not clear, as

Alan Marr shows in Chapter 8, precisely what is understood by this. Presumably the additional allowances are not merely for staying in teaching, but for the higher-quality teaching which would need evaluation, but which might be expected from experience. Similarly the committee approved of incremental enhancements and the extension of the national scale, but ducked the issue of what should be the criteria for receipt of any additional salary.

If senior teachers are to be paid for management, the senior chief inspector's report (1988–9) states unequivocally:

> The management of schools leaves much to be desired. In only about a third of those inspected was senior management judged to be particularly effective. The proportion of middle management so assessed was lower still. Effective senior management is characterised by clear objectives; sound planning; effective implementation; and review and evaluation. Such management is rare. Much more common is senior management communicating effectively but being much less successful in setting objectives; planning strategically; reviewing; evaluating; consulting staff, and providing clear remits for middle management.

If headteachers and other managers are to be paid for the quality of management, there is here another list of the characteristics which might be assessed; governors and LEAs should be able to recognize inadequate management. It also implies that there are few who would achieve the accolade of sustained levels of exceptional performance. Headteachers are in practice just as unaccountable as teachers.

There is in the Fourth Report (IAC 1991), inevitably, a chapter on appraisal:

> We have noted that effective management of school teachers requires detailed knowledge of their different strengths and weaknesses, and the development of individual career planning; that appraisal facilitates the systematic collection of detailed and consistent information about performance which can provide the necessary background for management decisions which will benefit both the whole school and individual teachers.
>
> (para 4.4)

The committee states that it was impressed on them this year 'that there is a need to reward good classroom teaching' (para

5.8), but goes very much further in their final section on changing attitudes:

> We believe the teaching profession needs to accept that a larger element of the pay bill made available to enhance the salaries of standard grade teachers should be related to performance... we have found resistance to salary differentiation solely on the basis of performance. One argument has been that the teaching profession is essentially 'collegiate' in nature, with the consequence that any move to differentiate salaries is divisive.
>
> (para 7.27)

The problem with the theory of collegiality is that it has produced the results described above. Standards of teaching and learning are inadequate.

> We have made it clear above that we consider this view to be misguided in principle... we are sensitive to concerns about how the award of additional discretionary payments related to performance would be determined in practice.
>
> (para 7.28)

The unions, in encouraging defensiveness, undermine the professional pride they seek to represent, and the morale which they claim to want to rescue from government attack. The difficulty is that sensitivities which exist and are acknowledged, are counterproductive.

'Appraisal provides a means of moving forward' (para 7.29). This is the central issue for the IAC.

> Appraisal also necessarily focuses on actual performance in the classroom, in the school and community more widely, and as a manager. The teachers' organizations have welcomed appraisal as a means of promoting staff development but have been concerned about direct links between performance assessed by appraisal and pay. We certainly do not envisage an automatic or precise relationship between appraisal and pay. But it seems to us that information about appraisal could properly be taken into account, along with other evidence, in taking decisions on whether to award discretionary payments. Indeed, it would be unfair to teachers to discount it, and we are pleased to see this is acknowledged in the Government's plans. But it would be better if information from appraisal were taken into account

overtly rather than covertly when considering performance for pay purposes.

(para 7.30)

This central argument the teacher unions have not dealt with. There does need to be a more sophisticated rationale for pay.

Perhaps therefore in the end it is a matter of what the other evidence might be. Since a successful appraisal system would have taken into account all the appropriate evidence, this might merely be a means of resolving the problem of how to bring in performance-related pay, based on appraisal, but somewhat covertly. When a culture of professional and personal development is established, and the whingeing about the current situation is reduced, including that of our teacher and political leaders, there are immense possibilities for real improvement in morale and pay.

KENSINGTON AND CHELSEA

The consultative document on *Performance-Related Pay for Headteachers and Deputy Headteachers* (Royal Borough of Kensington and Chelsea 1990) has had some publicity. Coopers & Lybrand were asked to carry out the review because their developmental work on local management of schools (LMS) was seen to be directly related to responsibility at school level, and the measurement of performance as required for performance related pay. The report (published on 1 February 1990) recognized the deep suspicion which the relationship between pay and performance had given rise to within the profession, though it was thought that there were signs that it was gaining a measure of acceptance. Coopers & Lybrand perceived a clear movement from the headteacher professional associations towards recognition that merit pay was, whether desirable or not, likely to happen.

One of the objectives of the Education Reform Act 1988 had been to stimulate increased quality of management and teaching, and thereby learning. The relationship between management or leadership, and responsibility, does need further clarification. Coopers & Lybrand found little empirical evidence that performance appraisal itself leads to improved performance, which must be a cause for concern for those who assume appraisal itself will improve standards. Their model proposed a much stronger role for the Chairs of governing bodies than the director of education judged appropriate. A job analysis would distinguish the respective responsibilities. A skills audit would assess the respective skills and abilities of headteachers and Chairs. This would lead to individual training needs analyses, and the planning of common training. This might involve, for example, interpersonal skills and team-building training to strengthen the relationship between headteachers and Chairs, an exciting prospect for some headteachers. Given this emphasis it is perhaps not surprising that the Chair of governors should play the leading role in appraising the headteacher. Given the complementary statutory responsibility of the LEA to evaluate and monitor performance, the detailed evaluation would be prepared by the director of education who would make recommendations to the Chair in a three-cornered appraisal.

A process based on objective-setting rather than personal characteristics was proposed. Supplementary measures would include quantitative performance indicators, qualitative evaluations and a school performance review. The significance of personal objectives would counter the argument that headteacher performance cannot be distinguished from that of the school or the staff as a whole, though a clear relationship does remain. The ten different aspects of performance significant for headteacher evaluation are

1 *School aims*   the headteacher's determination of the direction and ethos of the school; the development of an appraisal system
2 *Staff management*   the headteacher's ability to build a strong and effective school staff, to develop the skills, abilities and potential of the teaching and support staff
3 *Curriculum*   the effective delivery of the National Curriculum
4 *Teaching standards and pupil progress*   the quality of education delivery by teachers and of learning and general behaviour by pupils
5 *Governing bodies*   the nature and quality of advice and support given by the headteacher
6 *Parents*   strengthening parental links
7 *Maintaining body and other bodies*   performance with respect to LEA; relations with feeder schools; assessment might depend on market research testing perceptions of these relationships
8 *Resources*   making use of staff, financial and property resources of the school; include financial monitoring with a role for audit in assessing value for money

9 *Teaching* if a headteacher spends a substantial time in the classroom
10 *Personal development* development of particular skills, abilities, experience and knowledge, including participation in management development programmes.

The director of education and the chief personnel officer were developing a programme for assessing the skills of successful headteachers.

This model can be matched with that developed at the new Educational Assessment Centre at Oxford Polytechnic, which provides deputy heads and others with secondary headship potential with a diagnostic profile of their strengths and weaknesses across a series of generic management competences. The whole issue of management competencies and the Management Charter Initiative needs to be recognized. The parallel with SATs could be elaborated. This model is based on twelve key competences, which might be equally appropriate for measuring headship performance.

1 *Problem analysis* ability to seek out relevant data and analyse complex information to determine the important elements of a problem situation; searching for information with a purpose
2 *Judgement* ability to reach logical conclusion and make high-quality decisions based on available information; skill in identifying educational needs and setting priorities; ability to evaluate critically
3 *Organizational ability* ability to plan, schedule and control the work of others; skill in using resources in an optimal fashion; ability to deal with a volume of paperwork and heavy demands on one's time
4 *Decisiveness* ability to recognize when a decision is required (disregarding the quality of the decision) and to act quickly
5 *Leadership* ability to get others involved in solving problems; ability to recognize when a group requires direction, to interact with a group effectively and to guide them to the accomplishment of a task
6 *Sensitivity* ability to perceive the needs, concerns and personal problems of others; skill in resolving conflicts; tact in dealing with people from different backgrounds; ability to deal effectively with people concerning emotional issues; knowing what information to communicate and to whom

7 *Stress tolerance* ability to perform under pressure and during opposition; ability to think on one's feet
8 *Oral communication* ability to make a clear oral presentation of facts or ideas
9 *Written communication* ability to express ideas clearly in writing; to write appropriately for different audiences – students, teachers, parents, and so on.
10 *Range of interest* competence to discuss a variety of subjects: educational, political, current events, economic; desire to participate actively in events
11 *Personal motivation* need to achieve in all activities attempted; evidence that work is important to personal satisfaction; ability to be self-policing
12 *Educational values* possession of a well-reasoned educational philosophy; receptiveness to new ideas and change.

This contrasts with or complements the Kensington and Chelsea model, and shows how those preparing for headship will be able to demonstrate that they have the skills on which their performance will be assessed. Whether governors or LEAs would be able to evaluate headteacher performance for pay on this model is doubtful. The diagnostic profile, which is a basis for improvement, could also be built into the development of similar skills for teachers. It might be useful at this stage to consider one of the more exotic advertisements which has appeared in the *TES* (22 March 1991), and what it shows about the skills being sought.

Principal Post-16 Education – to £55,000
To establish an educational framework which encourages wider participation and high achievement through partnership with other providers and local communities. As a manager, visionary, and ambassador for the college, the appointee will be expected to deal with curriculum development, finance, quality assurance and personnel issues and to lead major policy initiatives.

An outstanding track record at senior management level in post-16 education and a strong commitment to the implementation of equality of opportunity are obvious prerequisites of the position. However, leadership, strategic management qualities, financial literacy, well-developed presentational skills, a sound grasp of promotion and marketing and the ability to initiate major processes of change are equally essential.

In Kensington and Chelsea, at the Educational Assessment Centre, and indeed in job advertisements, we have clearly entered very strongly and creatively into a world in which heads will be required to perform, and where evaluation of that performance and reward for excellence will first occur.

Coopers & Lybrand noted that 38 per cent of private sector headteachers often had a small proportion of their remuneration linked to a merit element. They insisted that the key argument was that relating pay to performance should bring significant benefits by stimulating performance. The responsibilities of headteachers were such that there must be a differentiation between them and other teachers. Their accountabilities were such that pay linked to performance was entirely logical. I would comment that the headteachers who think that they cannot work more effectively, with the concentration on improving in areas of weakness that performance-related pay will bring, are almost certainly insufficiently self-critical. It might be appropriate to ask the staffs of their schools about the quality of leadership, for example. Whether there was a complementary logic to this argument for teachers other than headteachers was left for the time being. There was no evidence presented for this key argument that performance-related pay would bring significant benefits in stimulating performance. Though the headteacher professional associations may be becoming more accepting of performance-related pay, it is perhaps only because they see this as the only means of significantly improving their pay.

Coopers & Lybrand identified two main routes for payment, either progression within a salary range, or a one-off bonus payment over and above base salary. The Royal Borough's existing salary policies were based on job evaluation using the proprietary scheme of Hay Management Consultants, which translates into a salary derived from their analysis of the management level salaries market. In this the wide salary range had a maximum of 35 per cent higher than the minimum. The objectives were agreed and recorded annually, and following a mid-year review, there was a performance review at the end of each year.

There were finally agreed five ratings for headteachers:

AA Exceptional: consistently exceeds expectations
A   Highly effective: standards for objectives exceeded
AB Effective: targets achieved

B   Less than effective: some objectives met
C   Unacceptable: fewer than half the objectives met.

In view of the desire to keep to the set national increments, a slightly revised version of the local performance-related pay matrix was used for headteachers, based on their position in the band for the school (see Table 12.1).

Table 12.1 Additional increments for headteachers

Assessed level	85–95%	96–105%	106–115%
AA	+4	+3	+2
A	+3	+2	+1
AB	+2	+1	no change
B	+1	no change	no change
C	no change	no change	no change

There was no forced distribution for council employees in general, but only about 5 per cent of all employees were expected to fall into the two extreme categories. Advancement into the upper third of their long range was restricted to those achieving A or AA ratings. The council also kept the ranges themselves up to date by increasing them in line with market trends. There were also one-off bonus payments of up to 3 per cent of salary for special achievements. There had been considerable consultation and training and seminars, in particular for the processes of setting objectives and reviewing performance.

The proposals for headteachers build on this experience. Individual objectives for the medium, three-year term would be firmly set in the context of the school development plan. The short-term objectives would derive from this and the headteacher's job description. The appraisers would review overall performance for the previous year, agree the coming year's objectives, and determine the criteria to be used in assessing them. There would be ongoing review and an annual formal appraisal exercise. This would start with the headteacher's self-assessment, and include consideration of quantitative performance indicators, qualitative evaluations or school performance review outputs. This process would lead to development discussions, pay decisions, agreed short-term objectives and counselling decisions. Coopers & Lybrand argued that the whole governing body, except the staff governors, should know the outcome of the performance assessment. At that time the director of education and the chief personnel officer thought that the results should be known only to the Chair of governors. Though Coopers & Lybrand recommended that the process should be voluntary and collaborative, the director of education and the chief personnel officer considered that the duty of the LEA to assess performance conferred a duty on headteachers to have their performance assessed. This would seem entirely reasonable. Responsibility for appraising the performance of headteachers and deputy heads should lie with the director of education and the Chair of governors, with the involvement of another headteacher if the appraisee requested it.

In Kensington and Chelsea over two-thirds of the headteachers have agreed to participate in the scheme, and are now on performance-related pay.

CAMBRIDGESHIRE

The principal accountabilities for Cambridgeshire headteachers are as follows.

1 *Policy advice*   develop and recommend education policies which will enable the governing body and the county council to meet their statutory obligations (for example, national policies for the curriculum), local needs and legitimate expectations
2 *Planning and budgeting*   direct the preparation of school development plans, programmes and budgets which will meet agreed policy objectives within prescribed cash limits
3 *Management and organization*   direct and keep under review the school's organization and the management of financial, staffing, accommodation and other resources in order to maximize efficiency and effectiveness in providing all pupils with high-quality teaching and learning in the context of an appropriate curriculum
4 *Monitoring/evaluation*   direct the internal monitoring of the quality of teaching and learning in the school to ensure that high standards are maintained which will meet the governors' objectives and the legitimate expectations of parents and pupils
5 *Joint planning and working*   promote joint planning and working with the county council and other agencies and the community in order to implement approved policies and maximize the use of resources and ideas

6 *Staff leadership and development* lead, direct and motivate staff throughout the school to ensure a high level of morale and performance in support of the school's objectives
7 *Pupil leadership and development* ensure the visibility of the role of headteacher in order to direct and motivate pupils throughout the school, having ultimate authority and responsibility for their progress, development and discipline to their parents, the governors and the county council
8 *Communication* ensure that the school's policies, purposes and achievements are effectively communicated within and outside the school in order to gain and increase the understanding of governors, the county council, staff, pupils and the public
9 *Community education* (where appropriate) direct the planning and delivery of community education within the agreed patch arrangements, so that the legitimate needs of the local population are met.

The proposed salary supplement from 1 September 1991 for the headteachers ranged from £1,941 to £2,973. The key contractual points included being subject to the council's system of performance management under which the headteacher would work to goals agreed with the chief education officer. The contract that headteachers would have with the authority is inevitably causing them considerable concern. It is not clear whether this will be successfully resolved, with one of the professional associations (AMMA) considering legal action because of the contractual implications. The additional element of pay linked to performance, if made, would be a single payment normally included with the June salary. The normal weekly hours of work would be thirty-seven, but it would be necessary to work longer hours and at weekends without extra pay, to meet the exigencies of the service. There would be thirty-five working days' holiday in addition to the eight statutory holidays. There are three possible schemes for the use of cars depending on whether a private vehicle is used, whether the employee participates in the lease car scheme, or whether the employee has a car provided within the lease car scheme at a reduced charge, up to 1,800cc for headteachers. The whole time of service must be devoted to the county council. Those involved must not engage in any other business, nor take up any additional appointment without the express consent of the chief education officer and/or Chair of governors.

Geoffrey Morris (chief education officer, Cambridgeshire) suggested (*TES* 22 March 1991) that the LEA of the future will have three roles: to determine the strategic patterns of local authority provision, to secure high standards of teaching and learning, and to distribute resources. Headteachers contribute to all three roles. They are relied on for policy development, they are the first line for quality assurance, and they will determine the size and nature of support services by their buying power. They are part of the senior management structure of the LEA, and hence their pay and conditions should reflect this. Headteachers in this role are seen as totally different from deputy heads. There is some evidence to suggest that deputy heads are trapped into excessively routine work as a result of inadequate planning by headteachers. This creates severe problems for the two headteacher professional associations, since they both, despite their titles, represent very significant numbers of deputy heads. The Secondary Heads' Association publication *If It Moves* (SHA 1989) shows the disillusionment of deputy heads at the many routine and humdrum activities with which they must become involved. Torrington and Weightman (1989) describe one school which showed three deputy heads 'holding highly paid positions all being underutilized and manifesting various degrees of dissatisfaction and sense of failure'. This was a fairly extreme example of the credibility problem: it was not uncommon. 'Seldom did we find a situation in which Deputies had full jobs and never did we find a situation in which three Deputies were actually needed'. (Torrington and Weightman 1989). In this case the deputy issue is complex.

LMS has not changed the dual accountability of headteachers to the LEA as well as the governing body. On this model there would appear to be no likelihood of a performance-related pay for teachers, or if so, there would be an entirely different rationale.

The Training Agency, in its publication series dealing with management development, *Investing in People*, examined *Performance Management: The Cambridgeshire Experience* (Training Agency 1990). This publication examines very fully the general principles of performance management which are now being applied to the education service. The aim of the county council was to 'value the development of employees as people, encouraging greater degrees of commitment, responsibility and personal awareness'. The system was intended to address four factors: cultural change, individual performance accountability, self-development and performance-related pay. The change to a performance-orientated culture was central. This is the culture which is being extended to the schools in Cambridgeshire by the assertion that the headteacher role is as defined. It would seem entirely logical to do so.

WESTMINSTER

Westminster's model is less fully worked out at present. The six-point scale ranges performance from faultless to inadequate. Increases are paid as one-off lump sums with the key objectives based directly on those outlined in the *Pay and Conditions* document covering general management, curriculum, pupils, staff, parents, governing body, external relations and personnel. At the start of each performance year the postholder and the Chair of governors, the assessor, in consultation with the director of education and leisure must agree the key objectives. It is expected that on average between ten and fifteen key objectives will be identified. This is significant in that the *Pay and Conditions* document presumably might later be used for teacher appraisal and performance-related pay.

Performance-related pay for headteachers is a reality at least in Kensington and Chelsea, though problems about conditions of service make the Cambridgeshire scheme less certain of widespread acceptance. How many headteachers will accept the new contracts remains unclear, although in Kensington and Chelsea over two-thirds had done so by June 1991. It is likely to be a rapidly increasing number if the experience in the education departments is paralleled. As the Management Charter Initiative develops it is likely that new standards of performance for educational managers will be easier to evaluate.

EDUCATION STOCK OWNERSHIP PLANS: SHARE OPTIONS FOR TEACHERS

Those involved in the education profession frequently fail to anticipate the next proposals of the secretary of state, because the long-term strategy has not been understood. The language that Lord Young used at the Department of Enterprise provides a rationale which has underpinned government policy making. Well before 1991 there were signs that some principals of further education colleges were finding their relationship with local authorities somewhat limiting. However, when the secretary of state announced that he was proposing to create a new independent sector for post-16 education, with funding coming from a new statutory funding council, there was again considerable surprise. What is interesting is how little attempt has been made to anticipate what, after the event, become apparently logical consequences of earlier political policy-making. It is now possible to recognize almost an inevitability about the process of educational policy-making deriving from Callaghan's Ruskin speech, and that it is genuinely about increasing standards as well as using resources efficiently.

A US proposal which might complement the rapid introduction of performance-related pay and deserves some consideration is an educational form of what North Americans call *Employee Stock Ownership Plans*. This is perhaps a logical development of the policy of privatization in the UK and an extension of the grant-maintained school model. Mann (1990) states quite unequivocally and accurately that national performance trends in the USA have shown little progress in improving reading or mathematics proficiency during the 1970s and 1980s. In the UK we have become entangled obsessively in arguments about whether standards have improved or not. Despite the evidence that there may have been a slight fall-back in reading standards during the 1980s, it is quite clear to anyone who examines the evidence seriously that standards have improved. If we take examination results, apparently the ultimate criterion, the percentage achieving five GCEs or GCSEs Grades A–C increased between 1979 and 1989 from 23 per cent to 32 per cent. In 1990 this increased again by 2.2 per cent, and there were further improvements in Advanced Level results following the change from GCE to GCSE. What is vastly more important, and still not sufficiently widely accepted by teachers, is that standards are not increasing at all quickly enough in Britain, they are much too low, and teachers can improve them substantially. This is perhaps now recognized in the post-16 age groups, though insufficiently in primary and secondary schools.

The response of those involved in education in the USA has been to deny the evidence, suggesting that the test measures the wrong things, and that teachers' salaries are inadequate. Both of these responses will be familiar, if the context is somewhat different. There is so much negative thinking that a commitment to a massive improvement in standards is constantly undermined. Business involvement in the USA has frequently been that of individuals committing themselves to working with specific groups of children, ignoring the other millions; there is a parallel with some heavy investments in city technology colleges, which can be seen as 'rescuing the survivors while the boat sinks, [or] putting new sails on the same leaky hull' (Mann 1990).

Mann sees US schools as overloaded with such projects, as is the case in the UK with the quiet desperation to establish yet more school-industry links, and using them as an excuse to fail to consider the need for real change. Testing in the UK is clearly a parallel development producing so many useless data that there is no time to improve standards. In any case teachers do not believe that they can transform levels of attainment in literacy and numeracy. There has been no improvement in the student achievement line as charted by the National Assessment of Educational Progress since 1971. All the federally supported projects, which parallel the National Curriculum and TVEI (Technical and Vocational Education Initiative) in Britain, site-based management, similar to LMS in Britain, and voucher plans, an extension of open enrolment in Britain, have had no effect at all on the central problem which, he suggests (and certainly I would agree), is teacher motivation. Teachers teach because of a love of children and because they enjoy their subject or they want to perform a public service. This impeccable altruism has had no effect on improving the level of performance. Committee meetings, similar to those held by governing bodies, flatter organization charts, similar to those implied by the Task Force, and parental choice among look-alike schools insulated by union power against the tonic of failure, have had no impact whatsoever in the USA. It is ironic that failing schools have provided the starting-point for many grant maintained schools. They may have equally little impact here unless these same issues are addressed.

Teacher unions in the USA also see their members as being the source of improvement, but the average teacher salary ($33,000 in 1990) changes only with seniority or accumulated graduate study. Effective and ineffective teachers are paid the same. The equivalent in education of Employee Stock Ownership Plans and an investment bank might, Mann (1990) suggests, be used to create real change by cutting through education's very strong bureaucracy, by offering rewards for hard work, risk, creativity, or success in getting the USA's students to a world-class science performance by the year 2000. Only improved teacher performance can conceivably achieve any of this. This form of performance-related pay would genuinely make teachers entrepreneurs.

Teachers, he suggests, might own the schools (Educators' School Ownership Plans), and have the additional motivation of reaping the profit benefits or loss consequences. This would be privatization with a social value in Britain perhaps, as opposed to donating the national industries at knock-down prices to the city. Teachers need not own the whole enterprise, nor need all their pay be so determined. There must, however, be a real connection between performance and pay. Employee stock option schemes work best in industry on a small scale and in desperate circumstances. This does describe the situation in a substantial portion of US public schools, and is approaching one-third of classrooms in Britain, according to HMI. Industry in the USA at present provides grants for improvement projects. However $250,000 could capitalize a modest incentive fund to pay teachers who help more children achieve more goals, work to good effect with priority groups and topics, recruit more students, reduce their own absenteeism and save substitution costs for example. Performance-related pay would be a more effective use of the money. Even the president of the American Federation of Teachers has proposed a not dissimilar scheme with a bonus of $15,000 to $30,000 to all those in a school which has had five years of sustained gains on 'good assessment measures'. I suspect that the NUT and NAS/UWT are not yet ready to make such proposals. Mann would see his alternative redirecting school improvement moneys used to little effect, as in city technology colleges, to focus incentives on system wide school improvement. Altruism, love of children and professional standards would be reinforced by financial incentives.

The present payment system provides very inadequate sanctions against poor performance. Those who become involved in profit or gain-sharing plans, however, would agree on goals, on how they could be measured, and how individual and organizational contributions could be recognized. Targets should be set below what the schools believe they can achieve in all innocent enthusiasm, but well above that assumed by conventional wisdom. There could be added value measures for children from the most or least privileged backgrounds. Both groups lose out in the American and British systems. It might be worth imposing similar measures on independent schools who take in pupils through the assisted places scheme, since there is no evidence that these pupils are achieving more highly than they would in maintained schools. The National Education Association was advertising last year with its slogan *Get Smart America: Invest in Education*. Investment in public schools did not, according to Mann, result in real choices between alternatives; a tangible pay-off, a dividend paid on time for teachers; or accountability, some real consequence for the teachers if the organization did not deliver. These proposals might take education in Britain into new areas, including one of at least two versions of the *Citizens' Charter*. I would suggest that they might be a logical consequence of policy-making developments during the 1980s.

In the enterprise culture people trade hard work and risk for bigger rewards. With school development plans appropriately focused such an approach would be possible for schools. Schools at present are 'risk-free, one-size-fits-all, take-it-or-leave-it enterprises' (Mann 1990) though perhaps enterprise, as the Department of Trade and Industry have redefined the word, would be an unsatisfactory word in the circumstances. An investment bank for education could pool venture capital for ideas that return private and public dividends. This might encourage movement to grant-maintained status if this is what the government wants. Those with better ideas would find their way through the education research, development and dissemination systems to achieve their rewards. The profit motive would augment, not replace altruism. Private money in the USA, but arguably central government money also in Britain, along the lines of TVEI, could lever systematic innovation and improved standards. School people with good ideas that can be refined and moved with market forces, and for-profit organizations would move into the school market because of the lowered capital costs. No US business had been persuaded to invest in the expertise and entrepreneurial leverage that an investment bank dedicated to education would provide. The impact of the many different quarter-million dollar grants to non-profit organizations for once-only demonstrations has not been very significant. Since the energy is undoubtedly there in education, genuine entrepreneurial incentives need to be added.

It should be clear that in 1991 US education financing of education is in much more serious trouble even than in Britain with the community charge capping uncertainties, and the burgeoning number of alternative methods for local government finance from the different political parties. A Republican governor in Massachusetts, a Democratic governor in New York, and an Independent governor in Connecticut are all cutting education budgets. California's governor has asked the legislature to suspend a law which guarantees 40 per cent of the state's outlays to education in order to solve the problem of a $12.6 billion budget shortfall (*Time International* 1991). There is an increasingly desperate anxiety in both countries to screw more value out of the decreasing amounts of money spent on education, since at least in the USA, and probably in the UK too, unless those who are paying are convinced that they are receiving value for money there will be less money available. In this international context the present situation in the UK has not yet reached the depths that have been seen in the USA, where there is a greater desperation about remaining a leading nation allied with this reduction of the funding to the education service that might make improvement possible. In the UK the government is trying, however inadequately, to ensure that the issue is taken seriously. It is absolutely clear that the only solution can be through higher performance by the teachers, however that is achieved. Mann's ideas may provide the basis for an experiment which will put teachers' performance at the centre as schools are run increasingly like businesses in order to provide a better education and higher standards. Though Mann may be considered something of an oddball in the USA, there is a logic about his proposals which suggests new ways of paying successful and highly achieving teachers for their performance.

CONCLUSION

One of the challenges of concluding a book like this is that government policy changes with now unsurprising frequency. National policies change with the results of elections, though with performance-related pay, the new salary flexibilities, LMS, and the changing culture of the public sector, it seems unlikely that performance-related pay will fade away. This will lead, first of all, to paying headteachers who produce the leadership to achieve the results that their parents, governors and local authorities (if these continue to exercise significant control) would demand. Then teachers whose appraisal shows they are achieving sustained levels of exceptional performance and making an outstanding contribution to improved performance will be paid more. This will change the culture.

The secretary of state, Kenneth Clarke, in an interview in *Education Guardian* (19 February 1991) made his own position clear:

The Prime Minister and I have a genuine interest in improving incentives for teachers who perform well. There does appear to be a nervousness about using incentive allowances and discretionary allowances on a performance-related basis.

In response to a direct question about how much of a good teacher's pay should be based on incentives:

I think the majority should be. In all organizations, pay is an important management tool to motivate the best of the staff to raise their performance. At the moment responsibilities tend to be invented to justify payment and where that happens it's weak management abdicating responsibilities.

He is right, and appraisal is the way this will be achieved. In a few years teachers will be enclosing their appraisal reports when seeking promotions, or more likely appraisal-related pay, in their own or other schools. The front page of *Education Guardian* (14 May 1991) reports on the headteacher paid by results at Dorridge Junior School, Solihull, and the headteacher and staff on performance-related pay at Kemnal Manor Boys School, Kent (reported more fully in Chapter 10). Performance-related pay is starting to spread throughout the system.

Meanwhile it would appear that large numbers of headteachers are negotiating salary top-ups for themselves. The National Association of Headteachers (NAHT) is advising its members to bargain, though the association secretary recognizes that there are great moral pressures on his members, who might think it is more necessary to spend the money on books and equipment. Lincolnshire has, perhaps uniquely, provided £100,000 for their sixty secondary and ninety primary schools with delegated budgets for salary increases. The Secondary Heads' Association (SHA) very strongly advises that a school pay policy should be created through normal staff consultations, partly perhaps because secrecy is unprofessional, and because the teacher unions have a right to see the school budget, but most particularly because it is good management practice. With performance-related pay this will become even more important.

At the same time headteachers and governors are genuinely concerned about the range of payments for which they are now responsible. Schools certainly need a pay policy to deal with the increasing number of discretionary allowances. The policy must be rational, linked to objective criteria when this is possible and easy to understand. Payments for outstanding ability as a classroom teacher will need to be soundly based but they must be made. In particular payment for performance presents a clear opportunity to recognize the contribution of women teachers, which the present system allows to continue to be relatively grossly underpaid. Accelerated progression must be linked to performance review. Incremental enhancements will need to be linked to a specific task and performance. The extension of the standard scale by the introduction of a local scale will also be selectively applied, and criteria for this will also need to be agreed and understood, and based on performance. The policy adopted must be capable of application to all who would qualify by reason of the objective criteria laid down. Without paying for high-quality performance, there will not be the significant further improvement in standards which is absolutely essential. What is needed is the determination by governors and headteachers to use the pay policy to improve performance. If this is not achieved pay will continue to decline relative to national averages. The present system of paying teachers for having a responsibility regardless of how successfully they carry it out, for qualifications often achieved many years previously regardless of whether they have been updated, for having experience without evaluating whether it is leading to improved quality, and without any judgement as to the quality of performance is distinctly unprofessional, indeed arguably pretty amateurish.

REFERENCES

Cambridgeshire County Council (1991) *Report to Committee*, Cambridge, 16 April.
DES (1990) *The Supply of Teachers for the 1990s*, London: HMSO.
IAC (1990) *Third Report of the Interim Advisory Committee on School Teachers' Pay and Conditions*, Cm 973 London: HMSO.
—— (1991) *Fourth Report of the Interim Advisory Committee on School Teachers' Pay and Conditions*, Cm 1415, London: HMSO.
Mann, D. (1990) Bankrolling educational entrepreneurs, *Education Week* 10(14).
Royal Borough of Kensington and Chelsea (1990) *Performance Related Pay for Headteachers and Deputy Headteachers*, consultative document: 1 February; report to Education and Libraries Committee: 8 November.
SHA (1989) *If It Moves*, London: Secondary Heads' Association.

TES (1991) Principal Post-16, *Times Educational Supplement* 22 March.
Time International (1991) Starving the schools, 15 April.
Torrington, D. and Weightman, J. (1989) *The Reality of School Management*, Oxford: Basil Blackwell.
Training Agency (1990) *Performance Management: The Cambridgeshire Experience*, London: Training Agency.

Index

absenteeism 121
accountability 124
age-weighted pupil count 93–4
Akers, J. 74
Alexander 96
alienation 120
allowances, *see* incentive allowances
appraisal 97, 99–100;
　advantages 175; or
　assessment 144;
　compulsory 92–3, 140;
　consensus on 134; criteria 93,
　116–18; frequency 145;
　governors role 140–1; heads 146;
　introduction of 139–40;
　judgemental versus
　developmental 136–7;
　Kingshurst 179; link with pay 9,
　186; nature and purpose 132–3,
　185; openness 143, 145; pilot
　study 133–6; and professional
　development 131, 141–2, 189–90;
　research project 132, 143–4, 148;
　and school aims 165; self- 137,
　144–5; and teacher
　recognition 135, 160
appraisal process 9–10, 173–4
appraisal systems, causes of
　failure 67–8; IBM 78–9; target-
　based 15
Assistant Masters Association
　(AMA) 95
Assistant Masters and Mistresses
　Association (AMMA) 111, 197

awards, cash 85–6

Bacharach, S. 43
Baker, K. 97, 100, 107, 139
Ball, C. 17
basic scale 91
Belgium 23, 26–8
Bolam, R. 134
Bolton, E. 174
bonuses 47, 63, 144, 172, 180
Boyer, E. 34
Bradley, H. 134
Burnham Committee 88–98;
　abolished 90, 107; set up 90

Callaghan, J. 200
Cambridgeshire 143, 146, 196–9
career, development 132–6, 141–2;
　idea of 125–30; structure 2–3, 8,
　31–2, 46–7, 51, 95, 187
Carlisle, M. 97
CBI report 11–12
city technology colleges
　(CTCs) 111, 143–4, 177–83
Clarke, K. 89, 108–10, 140, 205
classroom observation 137–8,
　168–70, 174
coaching 6–7
Cohen, D. 35, 39–42, 44–5
communications 70, 75–6, 121–2,
　161–2
contracts literature 39–41
Coopers and Lybrand 14, 190–6
Corbett, D. 40
corporate excellence 148

counselling 6–7
credibility gap 122
curriculum 165, 201
customer satisfaction share plan 85

de Gruchy 10
decision making 48–9, 121;
  decentralized 99–100, 116–17
Deming, W. 146–8
Denmark 23, 26–9
deputy heads 101, 104, 198
divisiveness 161

East Sussex education
  department 152–62;
  reaction 155–8; the
  scheme 153–5
Educational Assessment Centre
  model 192–3
efficiency 44–5
equity 160–1
equity shares 64, 85
equity theory 37
ESSO 6–7
expectancy theory 36–7

Fowler, A. 151
France 23–4, 26–32

Galbraith, J. K. 88
Germany 23, 25–9, 32
golden-age accounts 123
governors 140–1, 181, 190
Graham, D. 132, 134
Greece 23

headteachers 191–9; contracts 197;
  performance criteria 191–3;
  performance-related pay 5–6,
  146; rating 194–5; salaries 101,
  104
Her Majesty's Inspectors (HMI) 4,
  11, 134, 144, 174, 186, 202
Herzberg, F. 38
Hilsum, S. 92
hours of teaching 23–4; *see also* work
  load
Howarth, A. 9, 139

IBM 73–87; the company and its
  philosophy 73–6; internal
  communications 75–6; payment
  system 76–7, 81–6; performance
  planning 78–9; performance
  review 79–81; rating
  distributions 81
identity 118–20, 124–5, 129; life-
  cycle analysis 119
in-service training (INSET) 24,
  28–9, 31, 121, 125–6; in-service
  days 128; management
  training 129
incentive allowances (IAs) 7–8,
  101–5, 185, 187; criteria 92,
  103–5
incentive post system 3
incentive schemes 63, 85;
  design 4–5; effective 4–6;
  flexibility 4–5; pay and
  performance link 5; variation by
  seniority and function 6
incremental enhancement 104–5
industrial action 97
industrial relations 111–12
institutional develoment plans
  (IDPs) 126
Interim Advisory Committee
  (IAC) 6, 88, 90, 107, 114, 144;
  and pay flexibility 97–106;
  second report 141–2; third
  report 97, 141–2, 184–5; fourth
  report 186–90
investment bank 203
Italy 23–4, 25, 28–9

Jacobson, S. 5, 35, 43–5
Japan 4, 59, 146–7
job descriptions 123, 128, 174
job evaluation 159
Joseph, Sir K. 97, 131–2

Kemnal Manor Boys
  School 164–76, 205
Kensington and Chelsea 146,
  190–6
King, R. 49
Kingshurst 177–83; appraisal 179;
  salary structure 179–83; staffing
  structure 178

Kinnock, N. 88

LEAs, future role 198–9
Lipsky, D. 43
local management of schools (LMS) 100–1, 106, 190
local scales 144
Lortie, D. 38
Luxembourg 26–9

MacGregor, J. 108, 139–40
McMahon, A. 134
MacPhail-Wilcox, B. 49
Major, J. 94, 99
management consultants 14, 190
management discretion, salary increases 84
Mann, D. 200–4
market conditions 47, 95–6, 103
Marr, A. 188
Maughan, B. 20
merit pay 10; debate on 34–5; United States 34–51; *see also* performance-related pay
merit pay-systems 58–64; fixed performance related 59–60; merit only 62–3; performance rating and market movement 61–2; variable performance related 60
money motive 2, 36–8, 50
Monk, D. 35, 43–5
morale 120–5, 156, 187
Morris, G. 198
Mortimore, R. 18
motivation 2, 5, 36–8, 50, 106, 135, 156, 203
Murnane, R. 35, 39–42, 44–5

NAS 95
National Association of Headteachers (NAHT) 205
National Association of Schoolmasters Union of Women Teachers (NASUWT) 3, 4, 8, 108, 111, 134, 202
national negotiating rights 108
National Steering Group (NSG) 133–4, 139, 185

National Union of Teachers (NUT) 7–10, 91–5, 97, 108, 131, 134, 136, 202
Netherlands 24–8
Norway 23–5, 28

O'Kane 3
organizational structure, historical trends 12–14

parents', attitudes 20; choice 51
pay, differentials 91, 93–4, 98, 102–3, 106; flexibility 96–106, 111; public sector trends 107; satisfaction/dissatisfaction 86–7, 106, 120; *see also*, performance-related pay; salary
pay review body 13, 89, 108–12
performance, assessment 1–2; criteria 123; defined 159; long- and short-term 3; measurement 2, 87; planning 78–9; ranking 148; relative 19; review 79–81, 87
performance management 65–7, 69–70, 151–62
performance-related pay, in the 1980s 1–21, 56–7; costs and benefits of 39–41, 70–1; criteria 139; defined 1, 151; East Sussex education department 152–62; employee demand 58; failures 55–6, 158; industrial model 115; lessons so far 69–70; and performance management 55–71; private sector 55–71, 86; public sector 14–16; reasons for 57–8, 158–9; self defeating 143; theories of 35–41; types of 15; in US 41–51; *see also* merit pay systems; profit-related pay; salary
Perry, P. 148–9
personal accountability 2
personal development 156, 161; interview 168–70; questionnaire 166–8; *see* career

structure; professional development
piece-rate compensation 39–40, 50
primary sector 126–7
private sector 55–71; *see also* IBM
privatization 13–14
productivity 51
Professional Association of Teachers (PAT) 184, 186
professional culture 115–16, 118
professional development 132–6; and appraisal 131, 141–2, 189–90
professional and personal circumstances 116
professionalism 9
profit motive 203
profit-related pay 64–5
promotion chances 126
public sector 14–16, 107
pupil, accomplishment 40, 45–6; performance 10; self-esteem 17

ranking criteria 68–9
rating 194–5; distributions, IBM 81; drift 68; scales 1, 151
Reagan, R. 34
resource allocation between sectors 127–8
restructuring, reasons for 95–6
rewards, intrinsic and extrinsic 5, 38, 50
Rutter, M. 18–21
Rycroft, T. 12

salary, basic scale 91; basis of 147; components of basic 25–8, 30; extra payments 26–8; flexibility 171–2; heads and deputies 101, 104; increases 26, 28–31, 82–4; local scale 144; range 33; and redeployment or retraining 84–5; standard scale 91, 101–2, 105–6, 172; structure 7–8, 24–5, 179–83; *see also* merit pay systems; performance-related pay; profit-related pay
Saran, R. 93

SATs 17, 192
scarcity bonus 47; *see also* market conditions
Scholtes, P. R. 146–7
school effectiveness, variations in 17–21
school management 146, 188; *see also* local management of schools (LMS)
school manager 170–1
Secondary Heads' Association (SHA) 198, 205
secondary sector 127
service improvement 156
share options 199–204
sixth-form colleges 17
Smith, D. J. 17, 19–20
social inequality 17
Spain 26
stability 159–60
staff development, *see* career structure; professional development
standard scale 101–2, 105–6, 172; discretionary scale points 105; superstructure 91
standards, improved 200
Start, K. B. 92
stock ownership plans 199–204
students, *see* pupil

targets 2, 15, 138–9, 174
task analysis 118
teachers, confidence 12; effectiveness 45–6; efficiency 44–5; low expectations 4, 17, 19; performance measured 43–8; qualifications 22–3; responsibilities 30; role in decision making 48–9; scepticism 11–12
teaching evaluation 186
teaching load 23–4; *see also* work load
testing 17, 192, 201
Tomlinson, S. 17, 19–20
Torrington, D. 198

trade unions 13, 111, 189, 201; *see also* named unions
two-factor approach 38–9, 48

United States 5, 15, 34–51, 59, 144, 200–4
Urban, W. 41

vocational education 94

Vroom, V. 36

Weightman, J. 198
Westminster 146, 199
Wilson, B. 40
women teachers 126–8, 206
work quality 44
workload 23–4, 120, 123, 124

Young, Lord 199